Postcoloniality, Translation, and the Bible in Africa

Postcoloniality, Translation, and the Bible in Africa

EDITED BY

Musa W. Dube

AND

R. S. Wafula

PICKWICK Publications · Eugene, Oregon

POSTCOLONIALITY, TRANSLATION, AND THE BIBLE IN AFRICA

Pickwick Publications
An Imprint of Wipf and Stock Publishers
199 W. 8th Ave., Suite 3
Eugene, OR 97401

www.wipfandstock.com

PAPERBACK ISBN: 978-1-4982-9514-7
HARDCOVER ISBN: 978-1-4982-9516-1
EBOOK ISBN: 978-1-4982-9515-4

Cataloguing-in-Publication data:

Names: Dube, Musa W., editor | Wafula, R. S. (Robert Sammy), editor.

Title: Postcoloniality, translation, and the Bible in Africa / edited by Musa W. Dube and R. S. Wafula.

Description: Eugene, OR: Pickwick Publications, 2017 | Includes bibliographical references.

Identifiers: ISBN 978-1-4982-9514-7 (paperback) | ISBN 978-1-4982-9516-1 (hardcover) | ISBN 978-1-4982-9515-4 (ebook).

Subjects: LCSH: Bible—Postcolonial criticism | Postcolonialism—Africa, Sub-Saharan | Translation | Cultural Studies | Colonialism | Interpretation | Translation studies.

Classification: BS521.4 P51 2017 (print) | BS521.4 (ebook).

Manufactured in the U.S.A.   06/20/17

To our late parents
Mr Mfanyana J. Dube Tafa (1922–2017)
and
Joyce Nasimiyu (1946–1996)

Contents

vii

Part III: Savage Readings of Colonialized African Bibles

Contributors

Musa W. Dube a humbodltian awardee (2011), teaches biblical, gender, and research courses at the University of Botswana. Her area of specialization is the New Testament and her research interests include gender, postcolonial, translation and HIV and AIDS studies. Dube, who has written numerous articles and book chapters; co/authored and edited several anthologies, is Professor extraordinaire at the University of South Africa, Department of Biblical and Ancient Studies. She is the author of *Postcolonial Feminist Interpretation of the Bible* (Chalice Press, 2000). dubemw@mopipi.ub.bw.

Aloo Osotsi Mojola is currently serving as Professor and Chair of Theology, Biblical Studies and Philosophy at St Paul's University, Limuru, Kenya. He was previously a Lecturer in Philosophy at the University of Nairobi (1978–1983) and later served as Translation Consultant and as Africa Regional Translation Coordinator with the United Bible Societies. Prof. Mojola is the author of *God Speaks in Our Own Languages: A History of Bible Translation in East Africa from 1844 to 2010* (forthcoming ABS/SBL), among many other articles in various journals. aloo.mojola@gmail.com.

Malebogo Kgalemang is a Senior Lecturer in the Biblical Studies Unit of the Department of Theology and Religious Studies at the University of Botswana. Her research engages the Bible from postcolonial, gender, sexuality, and cultural studies. She has also taken a deep interest in the African novel especially novels that interweave the triad categories of postcolonialism, gender, and religion.

Johnson Kiriaku Kinyua is currently serving as a faculty of Religion and Theology at Saint Leo University (Center for Online Education, USA). He is also a PCUSA ordained minister serving as the Senior Pastor at Church of Amazing Grace International in Santa Ana, California. His recent publications include: *Introducing Ordinary African Readers' Hermeneutics* (London: Lang, 2011); in addition he is currently working on two other books for publication on "Bible Translation and Ideology" and "A History of the Gĩkũyũ Bible."

Gomang Seratwa, Ntloedibe-Kuswani is Senior Lecturer in Education Technology & Distance Education at the University of Botswana. She holds a PhD in Instructional Design Development & Evaluation from Syracuse University in New York. Her broad teaching and research interests is in educational technology with emphasis on reaching distance learners and transforming learning environments through using emerging technologies. Her publications in religion include three books entitled *Reflections on Religions—Books 1,2,3*; and the following book chapters: "Translating the Divine: The Case of Modimo in the Setswana Bible"; "Witchcraft as a Challenge to Batswana Ideas of Community and Relationships," in *Imagining Evil: Witchcraft Beliefs and Accusations in Contemporary Africa* (Africa World Press, 2007).

Dora Rudo Mbuwayesango is Iris and George E. Battle Professor of Old Testament Literature and Languages at Hood Theological Seminary. She is coeditor of *Postcolonial Perspectives in African Biblical Hermeneutics* (Atlanta: Society of Biblical Literature, 2012). She has contributed articles in journals and chapters in books including, most recently, "Sex and Sexuality in Biblical Narrative," in *The Oxford Handbook of Biblical Narrative* (Oxford: Oxford University Press, 2016).

Jeremy Punt is Professor of New Testament in the Faculty of Theology at Stellenbosch University in South Africa, and currently chairs the Old & New Testament Department. He holds a doctorate in New Testament (1999) and his research interests in biblical hermeneutics focuses on critical theory and the interpretation of the New Testament in Africa. He has recently published *Postcolonial Biblical Interpretation: Reframing Paul* (Brill, 2015) and regularly contributes to academic journals and book publications.

R. S. Wafula is Visiting Assistant Professor of Religion at Luther College, Decorah, Iowa, USA. He is the Author of *Biblical Representations of Moab: A Kenyan Postcolonial Reading* (New York: Lang, 2014); and "Power and Conflict Management: The Joban-God Talk," *Con-flict and Narrative: Explorations in Theory and Practice* 3 (2015) 1–21. He is also a co-author with Joseph Duggan of *Knowledge Activism Beyond Theory: A Worldwide Call for Action* (Borderless Press, 2016) and various other articles in edited volumes.

Acknowledgments

The editors and publishers wish to acknowledge the journals and books where these essays were published in earlier forms:

Chapter 1: **Musa W. Dube**, "Consuming A Colonial Cultural Bomb: Translating 'Badimo' into 'Demons' in Setswana Bible" was first published in *Journal for the Study of the New Testament* 73 (1999) 33–59.

Chapter 2: **Aloo Mojola**, "Postcolonial Translation Theory and the Swahili Bible" was first published in *Bible Translation & African Languages*, edited by Gosnell L. O. R. Yorke and Peter M. Renju, 77–104. Bible Translation in Africa. Nairobi: Acton, 2004.

Chapter 3: **Johnson Kiriaku Kinyua**, "A Postcolonial Analysis of Bible Translation and its Effectiveness in Shaping and Enhancing the Discourse of Colonialism and the Discourse of Resistance: The Gikuyu New Testament—A Case Study" was first published in *Black Theology: An International Journal* 11 (2013) 58–95.

CHAPTER 4: **Gomang Seratwa Ntloedibe-Kuswani**, "Translating the Divine: The Case of Modimo in the Setswana Bible" was first published in *Other Ways of Reading: African Women and the Bible,* edited by Musa Dube, 78–97. Global Perspectives on Biblical Scholarship 2. Atlanta: *Society of Biblical Literature*, 2001.

Chapter 5: **Dora R. Mbuwayesango,** "How Local Divine Powers Were Suppressed: The Case of Mwari of the Shona" was first published in *Other Ways of Reading: African Women and the Bible*, edited by Musa Dube, 63–77. Atlanta: Society of Biblical Literature, 2001.

Chapter 6: **Jeremy Punt**, "(Con)figuring Gender in Bible Translation: Cultural, Translational, and Gender Critical Intersections" was first published in *HTS Teologiese Studies/Theological Studies* 70.1 (2014) 1–10.

Chapter 7: **Musa W. Dube**, "The Bible in the Bush: The First 'Literate' Batswana Bible Readers." A longer version of this essay was first published in *Translation* 2 (2013) 79–103.

Abbreviations

BibInt	*Biblical Interpretation*
BFBS	British and Foreign Bible Society
BTB	*Biblical Theology Bulletin*
HTS	*Hervormde Teologiese Studies*
JAOS	*Journal of the American Oriental Society*
JBL	*Journal of Biblical Literature*
JIAI	*Journal of the International African Institute*
JIS	*Journal of Islamic Studies*
JRA	*Journal of Religion in Africa*
JRAS	*Journal of the Royal African Society*
JSOT	*Journal for the Study of the Old Testament*
JSNT	*Journal for the Study of the New Testament*
JT	*Journal of Translation*
JTSA	*Journal of Theology for South Africa*
KN	*Kikuyu News*
OBT	Overtures to Biblical Theology
SA	South Africa
T&S	*Theology & Sexuality*
TS	*Teologiese Studies / Theological Studies*
URJ	*UNISWA Research Journal*

INTRODUCTION

Silenced Nights, Bible Translation and the African Contact Zones

Musa W. Dube

In a hot December evening, there was an open air Christmas carol service in the main mall of Gaborone City, Botswana. I happened to be in the mall, and I happily joined the crowd, picking the handouts of Christmas hymns that were both in Setswana and English language. People sang in whatever language they felt comfortable with, or felt free to swing from one language to another. Soon we got to one of my favourite Christmas carols: "Silent Night, Holy Night."[1] I always found the melody of the hymn exceptionally beautiful; however, I was always intrigued by how the birth moment of Jesus was imagined as a "silent night!" Silence is not exactly the word to describe a moment of a woman birthing a child. Well, with the Setswana and English hymns in my hands, I began to sing along. As I looked closely into my hymns, I soon discovered that those who were singing in English were singing a different hymn from those who sang the carol in Setswana. Yes, I had known, forever, that the Setswana version begins by saying, "*Dumela Loseana*,"[2] that is, 'Hello infant" which is rather unrelated to the phrase 'Silent Night," that opens the stanzas of the English version. Yet I never thought much of it, or suspected that the whole translation had little or no relationship in meaning save for the tune, the focus on baby Jesus and one theme. Below, parallels of the English version, the Setswana Translation of Silent Night and a back to back translation of the Setswana version back into English, illustrates the point. My assumption here is that the Setswana version was translated from the English version.[3] A close

---

1. The hymn was composed by Father Joseph Mohr, (1792–1848) in German and was translated by John F. Young (1820–1885) into English.

2. "Dumela Loseana," is a Catholic Hymn 68 found in *Dithapelo le Difela tsa Bakatoloke* (Kimberly: Diocese of Kimberly, 1975) 476–77.

3. My assumption is based on the fact that the Christian mission of colonial times

scrutiny of these parallels, perhaps with the help of differently coloured high-lighters, will indicate if we have a synoptic gospels' problem, characterised by common sources here and there, sprinkled with individual uniqueness; or rather we are confronting a high Christological spiritual gospel of the Johannine style, that rewrites the story of Jesus to focus on his origin, identity and purpose. Or, are we even further down the road, confronting a Pauline's style that focuses on the death and resurrection of Jesus, without discussing his deeds and words.

The parallels of these translations are as follows:

English Translation Version	Setswana Translation	Back to Back Translation
Stanza 1	**Stanza 1**	**Stanza 1**
Silent night, holy night;	Dumela Loseana!	Hello infant
all is calm, all is bright;	O tswa kae, mme O mang?	Where are you from and who are you?
round yon virgin mother and child;	Ke tswa kgalalelong ya ga rre	I come from the glory of my Father
Holy infant, so tender and mild;	Ke tlogetse bogosi jame	I left my kingship
sleep in heavenly peace;	Ke Modimo morwa	I am God the son
sleep in heavenly peace.	Ke mmoloki wa lona	I am your saviour
Stanza 2	**Stanza 2**	**Stanza 2**
Silent night, holy night,	Dumela Loseana!	Hello infant
shepherds quake at the sight;	Ene Rraago ke mang?	Who is your Father?
glories stream from heaven afar, heavenly hosts sing Alleluia!	Rre ke motlhodi wa lefatshe	My Father is the Creator of the World
Christ the Savior is born,	Kgarebana Maria ke mme	Virgin Mary is my Mother
Christ the Savior is born!	Ke ngwana wa Modimo	I am a child of God
	Mme ke ngwana wa Motho	Yet also a child of a Human Being

in Botswana were largely, although not exclusively, English-based.

English Translation Version	Setswana Translation	Back to Back Translation
Stanza 3	**Stanza 3**	**Stanza 3**
Silent night, holy night,	Dumela Loseana!	Hello Infant
Son of God, love's pure light;	Otsile go dirang?	What have you come to do?
radiant beams from thy holy face	Go lo swela mo sefapanong	To die for you on the cross
with the dawn of redeeming grace,	Go boloka mewa tatlhegong	To save lost souls
Jesus, Lord, at thy birth,	Ke tsile go fenya baba botlhe ba lona	To conquer all your enemies
Jesus, Lord, at thy birth.		
Stanza 4	**Stanza 4**	**Stanza 4**
Silent night, holy night,	Dumela loseana!	Hello infant!
wondrous star, lend thy light;	O rata batho jang!	O how you love people
with the angels let us sing,	Ammaruri go go tshwanetse	Truly it suits you
Alleluia to our King;	Gore dipobiwa tsa lefatshe	That all creatures of the world
Christ the Savior is born,	Di go rate tsotlhe	Should all love you
Christ the Savior is born	Ka boinelo jotlhe	With all submission

A Talkative Baby Breaks the Silent Night

A close reading of the above parallels, indicates that whereas the English version of silent "Silent Night" described the night of Jesus' birth as "silent, holy, calm, bright, where a young mother and child were, and whereas it sought to describe the child, as tender and mild and to wish them a restful night, a back translation of the Setswana version into English is a world away from such a night. Yes it focuses on the baby Jesus, but not on the night of his birth. The first stanza of the Setswana version seeks to identify the origin and identity of the child, and certainly not on its silence. It assumes a narrative dialogue, where the child is greeted (hello infant/*Dumela Loseana*) and asked questions (where are you from?) And the child answers back, clarifying his identity, origin and purpose (I come from the glory of my father; I left my kinship, I am God the son; I am your saviour). The implied singer becomes the shadow dialogue partner with the infant—addressing, but above all being addressed by the infant.

Intrigued, we follow this Setswana version translator's rewriting to the second stanza. Here the English version of Silent Night zeros into the Lukan birth narratives (2:1-7) that speak of shepherds, glories from heaven and the praise of heavenly hosts, for "Christ the Savoir is born" on that night. The second stanza of Setswana version, on the other hand, features an articulate infant in dialogue with the implied singer/reader/audience. Again the implied singer/reader/audience begins by greeting the infant (*dumela loseana*) and takes up the subjects introduced by the infant in stanza one, asking: "Who is your father?" and the infant gives a rather long response that covers the rest of the stanza: "My Father is the Creator of the World. Virgin Mary is my Mother. I am a Child of God, yet I am also a child of a human being." No doubt infant Jesus is a theological giant discussing such concepts as soteriology, Christology and incarnation.

In the third stanza the implied interlocutor of the Setswana version of Silent Night salute (*dumela loseana*) the articulate baby Jesus and asks him a purpose-related question: "What have you come to do?" And baby Jesus responds, "To die for you on the cross; to save lost souls, I have come to conquer all your enemies." The third stanza of the English version of Silent Night, on the other hand, speaks of the "radiant beams of thy holy face, with dawn of redeeming grace; Jesus Lord at thy birth." It is a lofty praise-focused stanza. In the fourth stanza[4] of the Setswana version of silent night, baby Jesus is finally silent! The implied interlocutor salutes Jesus (*dumela loseana*) but he says nothing. Unperturbed the implied dialogue partner, exclaims, "Oh how you love people! Truly it suits you that all creatures of the world should love you, with all submission"! The implied singer/listener is now a convert, who invites others to the same path, declaring that "all creatures of the world should love and submit to Jesus!" The fourth stanza of English version, still insisting that it's a silent night, praises baby Jesus as a "wondrous star" and invites him to lend his light "with the dawn of redeeming grace," and turning from the child to the implied audience/people/singers,

---

4. Access to the original translation of Bishop John Young indicates that he had translated three stanzas. The fourth stanza is an addition whose author/translator is not known.

says, "With the angels let us sing alleluia to our King, Christ the Savior is born!"

The above case confirms what Translations Studies investigations have found; namely, that all translations are re/writings of the original text and that translators are writers, who are always driven by purpose, patrons, publishers, context, politics, ideologies, cultures, among other various factors, on the kind of re/writings they make. The power factor is central. Consequently, a major question is: to what degree does a particular translation rewrite its source text and what are the underlying forces? It is not a question of whether one can rewrite in translation, or not rewrite, rather it is a question of measuring the forms of rewritings, their ideological underpinnings and the power houses that propel particular translations, while discouraging certain types.

Accordingly, I became curious to find out how the first translator of Stille Nacht began the translator's journey of writing. The synoptic parallels again came handy, giving the reader a quick view and opportunity for close analysis. For the sake of those who cannot fully read German I asked my friend and colleague, Johanna Stiebert[5] to translate the original Stille Nacht, so Bishop Young's first translation into English and its writely moves can be observed.

The parallels are as follows:

Original Composition	First English Translation	Johanna Stiebert Translation
Stille nacht! Heilige Nacht! Alles schläft; einsam wacht Nur das traute heilige Paar. Holder Knab im lockigten Haar, Schlafe in himmlischer Ruh! Schlafe in himmlischer Ruh!	Silent night, holy night; all is calm, all is bright; round yon virgin mother and child; Holy infant, so tender and mild; sleep in heavenly peace; sleep in heavenly peace.	Silent/still night! Holy night! All is asleep; keeping a lonely watch is only the dear holy couple; beautiful boy-child with curled hair; Sleep in heavenly silence/stillness Sleep in heavenly silence/stillness

5. I am grateful to Stephanie Feder who also sent me her own translation of the "Stille Nacht."

Original Composition	First English Translation	Johanna Stiebert Translation
2. Stille Nacht! Heilige Nacht! Gottes Sohn, o wie lacht Lieb´ aus deinem göttlichen Mund, Da schlägt uns die rettende Stund. Jesus in deiner Geburt! Jesus in deiner Geburt!	Silent night, holy night, shepherds quake at the sight; glories stream from heaven afar, heavenly hosts sing Alleluia! Christ the Savior is born, Christ the Savior is born!	Silent/still night! Holy night Son of God, oh how it laughs forth dearly from your divine mouth that is when the saving hour chimes. Jesus in your birth/nativity Jesus in your birth/nativity!
3. Stille Nacht! Heilige Nacht! Die der Welt Heil gebracht, Aus des Himmels goldenen Höhn Uns der Gnaden Fülle läßt sehn: Jesum in Menschengestalt, Jesum in Menschengestalt	Silent night, holy night, Son of God, love's pure light; radiant beams from thy holy face with the dawn of redeeming grace, Jesus, Lord, at thy birth, Jesus, Lord, at thy birth.	Silent/still night! Holy night! Which brought to the world salvation/wholeness From the heaven's golden height letting us see mercy's fullness Jesus in human form Jesus in human form
4. Stille Nacht! Heilige Nacht! Wo sich heut alle Macht Väterlicher Liebe ergoß Und als Bruder huldvoll umschloß Jesus die Völker der Welt, Jesus die Völker der Welt.		Silent/still night! Holy night! Wherein today all might flowed forth fatherly love and a brother he graciously embraced Jesus the peoples of the world Jesus the peoples of the world

Original Composition	First English Translation	Johanna Stiebert Translation
5. Stille Nacht! Heilige Nacht! Lange schon uns bedacht, Als der Herr vom Grimme befreit In der Väter urgrauer Zeit Aller Welt Schonung verhieß, Aller Welt Schonung verhieß.		Still/Silent Night, Holy Night from long ago considerate of us wherein the Lord freed from grimness back in the distant times of the (fore) fathers predicting salvation for all the world ;Predicting salvation for all the world
6. Stille Nacht! Heilige Nacht! Hirten erst kundgemacht Durch der Engel Alleluja, Tönt es laut bei Ferne und Nah: Jesus der Retter ist da! Jesus der Retter ist da!		Silent night! Holy night! shepherds were first to proclaim through the angels' hallelujah it chimes loudly far and near Jesus the saviour is here Jesus the saviour is here!

Armed with multi-colored highlighters, one can now read the parallels from a synoptic problem approach. Here one assumes there were source/s that were used by the author (Bishop Young) and seeks to analyze how the source/s were used. It is assumed that Bishop Young's source was the original German composition by Father Mohr. As Johanna Stiebert's translation indicates, in the first stanza, Bishop Young kept the first lines, "Silent Night, Holy night" and the last ones; namely, "sleep in heavenly peace or stillness." He omitted the middle part, chopping off the beautiful boy's curly hair and replacing it with emphasis on calmness and brightness around the mother and child—a child who is described as tender and mild. In stanza two, Bishop Young's translation is best related to stanza six of the original composition, where shepherds and angels are mentioned. The last refrain, "Christ the savior is born" seems drawn from original stanza two, but with an addition of "savior," drawn from the stanza 6. In the Bishop Young's third stanza, what is drawn from the original source is the introductory refrain (Silent night, holy night) and the closing one (Jesus Lord at your birth). The middle part, as in the first stanza, is best seen as Bishop Young's addition. He speaks of "Son of God, love's pure light; radiant beams from his holy face, bringing, I presume, with it "the dawn of redeeming grace." On top to his omissions (of sentences and sections), additions, rearrangements, Bishop Young omitted three stanzas from the original source, as illustrated by the blank cubes in the parallels. An very common part of translational rewritings is to omit chunks of main sources, sometimes because they are held to be unacceptable to the new audience. Returning to address the synoptic problem of these translations; one asks the why questions: namely, why did Bishop Young, as an author-translator omit some aspects of the original source; add some of them and re-arrange others? What is his theological stand point and what informs it? Although, these questions demand that one must dig into Bishop Young's personal theology, socio-political context and his community of faith, narratively, one can discern a particular theological stance from his translation. The translation, it seems to me, sought to underline awe and glory of Jesus' arrival and his identity, which dramatically differs from the motivation of the Setswana translation.

In the above Setswana translation of Silent Night, the translator wrote in a colonial context and his/her driving interest was the economy of Christian conversion of the Other.[6] The Setswana translation was thus composed as a conversational pedagogical piece that seeks to instruct the implied Botswana reader/singer/audience about the origin, identity and purpose of Christ for them—as salvation. The hymn triumphatically ends with the anticipated Botswana singer/reader/audience who has been converted by baby Jesus now declaring, "*all* creatures of the world should *all* love you with *all* submission." Emphasis added. Cases of biblical translations as rewritings of both the original source and the target cultures guided by the economy of Christian conversion of the Other include, for example, the case of translating Badimo (Ancestors) into demons in the Setswana Bible (see the first chapter of this book); the case of translating Ngoma of the Kikuyu of Kenya into the devil (see Johnson Kinyua's chapter) and the case Latin American case analysed by David Caroll, which held that Panare killed Jesus.[7]

Whereas there are numerous reasons behind a translation of any text and various underlying power relations guiding them, in the modern colonial context, translation of biblical texts were driven by the economy of Christian conversion of the Other, well imbued with Eurocentric colonial perspectives. With racist Eurocentric perspectives that regarded Other cultures as inferior, to use a mild term, and deserving to be erased and replaced by the colonisers' cultures, translation of biblical texts in the modern

6. See Leshota, "Postcolonial Reading of the Nineteenth-Century Missionary Musical Texts," for a more comprehensive analysis of translation of Christian Hymns into indigenous languages during modern colonialism in Southern Africa.

7. Caroll, "Cultural Encroachment and Biblical Translation," 39–68.

colonial contact zone, to use Mary Louise Pratt's phrase, are therefore a theatrical performance of a colonial drama on the stage. Phil Noss points out that the Bible is the most translated book on earth (2007:1) while Giles Gravelle points out that it was during the height of modern colonialism that the bible was translated the most (2010:1-20). A combination of these observations is significant for research in biblical translation in the modern colonial contact zones.[8] Pratt defined the contact zone " the space of colonial encounters, the space in which people geographically and historically separated come into contact with each other to establish ongoing relations, usually involving conditions of cohesion, radical inequality, and intractable conflict."[1] She holds that contact zones are "social spaces where disparate cultures meet, clash, and grapple with each other, often in highly asymmetrical relations of domination and subordination—-like colonialism, slavery, or their aftermaths as they are lived out across the globe today."[9]

Contact zones are in-between spaces, generating hybrid identities and cultures. Colonial contact zones, as places where different cultures clash, are also unavoidably translational spaces, that seek to translate the colonised people, cultures and their lands into a new image of the coloniser. Such translations are neither copies of the original nor the targeted culture; rather they become new hybrid re-writings as attested by the above hymn. Since all translations are cases of various levels of power struggles between different forces, colonial Bible translations allow us to investigate the rewriting of other cultures, but also how the Other begun to re-write the translations and the translators for their own ends.[10] How have and how do biblical translation power struggles intersect with other cultures, race, gender, class, ethnicity, religion, anthropology, politics, geography in the contact zones are some of the questions addressed in translation studies and in this volume.

This volume is therefore, a transdisciplinary,[11] transnational and intersectional postcolonial approach to translated biblical texts. The volume represents an academic journey that began in 1995, when I accidentally discovered that colonial ideology had impacted biblical translations.[12] An

---

8. See Maluleke, "The Next Phase in the Vernacular Bible Discourse," 355–74.

9. Pratt, *Imperial Eyes*, 6.

10. See Dube, "Translating *Ngaka*," 157–72, on how the Batswana audience of Robert Moffat began to translate him, his books (Bible) and practices of healing or preaching into their cultural categories, regarding him (and his Jesus) as a *ngaka* (the indigenous healer), his preaching as divination, and his books as a divination set.

11. According to Arduini and Nergaard, "Translation," 8–15, "transdisciplinary opens up closed disciplines and inquires into translational features," 9

12. Dube, Consuming a Colonial Bomb Translating *Badimo* into 'Demons' in the Setswana Bible," *JSNT* 73 (1999) 33–59.

attempt to carry out a continent wide investigation, a decade and half ago, failed due to lack of biblically trained specialists on the continent.[13] However, in this past two decades, the number of academically trained African biblical scholars has been rising enabling this collection. It is to be expected that this volume contributes towards opening a crucial research area in the African continent and other continents postcoloniality and biblical translation. It features both established and young emerging scholars of the Bible.

While Translation Studies has grown into a huge academic discipline in the past four decades, studying translated works and taking a cultural turn (and several other turns), and although, as Phil Noss asserts that the Bible is the most translated book, both in time and space (2006:1), Translation Studies are yet to catch fire in mainstream biblical studies. Among mainstream biblical studies, there are handful volumes, which are few and far apart, that have been emerging. These include *Semeia Studies 76 edited* by Randall Bailey, Tina Pippin, RS Sugirtharajah, et al. *Race, Class, and the Politics of Bible Translation*. Atlanta, GA: Scholars Press, 1996; Athalya Brenner and Henten Jan W van, eds. *Bible Translation on the Threshold of the Twenty-First Century: Authority, Reception, Culture and Religion*. London, and New York, NY: Sheffield Academic Press, 2002; Semeia Studies 69 volume by Elliot, Scott S., and Roland Boer. *Ideology, Culture, and Translation*. Atlanta, GA: Society of Biblical Literature, 2012. The bulk of research in biblical studies is largely left to translation houses and their scholars, with limited interest from mainstream biblical studies. But given that the Bible has been widely translated over a wide space, time and under unequal power relations and across various cultures, translation studies, is minefield that is yet to be opened in biblical studies. This disinterest at best highlights that biblical studies remain Eurocentric, without fully taking into consideration the multiple boundaries that have been crossed by biblical texts, as well as the implication of biblical journeys for its academic study. This volume seeks to contribute towards this largely neglected area in mainstream biblical studies and to add to the above listed volumes.

Some Thematic Summaries of Sections

This volume is arranged in three sections although they overlap on several themes. The first section, consisting of three papers (Dube, Mojola and Johnson Kinyua), investigates the colonial context that generated most sub-Saharan Bibles. These papers analysis looks at various accompanying texts such

13. My call for papers ended up with only two papers: Seratwa Ntloedibe-Kuswani and Dora Mbuwayesango's paper featured in the second part of this volume.

as African languages, dictionaries, newsletters among others, thus placing the production of the translation of biblical text within wider literary and political contexts and the power dynamics that characterised the time. Aloo Mojola's paper, focusing on the historical and cultural setting that generated the Swahili Bible is an awesome investigation of multiple intersections over time and space. Swahili as hybrid Bantu language and culture, robing in many languages from the Arabs, Persia, Hindustan, Gujarat, Turkey, Malaysia, Portugal, Germany and the UK, made translation of the Bible a unique case to observe, given the colonial attitudes towards African concepts and languages, and how there was a shift of translational approaches from one missionary house to another and over different times. This was characterised by a tendency to over use Arabic words and religious concepts, to the extent that indigenous people could not read their own Swahili, which simultaneously led other missionaries to undertake counter translations—a process that kept going in circles. The best translations however, always had to contend with the prevailing power struggles in the region.

The second section features three papers (Ntloedibe Kuswani, Mbuwayesango and Punt). As said above, most Sub-Saharan biblical translations took place during the modern colonial period. But one must also underline that they were largely carried out by western male missionaries, who brought their own patriarchal perspective to African cultures. Many of these translations are being, or have already been, revised in various places mostly by indigenous male translators, under the tutelage of the former colonizers and their institutionalized theories. It follows that postcoloniality and patriarchy are central areas of research in African biblical translation studies. Chapters in this section, therefore, investigate the colonial and patriarchal translation theories, (See Seratwa Ntloedibe-Kuswani; Dora Mbuwayesango and Jeremy Punt's papers) renderings and their impact on the readers and their cultures, languages and gender relations. Some chapters chose some biblical passages to illustrate their cases and to highlight the changes made by colonial and patriarchal translators or by indigenous revisions.

Western feminist biblical scholars have problematized the male gender assigned to God's name, nouns, pronouns, metaphors and images in the English biblical translations.[14] Underlining that God is neither male nor female, they pointed out that the use of male gender in Bible translations maintains women's oppression and exclusion from social power. Suggestions for gender inclusive translations were proposed. Gender inclusive translation of God's name has, perhaps, found less acceptance, although gender

14. See Dube, "Towards Postcolonial Feminist Translations of the Bible," 215–39.

inclusive bible translations are available.[15] In most African cultures the De-
ity/God was not gendered as discussed by the papers of Seratwa Ntloedibe,
Dora Mbuwayesango and my opening paper of this volume. Colonial biblical translations, however, introduced male gender to the African Deity/
God and spiritual space. The process patriarchalized religious and social
spaces that were gender inclusive or flexible. The use of indigenous names
in biblical translations also became a tool of colonization that dispossessed
indigenous religions/cultures of their Deities, as some of the chapters in this
volume highlight, particularly Dora Mbuwayesango's paper.

The third section seeks to explore savage techniques of reading colonised African hybridised Biblical texts. Given that trained scholars of the
Bible in Africa began to emerge slowly in the past two decades, African
academic investigations of colonial translations are a new area of study.
Logically, the initial stage, which is yet to be fully explored, largely focuses
on exposing the colonial discourse and its representations of the Other in
biblical translations, as well as seeks to expose the power relationships that
informed colonial biblical translations. An area that is yet to be creatively
explored is the Third-Text, the hybridized-inculturated translations that are
results of colonial subversions; the use of African languages (that can only
inevitably bring in the feared African cultures into the Bible) and the indigenous readers' strategies. The third part of this volume, seeks to explore
how the use of African languages and concepts are inevitably rewriting the
biblical text and giving it a new meaning. Savage readings therefore seek
to courageously and creatively give interpretations of colonial Bibles that
highlight the multiple border-crossing of African cultural beliefs into the
translated biblical text and underline how African cultures have and continue to translate the meaning/use/impact of the biblical text in the process.
Such readings also depend on the oral cultures that African readers bring to
the text in the process of reading and the efforts of African creative writers,
who have attempted to wrest the translated biblical text from its colonizing
use. More work and creativity is needed in this area than stated by these
lines or represented in this volume.

Nonetheless, savage readings are illustrated by various papers in the
volume. In part one, whereas my paper, described colonial imbued bible
translations as tantamount to serving the colonised with a colonial bomb
for consumption meant to destroy their cultures, at the end of my research
it became clear that there were savage ways of eating up a bomb that is
supposed to destroy you. And so consuming a colonial bomb become a

---

15. A good example is The *New Testament and Psalms: An Inclusive Version* (New
York: Oxford University Press, 1995).

posture of savage resistance, as the readers insist on reading the colonial loaded versions in the process bringing in the Badimo (Ancestors) not as demons, but as friends with Jesus, together in the business of healing and empowering people. This strategy of reading used the Bible as a divination tool to diagonise people's life concerns and struggles and divination in the African cultures includes communing with Badimo (Ancestors). Healing people includes communing with Badimo (Ancestors) that is, reconciling people with the memories of their living dead community. Consuming a colonial cultural bomb through using the bible as divination tool thus becomes one savage way of handling a dangerous text that is supposed to explode your cultural beliefs and identity by finding ways of eating up a bomb. Consequently Johnson Kiriaku Kinyua argues that "translation . . . sometimes becomes a space of re-empowerment, transforming ordinary readers from passive victims of translation to active translators." Johnson Kiriaku Kinyua's a paper (featured in this volume), illustrates some examples of savage ways of reading by focusing on "ordinary readers," who assumed different ways of confronting colonial and colonising Bible. This includes the case of Charles M Kareri and Bildad Kaggia, who took it upon themselves to be active translators and to present their translations to translating houses, contesting overt colonial strategies.

As R. S. Wafula's concluding paper underlines, the resource of oral African cultures is a major base for counter-active savage readings. This best illustrated in my paper, "Bible in the Bush: The First literate Readers of the Bible," on how the Tiv of Nigeria took and rewrote *Hamlet* from Laura Bohannan to a point of no recognition, using their cultural perspective. The paper goes on to show that while the Batswana had no opportunity to participate in Robert Moffat's Setswana translation process, they protested at the translation's take of their language and concepts. Receiving an outright rejection from the concerned London Missionary Society led them to write back, asserting, "You should know that when we read our bibles, we change the words with our mouth! This savage strategy of reading denies that any written translation is final, nor does it have a final authority. Rather, the readers remain at liberty to rewrite the text on each point of reading using their mouths and drawing from their oral cultures. As long as oral cultures are alive in the memories of colonised communities, they remain a power house fuelling the consuming of the colonial cultural bombs in biblical translations.

Malebogo Kgalemang's chapter in this volume on novel translations presents another strategy of savage translations. Colonial and colonizing translations have been a fortress of carefully guarded practices that consists of western sponsors, well-resourced translation houses that have money and trained resource persons to carry out biblical translations worldwide as part of evangelism. The strategies of controlling the type of translation also included training their translators and consultants on particular ways of translating be its literal, formal or dynamic equivalence. Most translation consultants in the African translation projects still fly in from western metropolitan centres to check and validate translations carried out by mother-tongue personnel. Biblical translations have thus remained thoroughly centralised and proceeding according to the ideological posture of sponsoring translation houses. Anything to the contrary could be suppressed as illustrated by Bildad Kaggia's New Testament translations which Kinyua points out that, "it is not known if Kaggia's translation was ever considered." Novel translations, however, disburse with the hedged Bible translations by using the creative writing space and strategy to unleash savage translations of the biblical text. Ngugi wa Thiongo's novel translations, for example, are unbound by biblical translation houses. Kgalemang chapter highlights how Ngugi rewrites major Christian concepts and images, such as the cross and salvation. In the place of Jesus on the cross, he puts the devil on the cross. The description of the devil strongly befriends a white British colonial gentleman with his walking stick. In taking Jesus off the cross and sticking the devil on the cross, whose description is akin to a British white coloniser, Ngugi makes savage translation of the biblical story and Christian salvation. He argues that Jesus did not or does not deserve to be on the cross, rather the coloniser/imperialism must be crucified. If the coloniser is crucified, then the world will be saved from its evil power. Novel translations of the Bible in the African postcolonial context remain a major research area to explore and the strategies of resistance it offers.[16]

Pedagogical Implications

As I said elsewhere,[17] the postcolonial context and the historical dominance of colonised Bible translations have pedagogical implications. Whereas academic biblical studies were horned in the western centres, coincidentally during modern colonial times, postcoloniality demands that African biblical programs should review their programs. Western based academic

---

16. See Dube, Mbuvi, and Mbuwayesango, eds. *Postcolonial Perspectives in African Biblical Interpretations* (Atlanta: Society of Biblical Literature, 2012) 75–154.

17. See Dube, "The Scramble for Africa as the Biblical Scramble for Africa: Postcolonial Perspectives," Postcolonial Perspectives in African Biblical Interpretations (eds., Musa. W. Dube, Andrew Mbuvi, and Dora Mbuwayesango Atlanta: Society of Biblical Literature, 2012), 11–14.

biblical studies are Eurocentric, demanding that students should learn, on top of the ancient biblical languages, two more European languages. This leaves African students more versed in western languages than their own, a factor which makes them less competent to read their own Bibles and analyse them. In the light of the findings of Bible translations—and the fact that more work still needs to be done on both colonial Bibles and their revisions, it should be required that African Bible scholars should learn two African languages that were first used to translate the Bible in their regions. Further, in the globalised world, contact zones are ever multiplying, creating diasporised communities that live in the translational zone. Translation studies should no longer be in the periphery of African and biblical studies as a whole.

Bibliography

Arduini, Stefano, and Siri Nergaard. "Translation: A New Paradigm." *Translation Inaugural Issue* (2011) 8–15.

Bailey, Randall, et al. *Race, Class and Politics of Biblical Translation*. Semeia 76. Atlanta: Society Biblical Literature, 1996.

Benner, Athalya, and Jan W. van Henten. *Bible Translation on Threshold of the Twenty-First Century: Authority Reception and Religion*. Sheffield: Sheffield Academic, 2002.

Bohannan, Laura. "Shakespeare in the Bush." *Natural History* (1966) 1–14.

Carroll, Robert P. "Cultural Encroachment and Bible Translation: Observations on Elements of Violence, Race, and Class in Production of Bibles in Translation." *Semeia* 76 (1996) 39–54.

Dube, Musa W. "Consuming A Colonial Cultural Bomb: Translating *Badimo* into 'Demons' in the Setswana Bible." *Journal for the Study of the New Testament 73* (1999) 33–59.

————. "Towards Postcolonial Feminist Translations of the Bible." In *Reading Ideologies: Essays in Honor of Mary Ann Tolbert*, edited by Tat Siong Benny Liew, 215–39. Bible in the Modern World 40. Sheffield: Sheffield Phoenix, 2011.

Dube, Musa W., et al., eds. *Postcolonial Perspectives in African Biblical Interpretations*. Atlanta: Society of Biblical Literature, 2012.

Gentzler, Edwin. *Contemporary Translation Theories*. 2nd ed. Clevedon: Multilingual Matters, 2001.

Gravelle, Gilles. "Bible Translation in Historical Context: The Changing Role of Cross-Cultural Workers." *International Journal of Frontier Missiology* 27.1 (2010) 1–20.

Leshota, Paul. "Postcolonial Reading of the Nineteenth-Century Missionary Musical Texts." In *Black Theology International Journal* 12 (2014) 139–60.

Maluleke, Tinyiko S. "The Next Phase in the Vernacular Bible Discourse: Echoes From Hamanskraal." *Missionalia* 33 (2005) 355–74.

Noss, Phillip A., ed. A *History of Bible Translation*. Rome: Edizioni di Storia e Letteratura, 2007.

Pratt, Mary Louise. *Imperial Eyes: Travel Writing and Transculturation*. New York: Routledge, 1992.

PART I

The Colonial Discourse and African Bible Translations

1

Consuming a Colonial Cultural Bomb

Translating *Badimo* into "Demons" in the Setswana Bible[1]
(Matthew 8:28–34; 15:22; 10:8)

Musa W. Dube

> The domain in which the encounter with the mission made its deepest inroads into Setswana consciousness was that of literacy and learning. Those who chose to peruse the Setswana Bible learned more than the sacred story, more even than how to read. They were subjected to a form of cultural translation in which vernacular poetics were re-presented to them as a thin *sekgoa* narrative—and their language itself reduced to an instrument of imperial knowledge.[2]

Introduction: Language and the Art of Colonizing Minds and Spaces

Because colonizers tend to install their languages among the colonized, thus displacing the local ones, the subject of language is central to Postcolonial debates.[3] Questions such as why do the colonizers give their languages to their subjects? What happens to the languages of the colonized? What is lost when the colonized begin to speak, read and write in the colonizer's language and neglect own language? What strategies are adopted by the colonized to resist the imposition of the colonizer's language? These questions remain central to postcolonial debates. Frantz Fanon, a postcolonial critic of the sixties, addressed the issue of language back then. Fanon opened his book, *Black Skin, White Masks,* with a chapter on "where he stated that

---

1. The word Setswana denotes the language and culture of Botswana. The inhabitants, on the other hand, are Batswana (plural) and Motswana (singular).

2. Comaroff and Comaroff, *Of Revelation and Revolution,* 311.

3. Ashcroft, et al., *The Empire Writes Back,* 38–59.

3

he "ascribe [s] a basic importance to the phenomenon of language,"[4] for to speak a language is not only to use its syntax or to grasp its morphology, but it is 'above all to assume a culture, to support a civilization.'[5] Thirty years later, Ngugi wa Thiongo, one of the present-day postcolonial critics, echoes Fanon when he maintains that 'language carries culture, and culture carries the entire body of values by which we come to perceive our place in the world."[6] Their statements speak for themselves insofar as the imposition of the colonizer's language on the colonized and the loss of their own languages are concerned. The colonized, who speak, read and write in the colonizer's language, adopt the culture of their subjugators. They begin to perceive the world from the perspective of the subjugators. In this way, the colonizer takes possession of the geographical spaces and the minds of the colonized. The imposition of the language of the colonizer is thus an effective instrument for colonizing the minds of the subjugated, for it alienates them from their own cultures. On these grounds, Ngugi holds that:

> The biggest weapon wielded and actually daily unleashed by imperialism against that collective defiance [of the colonized] is the cultural bomb. The effect of a bomb is to annihilate a people's belief in their names, in their languages, in their environment, in their heritage of struggle, in their unity, in their capacities and ultimately in themselves.[7]

Ngugi describes colonization as a violent undertaking that proceeds by demolishing the cultural world views of the colonized. The suppression of their cultures "makes them want to see their past as one wasteland of non-achievement and it makes them want to distance themselves from that wasteland."[8] Describing the violence of colonialism on native cultures, Fanon holds that "Every colonized people—in other words, every people in whose soul an inferiority complex has been created by death and burial of its local cultural originality—finds itself face to face with the language of the civilizing nations."[9] Fanon equates colonization with the "death and burial" of one's culture. Fanon also regards the suppression of colonized cultures as a means to an end: it leaves the colonized confronted by the culture or

---

4. Fanon, *Black Skin, White Mask*, 17.

5. Ibid., 17–18.

6. Ngũgĩ wa Thiong'o, *Decolonising*, 16.

7. Ibid., 3.

8. Ibid.

9 Fanon, *Black Skin, White Mask*, 18.

the language of their subjugator. It serves, therefore, to clear the way for the implantation of the colonizers' language or culture.

Evidently, the explosion of the colonial cultural bomb shatters and alienates the colonial subjects from themselves, their lands and their cultures. But, more importantly, cultural colonization has ensured that the colonizers remain in power regardless of whether geographical and political independence has been won by colonized, or not. It ensures that the institutions of the colonized are generally permeated by the colonizer's world view, for the colonized subjects themselves embody the values of their subjugator and become the instruments of their own colonization. Language which is the crucible of culture is the effective instrument that constructs the colonized subject, as imitators, devotees and ambassadors of their oppressors, but, of course, not as equal subjects. This structural construction of the colonized subjects has indeed ensured that long after the colonizer's departure and absence from the former colonies, their domination is freely furthered by the colonized on themselves. It is also this aspect of colonialism that makes Postcolonial reading of texts a necessary exercise in what seems to be a largely post-independence era.

In this paper, I will examine the use of language to colonize from a slightly different angle. Most postcolonial debates focus on the imposition of the colonizer's language on the colonized, its impact on the colonized and the strategies of resistance, but I will examine the use of the language of the colonized to subjugate them. I will be examining "the colonization of local language[s]"[10] such that they no longer serve the interest of their original cultures, but indeed, become weapons that victimize the original speakers. This examination will look at the translations and definitions of words in the Setswana Bible and dictionaries, which were first carried out by London Missionary Society (henceforth, LMS) agents between 1829 and 1925. The first Setswana Bible and dictionary were subsequently revised by many other LMS agents and church missionaries of other societies. This paper will limit itself to the LMS work, for it was the most influential among Batswana who reside in the present-day Botswana. Although this paper will be specific to Botswana, I believe that such an investigation will be of interest to many other former colonized subjects who read colonial biblical translations and interpretations.

In assessing the colonization of the Setswana language, I will focus on the biblical and dictionary translations and definitions of "Ancestors" (*Badimo*), "doctor" (*Ngaka*), "diviner" (*Ngaka ya ditaola*), "demons and devils" (*mewa ee maswe*), terms that are all somewhat related to the divine arena. I

---

10. See Comaroff and Comaroff, *Of Revelation*, 218–20.

will pay attention to the time and ideology that informed their renderings as well the readers themselves. The Bible and dictionaries are treated together for they are closely interconnected: the dictionaries drew their vocabulary from the Setswana Bible. They were highlighting the response of the colonized, for a planted colonial cultural bomb may explode, but the scattering fragments of the colonized subjects continue to proclaim their existence even in their fragmentation. Indeed, to consume a colonial cultural bomb, or anything, is also an attempt to take power over something: it is a dangerous gesture of resistance. My exposition begins with my own story as a colonized subject and how I came to discover colonizing translations of the Setswana Bible only in 1995—after least twenty years of personal and academic biblical reading.

How I Discovered *Badimo* Dressed in the Skins of Demons

I was lucky to do my graduate studies during the reader age, when the theories of a neutral and expert reader had been sufficiently disputed in biblical studies. Taking advantage of this spirit, I returned home from my First World graduate school to read the Bible "with" Batswana women readers for my dissertation. I wanted to collect interpretations of Matt 15:21–28 and John 4:1–42 by women of African Independent Churches (henceforth, AICs).[11] These are readers with very low or no literacy skills, hence I decided to find a Setswana and Kalanga Bible for my field work.[12] I chose the local languages since most people with low levels of literacy can at least read or listen to their own languages.

Thus I first went to the Botswana Bible Society to buy Bibles. I found A. J. Wookey's Bible of 1908. Wookey's Bible was an upgraded version of Robert Moffat's Bible 1857. Wookey's Bible has remained the most popular version among Batswana ever since it's first printing. The recent 1992 Morolong Bible, which was produced by a group of Batswana, has yet to establish itself against Wookey's Bible of 1908. The second one was Sandilands' Setswana New Testament, which was launched in 1957 and was completed in 1970. The latter was sanctioned for centenary celebration of Robert Moffat's first Setswana Bible of 1857. The Sandilands version was accomplished through a number of Setswana scholars such as Moabi Kitchen. It is readable, for it is written in the orthography of the Setswana language

---

11. See Dube, "Readings of *Semoya*," 111–29, for some of the published account of their readings.

12. Kalanga is one of the many Bantu languages spoken in Botswana. It is different from Setswana and much closer to Shona, a language spoken in Zimbabwe.

of the present day in Botswana. Wookey's Bible, on the other hand, uses an old orthography and its Setswana language is a mixture of Sesotho and *Sepedi*, which are languages spoken in South Africa and Lesotho. The latter languages are different from the Setswana language spoken and written in present-day Botswana. It therefore made sense that I should use Sandiland's Centennial New Testament version. I also bought *Ndebo Mabuya*, a Kalanga Gospel of Mathew.

Armed with biblical texts written in the languages of my respondents, I began my fieldwork. But as soon as my Setswana speaking respondents heard me read from Sandiland's version, they said, '*O ko o mphe Baebele yame hoo. Eo ga ke utlwe sentle*', that is, 'Let me get my own Bible. I do not properly understand the Bible you are reading'. And yet this was the Bible written in our present-day Setswana language! What they brought out was Wookey's Bible. Here one must imagine a present-day English reader who maintains that they understand the King James Version better than contemporary versions. Similarly, when I read out *Ndebo Mbuyo* to my Kalanga respondents, my listeners/readers said, *Aito iwa. Maditole Baebele yangu*, that is, "I cannot understand that Bible. Let me get my own." Once again, they brought Wookey's Bible with its foreign and difficult Setswana language. This was particularly amazing, for most elderly Kalanga people are not good Setswana speakers. Moreover, most Kalanga speakers take great pride in their language, and they do not like to speak Setswana, which is our national language. In the case of these Kalanga readers, one must imagine a present-day non-English speaker who insists that s/he can understand the King James Version much better than modern English versions. While I had thought my respondents would welcome their own languages and understand them better, I had grossly miscalculated. My respondents had a close intimacy with Wookey's Bible, and reasonably so, for it had been the main Bible among Batswana for the past eighty years.

I must say I had always known that in many AICs in Botswana the South African languages, which were first used to translate the Bible, had become languages of worship. Many non-Sotho and non-Ndebele speakers of Botswana preach and pray in these languages once they enter church. Nonetheless, I did not expect readers/hearers to insist on these languages even when their own languages are now available in written forms. This, however, is a graphic example of what depending on a language other than your own at an institutional level can do to a reader. These AICs readers can rightfully be said to be regionally, colonized.

I went back to the Botswana Bible Society and bought Wookey's Bible for my fieldwork research. But here a minefield awaited me. I had trodden on dangerous and deadly ground. I found out that where the Canaanite woman said, "My daughter is severely possessed by demons," in Matt 15:22, it was translated *morwadiake o chwenwa thata ke Badimo, That is, "my daughter is severely possessed by the High Ones or Ancestors."* I was stunned. The word *Badimo* literally means the "High Ones" or "Ancestral Sprits" in Setswana cultures. *Badimo* are sacred personalities who are mediators between God and the living in Setswana cultures. They consist of dead members of the society and very old members of the family who are attributed divine status and sacred roles. *Badimo* hold the welfare of their survivors at heart, both at individual and community level. They bless the living and make sure that they are well provided for and successfully in their plans. They also punish those who neglect their social responsibilities and taboos, by removing their protective eye and leaving the concerned individual or society open to the attack of evil forces. In addition, that institution of *Badimo* serves as an institution of social memories cannot be overemphasized. *Badimo* are the thread that connects the present society and families with their past and are kept alive and actively involved in the events of contemporary society. *Badimo* therefore are sacred beings who regulate the norms of the society and ensure its stability or health. Yet here, in Wookey's Setswana Bible of 1908, the *Badimo* had been translated into "demons" and "devils."[13]

But this late discovery on my part begs an explanation. If Wookey's Bible had been in circulation for more than 80 years and had remained the main Bible until 1995, why had I not known that *Badimo* were devils and demons in the Setswana Bible despite my long years of reading the Bible? The answer to these questions points to my own colonization, which involved both church and academic structures.

To begin with my educational story: although I went to the so-called Setswana medium schools, all the subjects were taught in English except for the Setswana language itself. Like most students who undergo this national system of education, by the time I finished high school I found it easier to read and write in English than in Setswana. The problem of being a slow Setswana reader was further compounded by the fact that the circulating local Bible was written in a foreign Setswana and an old orthography. Further, my mother language is Ndebele and not Setswana. I could not be bothered

---

13. Although I had no access to Robert Moffat's original Setswana Bible, secondary sources trace the translation of *Badimo* into "demons" to him. See, for example, Comaroff and Comaroff, *Of Revolution*, 218. Further, Wookey, does not use the word *Badimo* for demons in the translated text of Mathew in his commentary, *Phuthololo Ea Efangeleo e e Kwadilweng ke Mathaiao.* He uses "modemona/Bademona" the hybrid word derived from "demon/s." But he uses the word *Badimo* to refer to demons when he comments on the verses (see p. 54). This suggests that the use of *Badimo* to refer to demons for demons, which Wookey maintained in his 1908 Bible, can be traced to Moffat himself, as attested by other secondary sources.

to read Wookey's Bible, which was the only complete Setswana Bible then, it follows that I used English Bibles.

When it came to church, my fellowship was primarily among the middle-class, educated young people, who felt more at home preaching and praying in English than in Setswana. In contrast to the AICs, who are largely of low class and low level of education, who use Sesotho and Ndebele/Zulu as their holy languages, English was the language of worship in my church. So when I returned from the USA, aware of my colonized biblical methods and schools of interpreting the Bible, I was determined to read the Bible 'with Batswana women' of the AICs. Thus I bought my first Setswana Bible. I rightly imagined AICs readers to be slightly insulated from colonial institutions and strategies of reading, since they are the resisting readers who historically walked out of the colonial missionary-founded churches to start their own. They walked out of these churches to read the Bible and worship God from their African cultural perspectives. AICs' Christian practitioners are also renowned for holding on to African cultural world views and infusing them with Christian perspectives. And yet I discovered *Badimo* sadly dressed in the skins of demons and devils in their favorite biblical text.

The Setswana Bible and
the Colonization of the Setswana Language

In my shock, I turned to other passages in Mathew to confirm my disbelief. I found the story of Jesus and the demoniac of Gadarene (Matt 8:28–34). There I found our sacred *Badimo* sacred in front of another divine being: they trembled and begged Jesus to leave them alone, to spare them or at least to cast them out to the pigs (vv. 29–31). And Jesus cast the *Badimo* out, sending them into pigs that ran away and drowned in the sea (v. 32). Here was a textual burial of *Badimo*! I turned to the commissioning of the disciples in Matt 10:1–15. There I found Jesus instructing the disciples to go out, preach, and heal and "cast out *Badimo*" (v. 8). This reading experience was chilling to say the least. My reading moment itself was a violent experience which accelerated heartbeat. The text exploded, shattering the very centre of my cultural world view. It invited me to see myself and my society as people who had believed in and depended on the demons and devils before the coming of Christianity. Could there be any more evidence for the dark and lost continent of Africa than the one I was reading in this Setswana Bible? It is important to name this translation, its aims, and how it achieves its purposes.

In this translation, the roles of *Badimo* are reinvented: *Badimo* are equated with demons and devils, when any Motswana reader expects them to be friends with Jesus, or with divine powers. The translation is a minefield planted in the Setswana cultural spaces, warning every Motswana Christian believer and reader of the Bible to stay away from the dangerous and deadly beliefs of Setswana. It marks boundaries and designates the Setswana cultural framework as a "dangerous, devil and death zone," to be avoided at all cost. The translation invites us, the Batswana biblical readers, to distance ourselves from *Badimo,* the demons, and to identify ourselves with Jesus, a Christian divine power. It achieves its aims through literary techniques of writing and characterization. The characterization maintains Jesus' holy role, but *Badimo* are given a new role, that of demons. The Comaroffs are correct to note that "Moffat's use of *Badimo* ('ancestors') to denote 'demons' . . . did violence to both biblical and conventional Tswana usage,"[14] Be that it may, the Christian tradition hardly lost anything central to its faith in this translation, while the Setswana tradition lost its very centre. The translation is, therefore, a structural device of alienating natives from their cultures, or what Ngugi describes as the colonizing art of making the colonized "see their past as one wasteland."[15] Who, indeed, would not want to distance her/himself from demons and devils?

At this stage of my reading I was an adequately educated biblical scholar, who could consult the Greek New Testament texts and lexicons for the "original" meanings of words. I was also sufficiently conscious of the politics of interpretation or translation. Yet I could not help but wonder about the oral readers who read or hear only the Setswana Bible. It was hard to avoid thinking about the Setswana readers/hearers who first read the Setswana Bible in 1857 and those who continued to read it for the next 150 years that followed: Did these Setswana readers/hearers discover their own *Badimo* as devils and demons? Did the written Setswana Bible prove to them that they were lost and knew no God, so much so that they venerated demons and devils as sacred beings? The implications and impact of these translations cannot be overemphasized for readers who were originally non-literate. As Tiffin and Lawson note, 'it is when the children (in both senses) of colonies read such texts and internalize their own subjection that the true work of colonial textuality is done.'[16] The construction therefore portrayed Setswana perspectives as evil powers, in order to promote the Christian and English

---

14. Comaroff and Comaroff, *Of Revelation,* 218.

15. Ngũgĩ wa Thiong'o, *Decolonising,* 3.

16. Chris Tiffin and Alan Lawson, *Describing Empire*, London: Routledge, 1994, 4.

world view as the necessary light. But who were these translators and what kind of era informed their thinking?

Reading the Translated Time and the Time of Translators

In 1840 Robert Moffat completed his Setswana New Testament translation and in 1857 he finished translating the Hebrew Bible. In 1908 A. J. Wookey produced the enduring revised version of Moffat's Bible. In 1870 John Brown compiled a Setswana dictionary, which drew most of its words from Moffat's Setswana Bible. He produced its revised version in 1895. His son Tom J. Brown brought forth an upgraded version in 1925. The latter remained the main dictionary until 1993, when Z. I. Matumo's version was published. What is significant in these dates is that the translations were carried out between the last half of the nineteenth century and the First World War. The latter half of the nineteenth century was the height of the British Empire, a time when the certainty of the empire seemed unquestionable. The First World War, however, heralded the revolt of the colonized voices, a period that has stretched to the nineties. How is this colonizer-colonized power struggle reflected in the Setswana Bible translations and dictionaries?

As the first writer of Setswana, Moffat's achievement was undoubtedly outstanding. Yet the Comaroffs tell us: "Those who chose to peruse the Setswana Bible learned more than the sacred story, more even than how to read. They were subjected to a form of *cultural translation* [emphasis mine] in which vernacular poetics were re-presented to them as a thin *sekgoa* narrative—and their language itself reduced to an instrument of imperial knowledge."[17]

The Comaroffs use the word *sekgoa* with a small (s) to describe the way European colonizing agents constructed themselves in the colonial frontiers against native cultures.[18] Moffat, the Browns and Wookey were missionaries who built schools, hospitals and churches for the natives. Yet their work was actively involved in the construction of *sekgoa* narrative. In short, they were men of their time and place: a time of European imperialism and a time of the glory of the British Empire. They were also well placed at the colonial frontier of Southern Africa. Accordingly, colonizing ideology found its way into their written accounts of Setswana language. As their translations of *Badimo* attest, they indeed 'reduced Setswana to an instrument of imperial

17. Comaroff and Comaroff, *Of Revelation*, 311.

18. Usually *Sekgoa* defines white Europeans (particularly the British) and their cultures.

knowledge.' Their translations seized the symbols that are central institutions of Setswana cultures and equated them to the evil powers.

I know that many have defended, and still vigorously defend, missionaries of colonial times, separating them from other colonizing agents and showing how they built schools, churches and hospitals for the natives; how they were often spokespersons for the natives against other colonizing agents of their time. Missionaries were certainly different from other colonial agents such as traders and politicians. This difference, however, does not exempt most, if any, missionaries of colonial times from the game of colonizing. What such arguments tend to overlook is that there are "diverse forms of the colonizing cultures."[19] In fact, missionaries of colonial times did not have to regard themselves openly or consciously as advancing the rule of their countries to be part of the colonizing squad, although many did. Missionaries of colonial times were inevitably colonizing agents. That is, we agree that missionaries were people who 'set out to save Africa [and other continents]: to make people the subjects of a worldwide Christian commonwealth', we should also agree that "in so doing they were self-consciously acting out a new vision of global history, setting up new frontiers of European consciousness, and naming new forms of humanity to be entered onto its map of the civilized mankind."[20] To establish any form of worldwide "commonwealth"—be it Christian, economic, political, social, ideological, environmental, military—always involves the suppression of cultural differences and the imposition of a few universal standards. It involves the promotion of certain powerful centres and the creation of some satellites cultures. Its establishment is accomplished through such institutions as schools, hospitals and trade centres, which become the crucible that proclaims and disseminates the colonizer's consciousness and finally establishes the institutions of the colonizer over against the native ones. These very institutions, which many missionary defenders are quick to remind us "civilized" or helped us, are the most important part of colonizing minds and spaces. Moffat, Wookey and Browns' work, for example, looks like an immense service to Batswana. Yet when put in its context, when its intentions are interrogated, and when its contents are examined, one realizes that their tasks were carried out to serve the establishment of a "worldwide Christian commonwealth," and that such a task entailed the "death and burial" of Setswana cultures in order to "[set] up new frontier of European consciousness."

19. Comaroff and Comaroff, *Of Revelation,* 313.
20. Ibid., 309.

The Colonization and Decolonization
of Setswana in the Dictionaries

As I have said, the compilation of the Setswana dictionary was interconnected with the Setswana Bible. The first dictionary was compiled in 1870 by John Brown and it was followed by revised versions in 1895, 1925 and 1993. The 1995 A. Kgasa and J. Tsonope[21] dictionary was the first to be produced outside LMS religious institutions. How, then, was the Setswana language colonized in these dictionaries? Can we also detect the forces of resistance and decolonization in these dictionaries? To answer these questions, I will comment on the structures, contents and definitions of words in the dictionaries.

To begin with the first question, both the first Setswana Bible and the first dictionary marked the beginning of the reconstitution of the Setswana language for services other than those of Batswana. Setswana was being transformed from an oral to a written language. Its written form, however, was designed to serve institutions other than those of Batswana. It served primarily in the mission schools, hospitals, church and colonial trade centres. These institutions set themselves against the local ones and competed with or replaced the established institutions of Batswana, such as *Bogwera* (boys' school), *Bojale* (girls' school) and *Bongaka* (healing institutions).[22] The written Setswana form was an instrument of disseminating a worldwide Christian commonwealth, European trade systems, and European medical and educational practices; by extension, it was employed to suppress its own cultural institutions.

Second, the structural organization of Brown's dictionary itself is instructive. The dictionary is divided into two parts. In the first part, its entries follow an English–Setswana language format: it lists English words first and explains them in Setswana, then in English. The structural organization presupposes readers who have an English vocabulary and who are looking for the meaning of their words in the Setswana language. These will be foreign English readers who have some interest in Batswana. Even though we can posit native Batswana readers, the dictionary portrays them as anglicized Batswana who will only read their language with and through the English language. On the issue of the intended readers, Tom J. Brown's instruction to his 1925 edition is explicit: "The Revs. John Brown and Alfred Wookey gave to their share of the work many years of willing service, in the hope

21. See Kgasa and Tsonope, *Tlhanodi ya Setswana*.

22. See Comaroff and Comaroff, *Of Revelatoin*, 206–38. The completion of local and missionary institutions of health and education were intense and are well documentation among various writers.

that it would prove useful to all Europeans, who were desirous of acquiring knowledge of the Secwana language and also to such Becwana[23] as were seeking to gain an acquaintance with English."[24]

Further, the structural arrangement of the dictionary itself symbolically captures the colonization of the Setswana language. The very placement of Setswana side by side with English structurally indicates that, as a language, Setswana no longer stands by itself. It is now a language that is enveloped by English. Moreover, English takes priority over it, since it is the language that is listed first and covers more space. Such a structural organization largely remained with us from 1870 to 1995, when A. Kgasa and J. Tsonope's *Tlhanodi ya Setswana* appeared.

Third, the colonization of the Setswana language is evident in the definitions ascribed to the listed words and the content of words in the different parts of the dictionary. To illustrate the former point I will look at the definition of *Badimo* and *Ngaka,* and some related words. Here we will see how the language itself was reduced "to an instrument of imperial knowledge" and agendas. The definition of a word *Badimo* and its centrality to Setswana cultures has already been explained above. *Ngaka* is not only a physician, rather, his/her role is priestly for s/he mediates between the living and the divine powers, *Badimo,* and *Ngaka* is in touch with *Badimo* on behalf of the society on issues of their welfare. Both *Badimo* and *Ngaka* are, therefore, central to Setswana religious thinking. Let us now look at how the dictionaries define these words. I will chronicle the words according to the order of publications available to me.

Content and Definitions in John Brown's Dictionary of 1895

In the first part of Brown's dictionary, "Ancestors" is defined as *Bagolo,*[25] which means "elders." "Ancestral Spirit" is not listed. Under the word "Spirit" Brown has a sub-entry of the phrase "evil spirits." According to Brown, the definition of "evil spirits" in Setswana is *badimo.*[26] Coming to the word "diviner-herbalist," Brown lists the word "diviner" and defines it as *moloi,* which means "wizard" or "sorcerer." He then lists the word "divination" and explains it as too, which means the practice of *boloi* or witchcraft.[27]

---

23. Please note that it took a while before the spellings became standardized. Thus Botswana was often spelled Becwana, Bechwana or Bechuna(land).

24. Brown, *Secwana Dictionary,* iii.

25. Ibid., 25.

26. Ibid., 203.

27. Ibid., 78, for the definitions of both "diviner" and "divination."

He also lists the word "doctor" and correctly defines it as "*Ñaka* [*ngaka*];[28] *moalahi*. To doctor, *alaha*; to doctor a person so as to protect him from danger, *upèlèla*."[29] It is significant that in the English part of the dictionary, Brown does not list the words "demon," "devil," and "Satan," a point which I will return to below.

Turning to the second part of Brown's dictionary (the Setswana part), the word *Badimo* is listed and flatly defined as "evil spirits."[30] Although he lists the word *moea*, "spirit," he does not list the phrase *moea oo maswe*, or "evil spirits." He also lists the word *modemona*, a hybrid word, drawn from "demon."[31] The word *diabolo* and *satane* hybrid words from devil and Satan are not listed. The word *Ngaka* or *naka*, meaning "doctor," is not listed. The word *naka*, is defined simply as "a pipe of dagga."[32] But the reader realizes that Brown knows that *naka* also means "doctor," for he defines "doctor" in the English part of his dictionary, using this word. What, then, is the significance of resisting to identify *naka* as a doctor in the Setswana part of the dictionary? This question will be clearer below.

With these definitions, Brown has subverted the Setswana language for imperial ends. If he wished to be fair to the Setswana language and culture, he could have defined the word "Ancestors" as both *bagolo* and *Badimo*. A diviner is also a *moloi* or wizard. A *ngaka* who is also a diviner in Setswana cultures is thus identified as an agent of the evil powers for English readers and Christianized Batswana. The omission of *Ngaka* in the Setswana part of the dictionary thus becomes clear: it is a categorical dismissal of his/her status. It is a denial that a doctor exists in Setswana cultures. Brown's refusal to recognize a diviner-herbalist as a doctor can be explained since we know that he defines a diviner as *moloi*, or wizard. Since a *Ngaka* is not only a physician but also a diviner with spiritual roles in Setswana cultures, Brown identifies him/her as a *moloi*; a real doctor is only the European type.

Turning to the context, is significant that Brown omits the words "Satan," "devil" and "demon" in the English part of the dictionary. This is particularly notable for a dictionary produced in a religious institution and whose main purpose was to evangelize the natives. The omission implies that the role of negative spiritual powers is played only by *Badimo* and found only in Setswana cultural thinking. The presentation purges English

28. Please, note that *naka/ngaka*, meaning "doctor" is another reflection of the fluidity of spelling before its current stabilization.

29. Brown, *Secwana Dictionary*, 79.

30. Ibid., 253.

31. Ibid., 374.

32. Ibid., 391.

language or culture of any knowledge of evil and pushes evil power onto Setswana cultures. Here we glean a *"sekgoa* narrative" that is the imperial construction and marketing of English (language) as a civilized, humane and Christian culture, over against colonized cultures that only appear as devilish, childish, and savage. This construction is glaringly attested to by the fact that Brown lists the hybrid word *modemona* in the Setswana part of the dictionary, while he does not list its proper form, "demon," in the English part of the dictionary. The omission that informed this *"sekgoa* narrative" reflects the thinking of the time and is well captured by Josiah Young's words of 1885. Young, a missionary of colonial times and at the height of British Empire confidently said:

> Is there room for reasonable doubt that this race . . . is destined to dispossess many races, assimilate others, and mold the remainder, until in a very true and important sense it has Anglo-Saxoned mankind? Already English language, saturated with Christian ideas gathering up into itself the thought of all ages is the great agent of Christian civilization throughout the world, at this moment molding character of half the human race.[33]

Young's eulogy of Anglo-Saxons displays no conflict between his Christian faith and the values or impact of imperialism on other races. The Anglo-Saxons' project of dispossessing, assimilating and molding foreign nations into Anglo-Saxons does not bother him as a missionary.

The mentality that freely dispossessed Batswana of their cultural agency can be fairly understood within this framework of thinking. But what is even more instructive here is Young's perception of English as a language and a culture. Young describes English as a language "saturated with Christian ideas" and "the great agent of Christian civilization." The English language is almost identical to Christianity in Young's description, which is why he finds the conversion of the world into Anglo-Saxon unproblematic. His words reflect the *"sekgoa* narrative" behind the dictionary entries that purged the English language of demons, devils and Satan, while it constructed Setswana counter culture, which is characterized as a realm of negative spiritual powers.

Turning to the local informants, it is inconceivable that any Motswana of Moffat, Brown and Wookey's day could have defined *Badimo* as evil spirits and *Ngaka* as a *moloi,* for the welfare of individuals and the society as a whole hinged and revolved on the loving care of *Badimo* and *Ngaka.* Another point which makes it very unlikely that Setswana informants could have likened demons to diviner-herbalist and *Badimo* pertains to the fact

---

33. Strong, "Josiah Strong on the Anglo-Saxon Destiny, 1885," 123.

that a *Ngaka* does not get spirit possessed or lose control at any point of her/his professional duties. In short, "Setswana did not include a tradition of possession or ecstasy."[34]

Although Ancestral Spirit possession is found in some Southern African cultures (*Nguni, Shona*), among Batswana speakers *Badimo* do not make their houses in people such that they lose control.[35] A *Ngaka* performs all her/his duties fully composed, even when s/he consults the divine power in Setswana cultures. It is also difficult to imagine that Moffat and Brown, who, together with other LMS agents, had been working among Batswana for at least fifty years, would have grossly misunderstood this particular aspect of Setswana cultures: the central aspect. What we are reading here is, therefore, a planted colonial cultural bomb, a cultural landmine. It is a deliberate design, aimed at exploding away the cultural validity of Setswana cultural spaces for the purposes of furthering a worldwide Christian commonwealth. It was a cultural landmine that marked Setswana cultural spaces as dangerous death zones to be totally avoided by Batswana Christian readers of the Bible. The establishment of a Christian commonwealth together with the accompanying European hospitals, schools, and trade necessitated this strategy for, unless the colonial missionaries defined other worlds as realms of evil, danger and death, it would be hard to justify their agenda. Brown's dismissal of Setswana cultures as a realm of evil spirits and wizards indeed reflects his time: he compiled his work at the height of the British Empire, when the imperial success seemed indisputable. This was a time when the so-called "savages" and "children" of colonies seemed destined to remain under the tutelage of the colonizer, but World War I would usher in a different era.[36]

Structure, Content and Definitions in Tom J. Brown's Version

Tom J. Brown's revised version of the Setswana dictionary was published in 1925, just after World War I. This was a time when the confidence of the empire was beginning to be shaken, both from inside and outside. The devastating war was a rude awakening that forced the colonizers to question their own civilization, for it graphically revealed that they were not all

34. See Comaroff and Comaroff, *Of Revelation*, 239.

35. Yet even among some Nguni groups, where Ancestral Spirits come and temporarily take possession of living human beings and speak their desires and give advice through them, they cannot be equated to demons, for evil spirits are institutionally debarred from possessing people.

36. The images are very common in the colonial literature. A good example here is Rudyard Kipling's poem, "The White Man's Burden: The United States and The Philippine Islands."

purged of demonic, satanic and demonic spirits. The war had torn the thin veil of "*sekgoa* narrative" apart and showed that there are evil spirits in the civilized continent of Europe. In addition, many colonized subjects began to insist on their autonomy. It would take several decades for most colonized countries to attain their political and geographical independence, but the ball had begun to roll. As we shall see that Tom J. Brown's dictionary reflects both the colonization of language and the tremors of decolonization in its structure, content and definitions of words.

To begin with the structure of the dictionary, there is a notable change. Whereas John Brown's dictionary begins with entries for English words, Tom Brown begins with Setswana words! While John Brown's dictionary is entitled *Secwana Dictionary: English–Setswana and Secwana–English*, the latter is entitled *Secwana Dictionary: Secwana–English and English–Setswana*. Nonetheless, the Setswana words are still defined in English. The Setswana language is still intertwined with English and is without an independence life of its own. When we look at the definitions of *Badimo* and *Ngaka* similar changes are discernable.

To start with the word *Badimo*, Tom Brown defines it as follows: "Spirits. Used generally of both good and bad spirits, but principally the latter."[37] He also lists the word Naka [*Ngaka*] and explains it as follows: "doctor: a witch doctor: a heathen doctor of any description."[38] In the second part of the dictionary (the English–Setswana part) Tom Brown lists the word "Ancestors," and, like the former Brown, translates it as *Bagolo; bagolwane*, meaning elders.[39] Here the word is stripped of Setswana religious tones. He also lists the "Spirit" and explains it as "departed spirits, *badimo*." It is notable that in the latter entry he has striven to be neutral by leaving out the qualifiers bad or good.

Tom Brown also lists the words "doctor," "diviner," and "divination." The word "doctor" is defined as follows: "A healer, *moalahi; a* native doctor, *mophekodi, naka: moloi*.[40] Divination is to practice *go laolo ka bola; go diha boitsaanape. (Nape* is one of the *Secwana* demi-gods)."[41] In short, divination is the art of getting in touch with *Nape*. Tom Brown goes on to define a diviner as a *Moitseanape*, which is a compound word made of *moitse* (one who knows) and *Nape*, the Setswana divine power.[42] It means one who knows or who is in touch with *Nape*. When one looks back to his first section of Setswana, one finds that he defines the word *Moitseanape* as

---

37. Brown, *Secwana Dictionary*, 13.
38. Ibid., 234.
39. Ibid., 345.
40. Ibid., 401.
41. Ibid.
42. Ibid., 400.

follows: "a diviner; a soothsayer; one familiar with Spirits: one who works divination; a magician."[43]

In Tom Brown's definitions we very much sense a colonial mentality that dismisses the local cultures and equates them with evil: *Badimo* are primarily "evil spirits"; *Ngaka* is still a "witch-doctor and heathen doctor of any description" and a diviner is a magician. But something has begun to happen. Tom Brown, unlike his father, lacks that categorical dismissal of Setswana cultures "as perfect specimens of absolute error, masterpieces of the hell's invention, which Christianity was simply called upon to oppose, uproot and destroy."[44] Here Tom Brown acknowledges *Badimo* as Spirits who have goodness. He acknowledges that there is a Setswana doctor, although he proceeds to qualify it from his colonizing perspective. A gleam of light is also discernable in his definitions of doctor, diviner and divination. The Setswana religious worldview no longer appears as an absolute realm of evil spirits, demons and wizards.

The content of Tom Brown's dictionary also reflects a different era. Like the former Brown, he lists the hybrid word *modemore* and explains it as "a demon."[45] He also omits *diabolo* and *satane*, hybrid words from "devil" and "Satan." But unlike the former Brown, Tom J. Brown includes the words "demon" and "devil" in the English Bible. He defines them as *moa oo mashwe* ("evil spirit") and *moea o mashwe; oo ga Dinwe* ("evil spirit"; "the spirit of an ogre") respectively. This inclusion reflects the tremors of decolonization that were beginning to shake the confidence of the empire in the post-World War I era.

Structure, Content, and Definition in Z. I. Matumo's Version

Although Z. I. Matumo's *Setswana English Setswana Dictionary* of 1993 was still produced within LMS institution, it was the first full-fledged revision of Tom J. Brown's edition by a Motswana. The preface states that "the whole of the earlier dictionary has been reviewed and there has been a careful study of definitions and a revision of grammatical apparatus in terms of the current understanding of the language."[46] As its title indicates, there is a change: the title privileges the local language, suggesting that English is now enveloped by Setswana. The title, however, is not matched by structure and contents for they still follow Tom J. Brown's arrangements of Setswana–English and English–Setswana categories (maybe in terms of the number of

43. Ibid., 205.

44. Gairdner, *An Account and Interpretation*, 137.

45. Brown, *Secwana Dictionary*, 198.

46. Derek Jones, "Preface," in Z. I. Matumo, *Setswana English Setswana Dictionary*. Gaborone, Macmillan, 1993, viii.

Setswana words and definitions). The Setswana language still does not have an independent life. As his definitions of words will show, Matumo is at once a decolonizing and colonized subject, like most postcolonial subjects.

How then did Matumo define the words *Badimo* and *Ngaka*? To begin with the former, Matumo defined *Badimo* as follows: "spirits; ancestors, ranging from one's parents who are alive to the dead and long forgotten ones: believed to influence or control events."[47] *Ngaka* is defined as "a doctor; a witch doctor; a physician; one who holds the highest university degree in any faculty."[48] *Moloi*, on the other hand is a "wizard: a witch; a poisoner; one who acts treacherously."[49] The hybrid words of *Modimona, Diabolo, Satane* are not listed. Turning to the English part of his dictionary, Matumo lists the word "Ancestors" and defines it as "*bagologolo; badimo*; the ancestors have responded, i.e. have heard people's prayers."[50] A diviner is defined as *Ngaka ya sedupe; moitseanape*, which means "a diviner-herbalist, clever person,"[51] A doctor is defined as "a healer, *moalafi, mophekodi: Ngaka ya moupo*; rain doctor, *moroka*; a witch doctor; *ngaka ya Moloi*."[52] Following his *predecessor*, he lists the words "devil" and "demon," but not Satan.[53] The devil is defined as "*mowa o o maswe*," that is, evil spirit. The word "demon" is defined in the same way.[54]

What is significant in Matumo's definitions? To begin with *Badimo*, his definition is a world apart from the Brown's definitions, who first defined *Badimo* as evil spirits and then as primarily evil spirits. In Matumo's definitions *Badimo* is part and parcel of Setswana family and society, ranging from the living to the dead. *Badimo* includes one's parents. In this English definition, Matumo does not suppress the religious meaning of *Badimo*, by simply defining the word as elders or ancient people. Rather, Matumo brings out its religious meaning by pointing out that these are sacred figures who answer prayers in Setswana cultures.

A significant aspect is also discernable in his definition of *Ngaka*. Matumo outlines a number of types of doctors, defining them according to their specialty or qualifications as healers, rainmakers, diagnosers of problems, and PhD holders. Matumo acknowledges that a doctor who tends to forget that his/her task is to save or enhance life and uses his/her knowledge to bring them harm is also to be included. Such a doctor would be called a

47. Matumo, *Setswana*, 10.

48. Matumo, *Setswana*, 281.

49. Ibid., 259.

50. Ibid., 463.

51. Ibid., 505.

52. Ibid., 506.

53. Ibid., 501.

54. Ibid., 499.

"witch doctor." But in Matumo's dictionary, a *Ngaka* is by no means identical to a *moloi* or a "witch doctor" as in the previous dictionaries. A wizard or *moloi* is one whose role is absolutely evil and his/her role is a world apart from the Setswana *Ngaka*, the diviner-herbalist. Further, in Matumo's definition evil powers are distinct from powers of good. The evil powers consist of demons and the devil found in the English vocabulary and *moloi* found in the Setswana language. These are not identical to *Badimo* and *Ngaka,* or the diviner as we have seen significant strides towards decolonize Setswana.

Matumo's efforts to decolonize the Setswana language have been continued by M. Kgasa and J. Tsonope's Setswana dictionary of 1995. The latter not only redefined the words according to Setswana understanding, but also restructured the dictionary. Unlike all other dictionaries that came before, the Kgasa and Tsonope dictionary does not treat the Setswana language side by side with English. For the first time, the Setswana language earned the right to stand by itself, after over a century (125 years) since the first dictionary appeared. This structural change is the most significant contribution of the Kgasa and Tsonope dictionary in the decolonization of the Setswana language.

Consuming the Colonial Cultural Bomb: Strategies of Resistance

As a colonized subject whose daily bread was that of consuming a different form of colonial cultural bomb (reading the English Bible and the Greek Bible), the cultural death of AICs Setswana Bible readers seemed certain to me. I could not see how they could ignore the fact that *Badimo* are negative spiritual powers in the Setswana Bible. Further, most AICs readers are hardly literate and have little or no way of researching the 'original' Greek meanings, or reading for themselves about the historical background that gave us the New Testament. What was given to them is what they received: It is the Word of God. AICs certainly marched out of missionary-founded churches, protesting against the white-only church leadership and preaching roles in colonial times. They started their own churches in search of autonomy, yet they still depended on the missionary Bible, for they had no financial power or academic skills to initiate their own Bible versions. Yet as I soon found out during my fieldwork research, they were not helpless consumers of the colonial cultural bomb. They managed to harness and redirect the energy of a destructive bomb for their own wellbeing. They did not observe the colonial boundaries that marked Setswana cultural spaces as a 'no-go dangerous death zone'. Instead, the readers rolled on minefields, detonating them with their methods of reading: namely, by divining through the Bible, reading the Spirit and through the Spirit, telling and retelling the text but hardly interpreting. While these methods are closely interconnected, I will focus on the method of divining through the Bible as a decolonizing strategy that reasserts the Setswana cultural agency.[55]

In Setswana cultures, divining is the skill of a trained diviner-herbalist (*ngaka*) who throws down a divining set to diagnose individual and community problems, their causes and solutions. The set can contain a minimum of four pieces, which represent key social relationships on their own, with the designs drawn on them and with the patterns they form in their fall, that is, their relationship to one another once they have been thrown down and with the directions they face. What a diviner-herbalist reads in the process of diagnosis is a combination of these aspects of the set. The point here is that a Setswana diviner-herbalist uses the divining set to get in touch with *Badimo*. They are asked to reveal the problem, the causes and the solutions through the divining set. Among the AICS, church leaders are also faith healers, who are consulted for various health issues. Instead of divining through a traditional set, they use the Bible. The structural similarities of the church and traditional institutions are evident in the healing practices and roles of spiritual leaders.[56] In a study where G. C. Oosthuizen focused on AICs faith-healers, he found that "there are a few who do not have the double-barrel approach, but none reject diviners, or oppose them."[57] Oosthuizen's respondents, who were themselves faith-healers, had this to say about their work: "[I] work under the power of the Holy Spirit but the Ancestors may be consulted"; another one said, "I . . . always start working as the prophet and if nothing happens then I would apply everything which a diviner would use because I am using both," and another one held that "I use *impepho* to dream and then the ancestors visit me; the cords on me fight illness and keep demons away, Then the Holy Spirit comes . . ."[58] These quotes from one study attest to a phenomenon that has been widely documented by AICs scholars; namely, that AICs freely draw from the Christian and African traditions in their business of maintaining life.

Accordingly, my arrival in AICs church compounds for field work research, on days and times when the worship service was not on, was often regarded as my wish to consult a faith-healer for her/his healing services. Thus when I was brought before them they treated me like any other consulting client: they handed me a closed Bible, asked me to hold it with my two hands,

---

55. Some Africans who first heard biblical reading and preaching immediately regarded it as divination. See Comaroff and Comaroff, *Of Revelation*, 229.

56. That AICs' theological practices draw from both Christian and African traditions is widely documented by scholars of these churches. AICs recognize Jesus and pay allegiance to African Ancestors at the same time. There are a few exceptions, but generally scholars agree that they are 'syncretistic'. See Oosthuizen, *The Healer-Prophet in Afro-Christian Churches*, 165–93.

57. Oosthuizen, *The Healer-Prophet*, 167.

58. Ibid., 166–67.

to open it and to hand whatever passage I opened to them. The business of healing was on! Had I complied, they would have diagnosed my life through reading whatever passage I happened to open. In Setswana cultural thinking good health is almost equivalent to healthy relationships and success, while ill health is also closely associated with unhealthy relationships and misfortune. To divine one's life, therefore, they would examine one's relationships: the unhealthy and healthy ones. Depending on what the passage reveals, through the help of divine powers, who are indispensable partners in these reading sessions, a problem is identified and solutions are advanced.

This usage of the Bible and method of reading is stunningly subversive to colonizing narrative designs. The AICs' readers resist the translation that turned *Badimo* into demons and devils in the Setswana Bible, the '*sekgoa* narrative' that constructed Christian and Setswana traditions as opposites.' Instead, they perceive the Bible from their own cultural perspectives as a book that diagnoses relationships and promotes the healing of relationships between people and the divine powers. Insofar as it is a book that detects bad relationships and recommends solutions that build for good relationships between people and divine powers, Batswana AICs readers see no differences between the biblical aims and their religious thinking. They see the Bible as a divining set. Hence once they were in control of biblical interpretation in their own churches, the Bible took its rightful place as one among many other divining sets. *Badimo* and Jesus/Holy Spirit also took their rightful place as divine powers that promoted good relationships and health in communities where the Bible is read. This AICs strategy of resistance entailed a method of reading the written Setswana language through and with the unwritten text of Setswana cultures. In short, while colonial missionaries took control of the written 'Setswana', they could not take control of the unwritten Setswana from the memories of Batswana readers and hearers. In this way, the Batswana AICs readers resurrected *Badim*o from the colonial grave site where they were buried; they detonated the minefields planted in their world views and reclaimed their cultural worlds as life-affirming spaces.

Conclusion

In this article, I have examined the Setswana biblical and dictionary texts, the age that informed its authors-readers (missionaries), how they reflect the colonization of the Setswana language and the methods of resistance adopted by Batswana readers and writers. I have treated translation and definitions of words as an interpretation, which allows us to see how the Setswana language was reconstructed for imperial ends. Missionary literacy works of translation have been shown to be heavily engaged in the colonization of the minds of natives and for advancing European imperial spaces. The death and burial of Setswana culture here was primarily championed through the colonization of their language such that it no longer served the interests of the original speakers. Instead the written form of language had equated their cultural beliefs with evil spirits, demons and wizardry. This colonization of Setswana was in itself the planting of a colonial cultural bomb, meant to clear the ground for the implantation of a worldwide Christian commonwealth and European consciousness. It was a minefield that marked Setswana cultural spaces as dangerous death zones, to be avoided by every intelligent Motswana reader or hearer of the translated text. Here as elsewhere, we realize that

> Imperial relations may have been established initially by guns, guile and disease, but they were maintained in their interpolative phase largely by textuality, both institutionally and informally. Colonialism (like its counterpart, racism) then, is an operation of discourse, and as an operation of discourse it interpolates colonial subjects by incorporating them in a system of representation. They are always already written by that system of representation.[59]

But as much as Batswana readers swallowed a colonial bomb for over a century and walked over cultural minefields, they also developed methods of resistance. The Setswana Bible that was once used to champion the degradation of *Badimo*, became now one of the divining sets, used to get in touch with *Badimo* and Jesus among the AICs' Bible readers. This method or reading among the AICs resists the suppression of diversity and cultivates liberating interdependency between the Christian and Setswana world views. It reads two canons simultaneously: the written and unwritten Setswana canons. The approach tears away the colonizing strategy that translated *Badimo* into evil spirits and demons in the Setswana Bible. But above all, divining through the Bible is a method that reconciles the divine with the divine: *Badimo* and Jesus are friends at last as they should be.[60]

Bibliography

Ashcorft, Bill, Gareth Griffiths, and Helen Tiffin, eds. *The Postcolonial Studies Reader.* London: Routledge, 1995.

59. Tiffin and Lawson, eds., *De-scribing Empire*, 3.

60. I am grateful to Tiro Sebina, Seratwe Ntloeedibe, Peter Mwikisa and Andrew Chebanne at the University of Botswana, my colleagues who read this article and gave me constructive feedback. *Le kamoso bagaetsho!*

———. *The Empire Writes Back: Theory and Practice in Postcolonial Literatures*. New York: Routledge, 1989.

Boehmer, Elleke. *Colonial and Postcolonial Literature*. Oxford: Oxford University Press, 1995.

Brown, John. *Secwana Dictionary: English–Secwana and Secwana–English*. Tiger Kloof: LMS Book Room, 1895.

Brown, Tom J. *Secwana Dictionary: Secwana–English and English–Secwana*. Tiger Kloof: LMS Book Room, 1925.

Comaroff, Jean, and John Comaroff. *Of Revelation and Revolution: Christianity, Colonialism and Consciousness in South Africa*. Chicago: University of Chicago Press, 1991.

Derek, Jones. "Preface." In Z. I. Matumo, *Setswana English, English Setswana Dictionary*. Gaborone: Macmillan, 1993.

Dube, Musa W. "Divining the Texts for International Relations (Mt. 15.21–28)." In *Transformative Encounters: Jesus and Women Re-viewed*, edited by Ingrid Rosa Kitzberger, 315–28. Biblical Interpretation Series 43. Leiden: Brill, 2000.

———. "Readings of *Semoya*: Batswana Women's Interpretations of Matt. 15.21–28." *Semeia* 73 (1966) 111–29.

Fanon, Frantz. *Black Skin, White Masks*. Translated by Richard Philcox. New York: Grove, 2008.

Gairdner, W. H. T. *An Account and Interpretation of the World Missionary Conference*. London: Oliphant & Ferrier, 1910.

Kgasa, Morulaganyi A., and Joseph Tsonope. *Thanodi ya Setswana*. Gaborone: Longman, 1995.

Ngubane, J. B. "Theological Roots of the AICs and their Challenges to Black Theology." In *The Unquestionable Right to Be Free: Black Theology from South Africa*, edited by Itumeleng Mosala and Buti Tlhagale, 71–100. Maryknoll, NY: Orbis, 1992.

Ngũgĩ wa Thiong'o. *Decolonizing the Mind: The Politics of Language in African Literature*. London: Curry, 1986.

Oosthuizen, Gerhardus C. *The Healer-Prophet in Afro-Christian Churches*. Studies in Christian Mission 3. Leiden: Brill, 1992.

Peek, Philip M., ed. *African Divination Systems: Ways of Knowing*. African Systems of Thought. Indianapolis: Indiana University Press, 1991.

Said, Edward W. *Culture and Imperialism*. New York: Knopf, 1993.

Sandilands, Alexander. *The History of the Setswana Bible*. Cape Town: Bible Society of South Africa, 1989.

Stoller, Paul. *Embodying Colonial Memories: Spirit Possession, Power and the Hauka in West Africa*. London: Routledge, 1995.

Strong, Josiah. "Josiah Strong on the Anglo-Saxon Destiny, 1885." In *The Imperialism Reader: Documents and Readings in Modern Expansion*, edited by Louis Synder, 123. New York: Van Nostrad, 1962.

Taussig, Michael T. *Shamanism, Colonialism and the Wild Man: A Study in Terror and Healing*. Chicago: University of Chicago Press, 1987.

Tiffin, Chris, and Alan Lawson, eds. *De-scribing Empire: Postcolonialism and Textuality*. London: Routledge, 1994.

Wookey, Alfred J. *Phuthololo Ea Efangeleo e Kwadilweng ke Mathaiao*. 2nd ed. Tiger Kloof: LMS Book Room, 1902.

2

Postcolonial Translation Theory and the Swahili Bible in East Africa

Some Critical Observations

Aloo Osotsi Mojola

Introduction

The late Anglo-Kenyan Swahili scholar James de Vere Allen, a former cura-
tor of the Lamu Museum on the Kenyan coast in his major work *Swahili
Origins—Swahili Culture and the Shungwaya Phenomenon*[1] makes the claim
that "There can be few historic peoples whose identity is as elusive as that
of the Swahilis." In this text he sets out to contribute to a solution of this
problem of the elusive identity and origins of the Swahili. Allen is part of
a string of both foreign and local writers to confront this problem, among
them C. H. Stigand, R. Coupland, G. S. P. Freeman-Grenville, James S.
Kirkman, A. H. J. Prins, Neville Chittick, Wilfred Whiteley, Derek Nurse
and Thomas Spear on the one hand and Mathias Mnyampala, Shihabuddin
Chiraghdin, Ibrahim N. Shariff, Alamin Mazrui, Ali Mazrui, Mohammed
H. Abdulaziz, Mohammed Hyder, Ahmed I. Salim, Mohamed Bakari on
the other hand, among others. The identity of the Swahili people of the East
African coast is certainly contentious and a subject of much debate. Allen
observes that, "For as long as written records exist, groups of Swahilis have
described themselves, not only as Mombasans (Swahili wa Mvita), Pateans
(wa Pate) Kilwans (wa Kilwa) or whatever, but also as Arabs (wa Arabu),
Persians (wa Shirazi) or something else—even, in at least one place, Portuguese (wa Reno)—rather than as Swahilis, and many still do so. Indeed, it is

1. Allen, *Swahili Origins*, 1.

26

doubtful whether even today most of the people would in all contexts accept the name Swahili."[2] This problem has been complicated in modern times by the emergence of the 'new Swahili' or what may simply be described as the 'Swahilization' of many families in a number of East and Central African urban centers as well as some rural areas. The epi-centre of this process may well be the present United Republic of Tanzania, comprising of former Tanganyika and the Islands of Zanzibar and Pemba.

After noting that "The Swahili people . . . entered the twentieth century with (1) an ancient tradition that no study of the history of Africa can ignore; (2) a centuries-old writing tradition that has further promoted the collective consciousness of the Swahili people and that has served to shed light on their history and civilization; and (3) a visible homogeneity of culture cemented by an Islamic ethos," Alamin M. Mazrui and Ibrahim Noor Shariff, themselves ethnic Swahili pose the problem of Swahili identity as follows: "with such a background, one would have thought that the identity of the Swahili people would never be a matter of debate nor an issue that might unsettle the tranquility of any informed mind." Situating this problem in the context of the Eurocentric, Arabocentric and the Afrocentric paradigms, vis-à-vis questions of race and ethnicity, Mazrui and Shariff's view in favour of the relative and dynamic nature of personal or ethnic identity seems a wise move. In this sense Swahili ethnicity is no different from that of other ethnic communities in the East African region such as the Mijikenda, the Abaluyia, the Chagga or the Kalenjin among others, a unity in diversity that is a dynamic function of historical, political, cultural, and linguistic as well as other factors.

Who is a Swahili? Early definitions of the Swahili tended to be heavily influenced by what Allen refers to as the 'Arab myth' or the 'Hamitic myth' or by the racist view that 'civilization' in Africa was a product of the lighter skinned peoples. Thus the history of the East coast of Africa, including that of the Swahili, was thought of in terms of outsiders, Arabs, Persians, Indians, Pakistanis, Chinese, Portuguese and so on. And so J. S. Kirkman would write that: "The historical monuments of East Africa belong not to the Africans but to the Arabs and Arabised Persians, mixed in blood with the African but in culture utterly apart from the Africans who surround them."[3] A. H. J. Prins' definition of the Swahili gives credence to this myth. Writing in 1967 he claimed that, "The Swahili are a typical cultural group in which henceforth the East African Arabs are to be considered as bearers of the culture par excellence and sociologically speaking as an upper status group within

2. Ibid.
3. Ibid., 6.

the whole 'ethnic' stock."[4] Others of this strain have viewed and defined the Swahili as an impure or hybrid race, as a mixture of African and Arab, as Arabised Africans or as Africanised Arabs, as non-African and foreigners, and as essentially a Muslim non-ethnic group, i.e. not a "tribe." Mazrui and Shariff[5] while accepting the Islamic component of the Swahili nevertheless reject the above as distortions resulting from centuries of Western bias and Eurocentric presuppositions. Similarly, Prof. Mohamed Abdulaziz[6] makes the point that what has given Swahili its great assimilating power in East Africa is "its Bantu-based culture." He sees its "Arab-Islamic component" as playing the role of "a strong cultural stimulus." Abdulaziz agrees that "Early historians writing about the East African coast often underplayed, and in some cases even denied, the African initiative in the formation of this literate urban culture. Yet it was precisely this indigenous base which gave Swahili culture its assimilating qualities."

It may be helpful to start off with Allen's definition of the Swahili. Allen proposes a pair of definitions of the Swahili as follows:[7]

a. a Swahili is a person who has made his/her home in or around one of the traditional Muslim settlements of the East African coast which were originally legitimized by their link with the Shungwaya alias Shirazi, or in one of the modern counterparts; whose lifestyle conforms to that of one of the sub-cultures existing there; and who has inherited or adopted the Swahili language as his/her preferred tongue;

b. a person is Swahilised to the extent that his/ her lifestyle conforms to that of one of the sub-cultures inhabiting the traditional Muslim settlements of the East African coast which were originally legitimized by their link with Shungwaya alias Shirazi, or their modern counterparts, and especially to the extent that he/she has adopted the Swahili language as his/her preferred tongue.

The first of Allen's definitions is based on the generally accepted fact that the original Swahili were coastal dwellers, predominantly Islamic in culture and religion, highly decentralized and who like their Bantu speaking Pokomo and Mijikenda neighbours for example, identified themselves more in terms of their coastal 'kaya' or settlements rather than in terms of their "Swahiliness." Each settlement or 'kaya' was associated with its own distinctive character and dialect of Swahili. Mohamed Bakari, a Kenyan

4. Ibid., 8.

5. Ibid.

6. Abdulaziz, "Tanzania's National Language Police," 173.

7. Allen, *Swahili Origins*, 259.

ethnic Swahili, in a recent linguistic study (1985) for example focuses on the following Kenyan Swahili dialects—Chi-Chifundi, Kivumba, Chi-Jomvu, Kimvita, Kiamu, Kitikuu and Kisiyu. Each of the communities who spoke these dialects had an associated settlement (kaya) or city-state as they are often described.[8]

The second of Allen's definitions is an acknowledgement of the phenomenon of "Swahilization" which has extended well beyond the original Swahili coastal settlements. It is interesting to note that in the past Swahilization was not only closely linked to Islamization but also to Arabization. Increasingly however, current Swahilization trends, as is to be observed for example in Tanzania, indicate a delinking of Swahilization with these or other related processes. Mazrui and Mazrui[9] see this as an aspect of what they term "detribalization." As already indicated, groups of people who describe themselves as Swahili are to be found in numerous urban settlements in both East and Central Africa. The degree to which the lifestyle, culture and religion of any of these groups conforms to that of the classic Swahili is variable and not necessarily uniform. Moreover, the "Swahilization" of Tanzania as hinted to above pushes the meaning of this second definition beyond its traditional limits. Here the Swahilization should not be understood as an aspect of "retribalization" but rather as the formation of a pan-national consciousness and identity. In the Tanzanian sense, a Mswahili is any African who speaks Swahili as his dominant means of social discourse, a phenomenon that was reinforced during the Tanzanian Socialist (Ujamaa) era, when Swahili was elevated to the status of official and national language and effectively became the medium of official government communication as well as the medium of instruction in all primary schools and to a certain extent in secondary schools throughout the country. The impact of this decision on the development of new terminology in all scientific and technological fields was astounding. In Kenya and elsewhere in the East African region, "swahilization" in the Tanzanian sense is not pronounced. Thus for example in Kenya, there are some who hold the view that, "There is no such thing as Swahili tribe or group, the term is loosely applied to a variety of people who live on Kenya's coast who are linked only by their common language and to some extent, a common religion—Islam."[10]

8. See for example Abungu, "City States of the East African Coast."

9. Mazrui and Mazrui, *Swahili State & Society*, 1–8.

10. Mazrui and Shariff, *The Swahili Idiom and Identity*, 44.

The Swahili Language

There is no doubt that the Swahili language is central to any definition of what it means to be Swahili, even while granting that there might be some ethnic Swahili who may not speak their language. There are of course millions more who speak Swahili but who do not so identify themselves. This should not be surprising given that Swahili is one of the most widely spoken lingua francas in Africa. Estimations of Swahili speakers vary from as 50 to 80 million people. Obviously, this figure includes people whose command of Swahili varies from mother-tongue competence to mere functional use in limited areas. Wilfred Whiteley[11] identifies at least four main groups of Swahili speakers:

> first those who speak Swahili as a 'mother' tongue, who probably do not number more than a million and who live mainly along the East African littoral, on the offshore islands of Zanzibar, Pemba, Mafia, the Comoros, and a number of inland towns. These Swahili pools were left behind when the tide of Arab trade receded in the nineteenth century, places like Tabora, Ujiji, Bujumbura, as well as isolated trading settlements in Zambia, and along the Congo river. Second those who acquire it as a second language and use it for much of their daily life. There are certainly in excess of ten million in this group, living in the United Republic of Tanzania and in the Bantu speaking areas of Kenya. Third, a group, probably in excess of a million, who regularly use the language to a limited extent. This group is located in Uganda, the Nilotic speaking areas of Kenya. and parts of the Congo-Kinshasa. Finally there are those with a very limited control of the language who use it only sporadically. They are mainly located along the periphery of the main Swahili-speaking areas, in southern Somalia, northern Mozambique, parts of Rwanda, Burundi, and the western areas of the Congo around Kinshasa, the capital.

It is noteworthy that about thirty years later since Whiteley made this observation, the demographic situation has greatly changed and the numbers increased, hence the high estimates of the number of current Swahili speakers. It should be noted further that Whiteley does not mention Malawi, a country neighbouring Tanzania where there are many Swahili speakers. Neither does he mention pockets of Swahili speakers in southern Sudan or those in southern African countries such as South Africa or Namibia.

---

11. Whiteley, *Swahili*, 3.

Swahili speakers prior to the standardization of Swahili by the colonial British government in East Africa from the 1920s onwards did not, as a matter of fact, speak a single variety of their language. As indicated above, each 'Swahili' settlement was associated with its own variety or dialect of this cluster of languages now commonly referred to as Ki-Swahili. (This situation is typical of many languages or dialect clusters in East Africa characterized as they are by 'language continua'. In fact according to Professor Mohamed Abdulaziz,[12] "Present institutionalized names of languages would seem not to be based on any scientific criteria. Some of them are comparatively recent names, and by no means the original names of the languages as known by the speakers. Kinyamwezi and Kisukuma . . . provide a good illustration of the difficulties involved in deciding what constitute languages and language communities." In Tanzania, for example, the Chagga constitute a classic case of a people who currently consider themselves a single ethnic community but who speak dialects that are not always mutually intelligible. Thus the Machame and Rombo, who form part of the Chagga dialect cluster, speak mutually unintelligible dialects, although both identify themselves as Chagga.[13] Interestingly, the Machame-Chagga and their Meru, non-Chagga neighbours speak mutually intelligible dialects. In Kenya the present author's own ethnic community—the Abaluyia comprise 17 or so dialects in this linguistic cluster, with intelligibility among any two of them ranging from very high to extremely low. Yet the Abaluyia currently identify themselves as one people![14] Such examples can be multiplied many times over. In reality however these new groupings, linguistic as well as ethnic, are to a greater or lesser extent, colonial inventions more or less like most countries in Africa, the Asia-Pacific region or the Americas are colonial creations and inventions, brought into existence without representation consequent and subsequent to the Berlin conference!

In the case of Swahili, scholars recognize three major dialect clusters—a northern, central and southern, spread out along the East African coast, stretching from Somalia in the north to Mozambique in the south. Whiteley[15] notes that:

> The northern cluster comprises the dialects of communities living around Lamu and Pate on the northern coasts of Kenya (Ki-Amu, Ki-Shela, Ki-Pate, Ki-Siu), together with that of the Bajun (Ki-Tikuu), who stretch northwards into Somalia. The . . .

12. In ibid., 161.
13. See Mojola, "The Chaga Scape-Goat Purification."
14. See Kanyoro, *Unity in Diversity*.
15. Whiteley, *Swahili*, 4.

dialect of Brava (Chi-Miini) is best regarded as a sub-group of this cluster. The central cluster comprises the dialects of Vanga (Ki-Vumba) and Mtang'ata (Ki-Mtang'ata), located on the southern Kenya and northern Tanzanian coasts respectively. To these must be added the various dialects of Pemba, and the two major rural dialects of Zanzibar (Ki-Tumbatu and Ki-Hadimu). The southern cluster comprises the dialects of the Tanzanian coast south of Bagamoyo, including the island of Mafia, and the dialect of Zanzibar town, which was subsequently chosen to be the 'Standard' form of the language. To these must be added the 'bridge' dialects in and around Mombasa (Ki-Mvita, Chi-Jomvu, Ki-Ngare, with Chi-Chifundi farther to the south), which share some northern and some central feature. The dialects of the Comoro Islands, however, require separate groupings (Ki-Nzwani, Shi-Ngazija).

Edgar Polome,[16] Derek Nurse, and Thomas Spear[17] as well as other leading Swahili scholars give, with minor variations here and there, essentially the same list of recognized nineteenth- and early twentieth-century Swahili dialects on the eastern African coast and the neighbouring islands. Many of these are in serious decline, but quite a number are still alive and well and can still be heard by any interested visitor. Evidence of the long ancestry of some of these dialects has been preserved for posterity in the recorded literature of these Swahili speakers.[18] Although current Swahili writings employ the Roman script, a practice that was established during the colonial period, classical Swahili writings some dating as far back as the ninth century CE or thereabouts, such as the famous epic of Fumo Liyongo, or those composed somewhat later, such as that of Al Inkishafi, Mwana Kupona, or the nationalist poetry of Muyaka bin Haji of Mombasa, it should be noted that classical Swahili literature was originally written in Arabic script.

The need to standardize Swahili was no doubt closely intertwined with its expanded use as a lingua franca in the region, its use for trade in the East African hinterland stretching into the interior of the Congo, as well as its use for educational and religious purposes. Trade between the coast and interior is age old but was probably intensified by the coming of Arab and other Asiatic traders.[19] The dark era of the slave trade was a culmination of

16. Polome, *Swahili Langauge Handbook,* 19–25.

17. Nurse and Spear, *The Swahili,* 57–67.

18. See, for example Jan Knappert's *Four Centuries of Swahili Verse*; or Mulokozi and Sengo's *History of Kiswahili Poetry AD 1000–2000*; or M. M. Mulokozi's recent *Tenzi Tatu za Kale.*

19. See Mutoro, "Precolonial Trading Systems."

this process. The notorious Afro-Arab slave trader Hamed bin Muhammed el Murjebi commonly known as Tippu Tip, typifies the evils of this period. His activities as well as those of his ilk, set in process the Swahilization as well as the Islamization of the interior to various degrees. These processes were, however, in themselves independent of this evil. The Swahilization process was promoted to varying extents by groups of mainly European and American adventurers, travelers and researchers, such as David Livingstone, David Morton Stanley, and others. For example, when Stanley visited Kabaka Mutesa the King of Buganda at his palace in Kampala in April 1875 during his second Trans-Africa Expedition of 1874–1877 (his first expedition of 1871–72 had been in search of Dr. Livingstone), he found Swahili interpreters at the court where the main medium of communication was Luganda—the language of the Buganda kingdom. It is interesting to note that Stanley was accompanied by two Swahili speaking guides, namely Robert Feruzi and Scorpion Maftaa, freed slaves from Zanzibar trained at the Christian mission school there. It is reported that Stanley left Maftaa behind in Buganda to teach the Kabaka about the Whiteman's Book[20] presumably in Swahili.

Use of Swahili in the hinterland was however intensified and extended during the colonial period through the roles and activities of German and British colonial agents as well as those of their native Swahili or Swahili-speaking collaborators, "such auxiliaries as soldiers, teachers, policemen, guides, interpreters, junior administrative officers . . ."[21] Nevertheless its adoption and widespread use by the missionaries during the colonial period is what provided the major impetus and motivation for expansion in the interior as a lingua franca. The missionaries transformed Swahili into the major medium and tool for promoting and advancing their educational and religious goals in the region, eventually making it indispensable for use in the school and the church. But before this goal could be realized they needed to create a single standard orthography as well as a single standard Swahili out of the many existing and competing varieties. The Education Conference held in Dar es Salaam from the 6th to 9th October 1925, was the precursor of the East African Swahili Committee, a committee devoted to the task of standardizing the language and its orthography, preparing standard dictionaries and grammars, promoting and publishing literature and textbooks in the new standard. The widely used Fredrick Johnson's *A Standard Swahili–English, Standard English–Swahili Dictionaries* (1939)

---

20. See Tuma and Mutibwa, *A Century of Christianity in Uganda*, 93.

21. Abdulaziz, "Tanzania's National Language Police and the Rise of Swahili Political Culture," 162.

based on the work of Arthur C. Madan were in fact produced under the aegis of this Committee. To be effective the British colonial government, the imperial power in Kenya, Tanganyika, Uganda and Zanzibar gave the power of imprimatur to this Committee. In this way it was possible to control and influence the form and substance of Swahili used in the major public media of the day in this region.

The first meeting of the East African Swahili Committee, also known as the Inter-territorial Language (Swahili) Committee to the East African Dependencies was held on 1 January 1930. One of its most important resolutions was its ratification of the choice of Kiunguja (the Swahili of Zanzibar) as the dialect of Swahili standardization, a decision that was strongly disputed by defenders of other Swahili dialects notably Kiamu (the Swahili of Lamu) and Kimvita (the Swahili of Mombasa). These latter two were hitherto the most prestigious dialects of classical Swahili poetry. The 1925 Dar es Salaam conference had recommended the choice of Kiunguja as the basis for standardizing Swahili. It was however left to the Mombasa conference of 1928 to formally endorse that recommendation. The main contending dialects were those of Mombasa and Zanzibar, the two major urban centers of the region. The missionaries of the Church Missionary Society (CMS) with their headquarters in Mombasa naturally put their weight behind Kimvita—the Mombasa dialect, while the missionaries of the Universities Mission to Central Africa (UMCA) put their weight behind Kiunguja—the Zanzibar dialect. With the Kenyan delegates at the conference divided between Kiamu and Kimvita, the Tanganyika and Zanzibar delegates were able to score an easy win. Mbaabu (1996:68) reports that:

> The chief supporter of Kimvita, Canon Crawford of Kenya, having spent all his life in Kimvita speaking areas, spoke very strongly for Kimvita since, like other supporters of Kimvita, he did not know another dialect. When a vote was taken and it went in favour of Kiunguja, Canon Crawford was so overcome with grief that he burst into tears and had to be led out of the conference room.

The reasons for the choice of the Swahili of Zanzibar (Kiunguja) as the basis for standardizing Swahili are understandable. Zanzibar had been for many years the Sultan's power base as well as the major political and Islamic religious centre in the East African region. At Zanzibar was to be found the biggest slave market in the whole region, making it the leading business and commercial centre in this part of the world. No wonder nearly all expeditions and travels to the East African interior started here in Zanzibar. Advantages accruing to Kiunguja from all these factors are obvious.

Language prestige and power go hand in hand. The choice left much bitterness among the colonial scholars and missionaries from these two areas. Whiteley[22] observes that:

> This was doubly unfortunate: the richness of the historical and literary traditions of Mombasa and the northern coast, together with their links with Islam, seemed to offer little of relevance to the rest of Kenya, which tended to look towards the Swahili of Tanganyika; but the south lacked any such traditions, and their absence from school syllabuses in both Tanganyika and Kenya certainly impoverished the Swahili Courses of several generations of students. Against this, however, the adoption of a variety closely akin to varieties of the language already spoken over large areas of inland Tanganyika contributed powerfully to its rapid acceptance.

For example writing in defense of the Swahili of Mombasa (Ki-Mvita), Canon W.E. Taylor (the main translator of the Bible in the Swahili of Mombasa, described by Frankl,[23] as "England's greatest Swahili scholar") argued that Kimvita was far superior to Kiunguja and all other Swahili dialects because of its being a central dialect:

> Central because while the genius of the Mombasa dialect eschews the blemishes and excrescences which are to be found in the others—the too patent crudities, ambiguities, and corruptions of the careless South, and the needless complications and iron bound archaisms of the too conservative islanders of the North—the Mombasa speech, in its purity displays and cultivates to the full all their respective excellence . . . the Mombasian or Kimvita is the dialect considered of all others the best fitted for accurate statement and grave discussion—the Swahili for prose per excellence.[24]

Missionary Johannes Krapf writing earlier did not think much of Zanzibar Swahili either. Although he admitted its widespread use far into the interior and by a wide range of speakers he still held that: "Kiswahili spoken at Zanzibar has a large infusion of Arabic and other foreign words. The Mombasians therefore consider the dialect of Zanzibar as the maneno ya kijingajinga, i.e. the language of the ignorant people, or the newly arrived

22. Whiteley, *Swahili*, 81.

23. Frankl, "Siku ya Mwaka," 125.

24. Quoted in Mbaabu, *Language Policy in East Africa*, 66–67.

slaves and other foreigners . . ."[25] The Swahili lexicographer, A. C. Madan seems to accept this view. For him:

> "The dialect has no literary standard. Its vocabulary is ill-defined and fluctuating, the proportion of Arabic words (for example) varying largely in different sections of its very mixed population, while words from every dialect use between the coast and the Great Central Lakes, and from Delgoa to further India, from time to time assent their claim to be incorporated in it and even a certain proportion from the languages of modern Europe.[26]

This is not the place to get into the full story of the standardization of Swahili. It should be interesting though to take note of a statement found in the *Bulletin of the East African Interterritorial Language (Swahili) Committee* of 1934 in which a committee member expresses the following view on the new Standard Swahili:

> We have standardized Swahili and in the process Swahili seems to have become a new language. While, doubtless, all are ready to admit that Swahili, like any other language is bound to develop and grow, in form, idiom and vocabulary, as a result of the impact of the civilizations of the immigrant communities, yet surely the development must come from the Swahili mind, and must not be superimposed on them from without. But that is just what we have tried, and are still trying to do, with the result that we are in the somewhat ludicrous position of teaching Swahilis their own language through the medium of books, many of which are not Swahili in form or content, and whose language has but little resemblance to the spoken tongue. We are perhaps too apt to overlook the fact that the people themselves are not only capable of adapting their language to modern needs, but are doing so with amazing rapidity.[27]

The Translation of the Bible in Swahili

P. J. L. Frankl,[28] a British scholar, in consultation with Yahya Ali Omar, an ethnic Mombasa Swahili, make the claim that: "Islam has for countless generations permeated the lives of the Swahili people from cradle to grave, just

---

25. Quoted in Ibid., 66.

26. Ibid.

27. Quoted in Whiteley, *Swahili*, 85.

28. Frank, "The Word for 'God' in Swahili," 207.

as it permeated their speech from *alifu* to *yee* (from 'A' to 'Z')," and that "unlike the Swahili of second language speakers, the speech of the Swahili people has evolved wholly within the world of Islam . . ." Obviously this claim raises serious questions about the Swahili language and what it means in general for a language to be an Islamic language. Elaborating somewhat on this Frankl and Omar[29] argue that "the language and literature of the Swahili may be described as 'Islamic' neither on account of the script . . . nor because of Arabic loan words . . . but because for very many generations the Swahili people have been virtually exclusively Muslim, and for them, as for all long established Muslim societies, speech reflects a way of life in which there is no distinction, at any rate not in theory, between sacred and secular. Thus to suggest that the contemporary speech of the Swahili people can be described as 'Islamic' is to make a statement about Swahili culture rather than about Swahili syntax . . ." It could be argued in response that Frankl and Omar are confusing language and culture, and that to know a language does not entail knowing its culture. Perhaps in a deeper sense what Frankl and Omar are suggesting is that meanings in every language are only possible on the basis of a given interpretive grid or belief system, or world view. In the case of ethnic Swahili that grid is Islam.

André Lefevere in his article "Composing the Other"[30] probably has this problem in mind. There he contends that "people who translate texts do not, first and foremost, think on the linguistic level, the level of the translation of individual words and phrases. Rather, they think first in terms of . . . two grids."[31] Although Lefevere speaks of two grids, there may in fact be more grids at play.[32] Lefevere's two grids, which he terms a conceptual and a textual grid are, as he claims, intertwined. The textual grid relates to the text and its literary signs, markers, genres, types, stylistic conventions, etc. "designed to elicit certain reactions on the reader's part, and that the success of communication depends on both the writer and reader of the text agreeing to play their assigned parts in connection with those markers . . ."[33] The conceptual grid on the other hand could refer to one's perspective, world view or even to one's cultural and religious assumptions. Lefevere reformulates this as "the most important problem in all translating and in all attempts at cross-cultural understanding: Can culture A ever really understand culture B on that culture's (i.e. B's) own terms? Or do the grids always

---

29. Ibid., 206.

30. In Bassnett and Trivedi, eds., *Postcolonial Translation,* 75–94.

31. Ibid., 76.

32. On this point see Tim Wilt 2000.

33. Ibid.

define the ways in which cultures will be able to understand each other? Are the grids . . . the prerequisite for all understanding?"[34] Lefevere believes that this problem could be overcome if we invest hugely in a 're-education/ re-socialization' programme that is necessary if "we are ever to arrive at the goal of understanding other cultures 'on their own terms.'"[35]

How does this apply to the translation of the Swahili Bible? The Christian missionaries who took the challenge to translate the Bible in Swahili had to contend with the problem of operating with grids that were not only different from their own but also different from one another and often conflicting. Or as Adrian Hastings has put it: "Christians had to decide their faith in terms of words and concepts whose usage and meaning hitherto had other purposes and other senses."[36] In the case of Swahili, Farouk[37] points out that initially Islam faced the daunting task of formulating its own theological concepts and terms in Swahili. Later Christianity had to do the same, but this time having to contend with both the Islamic Arabic heritage and world view as well as with the underlying original Swahili Bantu heritage and religio-cultural world view. This dual heritage could not be brushed aside. It is not clear that the early missionary translators who undertook this task realized the magnitude of what was before them.

The first Christian missionary to undertake this task in this region was Dr. Johann Ludwig Krapf. He landed in Zanzibar on January 7, 1844, and set foot in Mombasa on May 5, 1844. Ype Schaaf in his book *On Their Way Rejoicing—The History and Role of the Bible in Africa*[38] makes the unconvincing claim that: "By October 1844 he (Krapf) had completed not only a Swahili grammar and dictionary, but also the New Testament and Genesis." How is this kind of output possible? Is it possible to master a language in that time frame and produce reliable and acceptable or authoritative works in it? Can the quality of such works be trusted? W. B Anderson[39] allows for more time and is probably closer to the truth. He writes: "By 1846 when his colleague Johann Rebmann arrived, Krapf had translated most of the New Testament into Swahili."

In addition to the above, soon after his arrival in Mombasa, Krapf is also said to have started translating the biblical book of Genesis into Mombasa Swahili (Kimvita), with the assistance of a Muslim *kadhi* or judge—a certain

34. Ibid., 77.

35. Ibid.

36. Quoted in Topan, "Swahili as a Religious Language," 334.

37. Ibid.

38. Schaaf, *On Their Way Rejoicing*, 75.

39. W. B. Anderson, 1977: 2.

Ali bin Mohedin. However, only three chapters of Krapf's translation of the book of Genesis were actually published. These appeared in the *Journal of the American Oriental Society*.[40] Now, although Krapf's New Testament in Kimvita Swahili was completed, it has never in fact been published. Ype Schaff[41] writes that it "proved not to be usable, because it was the Swahili of the Arabs and not that of the Africans." After retirement in Germany, Krapf continued reworking and improving his Swahili NT. All was however not lost, Krapf was able to pass his NT to Bishop Edward Steere, the leading and pioneer translator of the Bible in Kiunguja Swahili. The influence of Krapf's pioneering translation of the Scriptures and of his groundbreaking Swahili research is undeniable.

It is not clear to what extent Krapf delved into the cultural and religious systems of the Swahili, and to what extent he mastered the Swahili language with all its historical and linguistic complexities. To what extent did he for example impose his own Germanic cultural and religious presuppositions onto the Swahili grids and frames? Krapf was a very prolific and indefatigable researcher. His *Outline of the Elements of the Ki-Suaheli Language with Special Reference to the Kinika Dialect* (1850), as well as his *A Dictionary of the Swahili Language* (1882) are an important and lasting contribution to Swahili diachronic linguistics and lexicography.

Although Krapf pioneered the work of translating the Bible into Kimvita Swahili, it was left to Canon W. E. Taylor and his colleague H. K. Binns to complete the task. The New Testament was published in 1909 and the Old Testament five years later in 1914. As already noted the future did not lie with these translations in Kimvita Swahili, even though this was the dialect of Muyaka bin Haji of Mombasa (1776–1840), one of the most celebrated nationalist poets of the East African coast.[42] It is not surprising that Canon Taylor steeped himself thoroughly in the literature of the northern poets. It is to Mwalimu Sikujua bin Abdullah and Canon Taylor that we owe the present annotated collection of Muyaka's poetry in Romanized script. Prof. Abdulaziz acknowledges: "To these two men the verses of Muyaka owe their survival." No wonder Abdulaziz himself a Mombasan, and an ethnic Swahili linguist and expert on Muyaka's poetry dedicated his book to these two men "for their selfless enterprise in collecting and writing down these verses of

40. Vol. 1, 1849: 261–74. Printed in Bombay, India. A copy of this journal can be viewed at the London School of Oriental and African Studies library.

41. 1994:76.

42. See Abdulaziz, *Muyaka*.

Muyaka."[43] The involvement of a Swahilist scholar of Canon Taylor's caliber obviously contributed to the quality of the Bible in Kimvita Swahili.

It was however Bishop Edward Steere and his colleagues in Zanzibar who are credited with producing the first Bible in East Africa in Kiunguja, the Swahili of Zanzibar. These missionaries of the UMCA were graduates of the best British universities of the time—Oxford, Cambridge, and Edinburgh and were destined to make a real contribution to Swahili studies. Thus E. Steere's Swahili grammar or Arthur C. Madan's dictionary have been widely accepted as authoritative texts and widely used until recent times. Of Madan, a Chronicler of the UMCA, Blood, wrote: "A student of Christ Church, Oxford, he joined the Mission and went out to Zanzibar to work under Bishop Steere in 1880. He was pre-eminently the 'scholar' of the Mission and during the sixteen years that he served in Zanzibar 'carried on Bishop Steere's work in Swahili and has enriched . . . all East Africa with many valuable works."[44] In a foreword to Frederick Johnson's *A Standard Swahili-English Dictionary* (which is 'founded on *Madan's Swahili-English Dictionary*) the Anglican Bishop of Zanzibar put it that: "The Universities Mission to Central Africa has been allowed to have an important share in the discovery and elucidation of the Swahili language, and in this connection the names of Steere and Madan can never be forgotten. They were not merely pioneers but scholars, and this fact has given a lasting permanence to their labours."

It is interesting that these UMCA men always took pride in their scholarship. Thus for example in an argument between Canon Hebert E. Butcher of Mombasa and Canon Augustine B. Hellier of Zanzibar, the two translators of the main standard Swahili Bible, i.e. the Swahili Union Version Bible, a lot of emotion was generated. Clearly the difficult and demanding task of translating the Swahili Bible in the new Standard variety was not easy! Moreover for the CMS men from Mombasa, the choice of Zanzibar Swahili as the base for the new standard was simply wrong. The UMCA men from Zanzibar obviously thought otherwise. Disagreement was not just on lexical, grammatical, orthographical matters but also on exegetical matters as well. Obviously the accomplishment of this task required a lot of patience, give and take as well as mutual respect. This was not always possible. For example Canon Hellier wrote to Canon Coleman: "Nobody can produce agreement between us on such a point . . ."[45] In his counter-response to Canon Coleman, Canon Butcher wrote: "The position with regard to these

43. Ibid., 3.

44. Blood, *The History of the Universities Mission to Central Africa*, 151.

45. See Mojola, "The Chagga Scape-Goat Purification," 70–71.

Psalms is a bit complicated as they are almost solely Canon Hellier's work . . ."[46] Meanwhile Canon Broomfield, UMCA Secretary in London writing to A. Wilkinson, British and Foreign Bible Society (BFBS) General Secretary wrote: "I feel that final decisions should rest with Hellier. After all, he is a scholar, and I do not think Messrs. Butcher and Pittway for instance would make that claim for themselves. At one of our meetings to discuss NT translation they admitted that they knew practically no Greek."[47] Earlier writing to E. W. Smith of the BFBS, Broomfield complained: "as far as Swahili as we know it is concerned, the present Zanzibar version is much better than that written by our friends in Kenya . . . In a word, it seems to us that Messrs. Butcher and Pittway and Miss Deed are not Swahili scholars of the same caliber as those responsible for the present Zanzibar version."[48] Rev. G. Capon of CMS Limuru, Kenya, in defense of his Mombasa friends, wrote to Rev. H. D. Hooper of CMS, London on 17.1.1941 as follows: "a fairly close study of Hellier's work makes me very doubtful whether he should be an assessor over Butcher, or indeed over anybody else at all . . ."[49]

There is no question that the translators of yesterday were no different from those of today. Neither can it be claimed that missionary translators were in a class of their own, simply because their translations broke the ground and are in many places revered and placed on a pedestal, as is the case with the present Swahili Union Version (SUV). It is clear that like today's translators personal, academic, denominational, and doctrinal sensitivities bedeviled the translation teams of yesterday. Canon Hellier's subsequent mental breakdown in England was probably due to the many strains and stresses he suffered in the course of his work as the chief translator to the Swahili Union Version. Canon Hellier never forgot his native collaborators. He specially wrote to the BFBS, the publishers of the SUV on 15.9.1952 to send a copy of the first edition of the SUV from the press to Rev Paulo Kihampa because "he made some original and really helpful remarks in the discussion and I felt that for a native he was quite outstanding."[50] It is a miracle of grace that these human frailties resulted in such a great translation. Clearly the BFBS was correct in claiming in a letter written to the widow of Canon Hubert John Edwin Butcher (1879–1956) at his death

46. Ibid.
47. Ibid.
48. Ibid.
49. Ibid.
50. Ibid.

that: "The Union Swahili Version has already taken its place as one of the monumental achievements of the Bible Society . . ."[51]

Translators of the Bible in Mombasa Swahili (the men from CMS - Krapf and Rebmann to Taylor and Binns) and those of the Bible in Zanzibar Swahili (the men from UMCA - Steere and his colleagues) were clearly scholars steeped in the study of the culture and dialects in which they worked as well as its literature. Steere's Bible of 1891 (NT 1879) was widely used throughout the region. It was the Bible that the first missionaries in the hinterland and as far away as Buganda and indeed the whole Great Lakes region used. Its impact on Bible translations in other languages of this region such as Luganda (Bible 1896), Chiyao (NT 1907, Bible 1920), Cigogo (NT 1899), Runyoro-Rutoro (NT1905, Bible 1912) Kitaveta (NT 1906), Giriama (NT 1901, Bible 1908) among others is evident. Taylor's Bible in Mombasa Swahili which came out in 1914 (NT 1909) was not as widely used in the region as Steere. Moreover, as already noted its impact was drastically reduced by the decision to create a regional Swahili Standard from the 1930s onwards that virtually bypassed it. Adrian Hastings has this situation in mind when he writes:

> In many parts of East Africa, including Buganda, missionary teaching was initially imparted either through the medium of Swahili, or in a local language much affected by Swahili borrowings. Reasons for this were several. Swahili being a coastal language its missionary use preceded that of any other language by decades. Up-country missionaries . . . had Swahili grammars, dictionaries and Bibles to make use of in coping with their own still unwritten but kindred languages.[52]

Working however in a Swahili Muslim environment, Krapf and Rebmann, Taylor and Binns, Steere and his colleagues, all heavily relied on Swahili Muslims for their knowledge of the language and its underlying religious and cultural life. This no doubt affected and impacted on their respective translations. It is not surprising that Islamic terminology and concepts were adopted and used extensively in the translations. All three Swahili Bibles mentioned above namely Steere's Bible of 1891, Taylor's Bible of 1914 and Hellier and Butcher's Swahili Union Version of 1952 were produced, as already noted, with primarily an ethnic Swahili target audience in mind. Of course, first language speakers were envisaged as well but they were not primary. These missionary translators were to all intents and purposes resident

51. Ibid.

52. Hastings 115, quoted in Frankl and Omar, "The Idea of 'The Holy' in Swahili," 112.

at the coast among Swahili-speaking heavily Islamised people. It is therefore safe to conclude that these translations reflected something of the Islamic culture of the ethnic Swahili people. This influence is patently evident in the generous use of Islamic religious terms in these translations, even in cases where suitable Swahili terms of Bantu origin exist. For example, words for priest, prophet, spirit, holy, sacrifice, altar, offering, life, blood, impure, sin, cleanse, condemn, believe, faith, hope, human being, good news, book, psalm, glory, blessed, earth, and numerous others, in these translations are all derived from Arabic. Even in cases where a particular term was not in use in Swahili Islamic discourse, these translators invented one derived from the Arabic. In this connection Frankl and Omar write:

> The available evidence, which dated from the mid-nineteenth century, suggests that the Swahili people had no need of a word for 'holy' to express their sense of 'The Holy'. In order to translate the word 'holy' for speakers of *kiMisheni* (the Swahili spoken by European-Christian missionaries and their followers) a Swahili word *takatifu* was derived to translate 'holy'—this probably occurred in the late 1850s or in the 1860s. But the Swahili language has a genius for absorbing new words, and so since the second World War, the *maShekhe* have used the 'Christian' *takatifu* in their qur'anic interpretations for the qur'anic words derived from the Arabic consonanta; root *q d s*. Whatever the origin of *takatifu* as a printed word, it is true to say that in their conversations of Swahili folk *takatifu* has been until recently a word unknown and therefore a word unheard.[53]

Through the influence of these translations the word *takatifu* was widely adopted in numerous translations of the Bible in the East African Bantu languages. Hastings draws attention to this in the case of the Luganda. He writes:

> In Luganda *takatifu* was at first only one of many Swahili words employed . . . Between 1908 and 1912, however, there was a systematic removal of unnecessary Swahilisms from Christian Luganda undertaken by both Protestants and Catholics. Swahili had come to be regarded as an alien and—perhaps also—a threateningly Muslim language . . . *Takatifu* was at this point changed to the indigenous *tukirivu or tukuvu*.[54]

---

53. Frankl and Omar, "The Idea of 'The Holy' in Swahili," 113.

54. Ibid.

Farouk Topan[55] notes that "almost all major terms for an Islamic discourse in Swahili are derived from Arabic." No wonder a number of writers, among them Ali Mazrui and Pio Zirimu (1990), speak of Swahili as an Islamic language or an Afro-Islamic language. It seems that when the original Swahili Bantu culture was Islamized, the Bantu religious component was transformed and given a new linguistic component. This process never completely eliminated the original Bantu factor. Inspite of the power of Islamic transformation, the Swahili Bantu name for God, Mungu, which Swahili shares with a number of other Bantu languages in the region[56] still dominates in Swahili Islamic discourse.[57] Farouk Topan thinks that the process of Islamizing Swahili Bantu religious discourse and terminology could have proceeded as follows:

i. the original Arabic term was Swahilized, eg. Ruh (Arabic) à Roho (Swahili)

ii. the original Arabic term was Swahilized and, additionally, given a Bantu synonym, eg. Rasul (Arabic) à rasuli/ mtume (Swahili)

iii. the original Arabic term was generally not adopted but the concept was given a Swahili term, eg. Mungu was preferred to Allah.[58]

It should be noted that even when a term from the Bantu was retained, if it related to the religious sphere it was given Islamic meaning. Thus Mungu (Allah) in Swahili Islamic discourse is always qualified as 'Mwenyezi' Mungu. Farouk Topan[59] correctly notes that 'Mwenyezi' is: "a compound of Swahili and Arabic elements respectively: *mwenye* denoting 'possessor' and *ezi* (from *'izza*), 'power' and 'might'. The full phrase is taken to express the omnipotence, sovereignty and regality of the Almighty." Mazrui and Mazrui[60] exemplify this process by offering a few more examples as follows: "The word for God in Kiswahili (*M'ngu* or *Mungu*) comes from Bantu, whereas the word for angels (*malaika*) comes from Arabic. The word for the heavens (*mbingu*) comes from Bantu whereas the word for earth, especially when used religiously (*ardhi*), comes from Arabic. The word for a holy prophet (*mtume*) comes from Bantu, whereas the word for a devil in a religious sense (*shetani*) comes from Arabic. Curiously enough, the words for paradise and

---

55. Topan, "Swahili as a Religious Language," 335.

56. See Mojola, "A Female God in East Africa."

57. See article on this by Frankl, "The Word for 'God' in Swahili," 202–11.

58. Topan, "Swahili as a Religious Language," 335.

59. Ibid., 336.

60. Mazrui and Mazrui, *Swahili State & Society*, 22.

hell (*pepo* and *moto*) come from Bantu, whereas the word for the hereafter as a whole (*akhera* or *ahera*) comes from Arabic." In general, however, it could be argued that Swahili seems to have synonyms or alternative ways of expressing many of the ideas for which the Arabic term or word is now dominant, unless of course the term in question is about entities or realities that were absent in the original Bantu world.

Krapf, Taylor, Steere, and their collaborators and even Butcher and Hellier later apparently had no problem with the Arabic-Islamic component of Swahili or its suitability as a medium for expressing Christian ideas. On the contrary this component made their task lighter. They did not have to struggle to look for, to invent or to create suitable Bantu words for expressing Christian concepts and ideas. Krapf spoke for the rest when he pointed to the fact that this Arabic-Islamic component of Swahili "affords to the translator the resource of being able to adopt at will an Arabic word when in difficulty for a proper expression in Kisuaheli (sic)."[61] And as already indicated this Arabisation of Swahili Bantu well into the translation of the Christian Scriptures was extended to quite a number of the languages of the East African hinterland. Naturally this posed a problem. It was the German Lutheran missionary Dr. Karl Roehl who took the bull by the horns. To what extent should the Christian missionaries facilitate an Arabisation programme while promoting a parallel programme of Christianising the local cultures and languages? Topan[62] has put it well: "If Swahili, as a lingua franca had to be used, then it had to be de-Arabised "or freed from its Arabic character. In fact, Roehl refused to collaborate with the British team of Butcher and Hellier on the translation of the Swahili Union Bible precisely on the issue of what he felt was its excessive use of Arabic words. Roehl's idea was to substitute Bantu words wherever possible for Arabic words. The British members were of the view that "this limits the possibility of bringing out the meaning of the sacred text, especially if words which have been for a long time in use are replaced by less meaningful words."[63] (A first tentative edition of the proposed joint union version had been translated by Godfrey Dale (UMCA—Zanzibar) and revised by G. Pittway and H. J. Butcher (CMS—Mombasa) and published by the BFBS, London in 1934. Dr. Roehl rejected this test portion presented as a model on the grounds that it contained "so many Arabic words."[64] It should be noted here that although Swahili has borrowed heavily from Arabic, a situation that has given

61. Krapf 1882, xii, quoted in Topan, "Swahili as a Religious Language," 338.

62. Ibid., 339.

63. See Mojola, "A Female God in East Africa," 70.

64. Ibid.

the false impression that it is closer to Arabic and related Semitic languages, it is actually in every respect a Bantu language—in terms of its syntax, its morphology and phonology, its core lexicon which is closely related to Pro-Bantu, and its links to the neighbouring Bantu languages. For example, it is much easier for a speaker of a related Bantu language to learn Swahili than say for a speaker of Arabic or related Semitic languages. In fact, Swahili did not borrow words exclusively from Arabic but from all the languages that it came into contact with. Freeman Greenville estimated that "'20 to 30 percent of the (language) is composed of loan words' that come from such disparate areas as Persia, Hindustan, Gujarat, Turkey, Malaysia, Portugal, Germany and of course, England . . . Some words, too, are from 'special Arabian dialects.'"[65] Romero herself thinks that: "All of the words referring to Islam and religion, of course, are Arabic."[66] This is clearly false, as can be seen from the fact discussed here that the key word for the deity in Swahili is Bantu and shared by other related Bantu languages.

Dr. Karl Roehl embarked on his own translation reflecting his convictions. In his Bible translation project he aimed not only to fully utilize the Kiunguja Swahili as a base, but also to go beyond it in capturing its expanded use and function in the interior. He aimed at minimizing its Arabic lexical borrowings while at the same time maximizing the use of its Bantu lexical roots as reflected by usage in the interior of mainland Tanganyika. Roehl was a missionary of the Bethel Mission of the German Lutheran Church who had previously translated the New Testament into Kishambala. For his Swahili translation of the Bible he started by revising an earlier translation of the New Testament done by a fellow German missionary, Martin Klamroth of the Berlin Missionary Society. This translation was on behalf of four German missionary societies, namely the Berlin Mission, the Bielefeld Mission, the Leipzig Mission and the Moravian Mission. At meetings held in August and October 1914 representatives of these missions resolved to sponsor "a new translation, of the Scriptures in Swahili suitable for use throughout German East Africa" and whose "main object was to purify Swahili as a Bantu language, by eliminating the majority of the Zanzibar Arabic words, which are either not used, or only imperfectly understood, by the natives on the coast, and are quite unintelligible to those in the interior."[67]

Martin Klamroth with the help of some of his colleagues, and with some linguistic assistance and advice from Prof Carl F. M. Meinhof of Hamburg, completed the New Testament in 1914 but the outbreak of the War

---

65. Quoted in Romero, *Lamu*, 3.

66. Ibid.

67. See Mojola, "The Chagga Scape-Goat Purification," 68.

made its publication impossible. After the War, in the mid-1920s, Roehl commenced work on the revision of the Klamroth translation at Dar es Salaam. It was reported by Prof Dietrich Westermann in 1926 that this translation was "especially adapted to the Swahili as spoken in the interior. Many Arab words have been replaced by authentic Swahili words. It is written in the orthography officially adopted by the Government."[68] Attempts by the BFBS to enlist the help of the Germans and Dr. Roehl in launching a common union translation in standard Swahili for the whole of East Africa proved unsuccessful. Roehl's version of the New Testament in Swahili was eventually published in 1930 and the complete Bible containing both the New and Old Testaments in 1937 by the Württemberg Bible Society in Stuttgart, Germany. Dr. Roehl had been assisted by Pastor Martin Nganisya and Mwalimu Andrea Ndekeja.

The Stuttgart Society observed: "Our Swahili Bible is, as far as we know, the first edition of the Bible in a standardized Swahili written in the standardized orthography."[69] This Bible had as its target audience "all the Christian people in the whole East and Central Africa."[70] Rev H. Scholten, the Secretary of the Tanganyika Missionary Council writing about this translation observed as follows: "I still regret that two translations of the Swahili Bible will follow each other in short periods, but I do think that Dr. Roehl has done a great piece of work. I hardly doubt that his version of the Old Testament will be easily surpassed."[71]

The fate of the Roehl Bible was short lived even though it was considered a first class translation. With the fall of the Germans and the establishment of British hegemony in East Africa, the Roehl Bible did not receive much support. The influence of the British and Foreign Bible Society in East Africa saw to it that the Roehl Bible did not supplant the Swahili Union Version. As a result after it was printed in 1937, it was reprinted some years later in 1961. With the Roehl Bible out of print and with most of its champions gone, the arrival of a new General Secretary at the Bible Society of Tanzania, an ardent supporter of the Roehl translation, changed the situation. He had a new edition printed in 1995 and a reprint of this again in 1999. Some observers attribute the support of the Swahili Union Version by the establishment to its strong endorsement by the two main British Anglican missions, namely the CMS and the UMCA, as well as to its promotion by its publisher the BFBS. Now although the Roehl Bible had the support of

68. Ibid., 69.

69. Ibid.

70. Ibid.

71. Ibid.

the numerically stronger Tanzanian Lutheran church, it lacked the requisite institutional support by the powers that be. The whole matter boils down to a question of the dynamics of power in the East African Dependencies in the era of *pax Britannica*. Roehl's open agenda of de-Arabising Swahili was lost in the mist of power and church politics.

The first Bible in Swahili translated by East Africans themselves is the Biblia Habari Njema (NT 1977, Bible 1995). It is a "Common Language" Swahili translation, in everyday standard and current Swahili. It was however, not translated by the ethnic Swahili themselves, but nevertheless by East African speakers of the standard form of Swahili as currently used. This is in itself is an interesting commentary on the dynamics of Swahili use today. Translation work on this version was started in 1973 with the following participating as translators at different times—Peter Renju (RC), Cosmas Haule (RC), Jared Mwanjalla (Anglican), David Mhina (Anglican), Amon Mahava (Lutheran), Ammon Oendo (SDA), Douglas Waruta (Baptist) and Leonidas Kalugila (Lutheran). The first test portion of this translation, the Gospel of Luke appeared in 1975 jointly published by the Bible Societies of Kenya and Tanzania. The New Testament followed three years later in 1977 to an enthusiastic reception. It has since become a best seller in the region. The complete Bible was released simultaneously in Kenya and Tanzania on 24 March, 1996 in two editions, namely one with the Deutero-canonical books and the other without them. The launching dedication ceremony in Tanzania was held in the little backwater town of Manyoni, on the old slave route and on the main central railway line to Western Tanganyika. The choice of Manyoni is interesting and significant. Perhaps the idea was to make a symbolic statement delinking modern standard Swahili from the 'original' Swahili dialects of the East African littoral and of the traditional Swahili Islamic 'kaya' or settlements. The language of Biblia Habari Njema was predominantly Swahili as currently spoken especially in Tanzania and as taught in institutions throughout the region as the standard form of the language. It is interesting to note that the translation freely employed the terminology created and popularized by the Socialist government of Tanzania at the time. However the old Roehl agenda of de-Arabising standard Swahili was not taken up. Thus where Roehl uses, for example, the terms *kumtegemea Mungu, tambiko,* or *matoleo* (ie. Faith, sacrifice, or offering, respectively), Biblia Habari Njema uses the traditional Swahili Arabic terms, going back to Taylor and Steere (ie. Imani, dhabihu or sadaka). Roehll's terms are perfectly good Swahili Bantu words going back to the roots of Swahili Bantu religions. Their use in Biblia Habari Njema would certainly have advanced the cause of inculturation or indigenization, at least as far as it relates to the current non-ethnic, non-Muslim current Swahili speaker who is now the majority target user.[72] In general however, Roehl's agenda of de-Arabising standard Swahili has been bypassed by the current practice of borrowing heavily from Bantu languages first and thereafter from foreign languages. In the area of science and technology for example modern standard Swahili has borrowed heavily from the English. Borrowings from Arabic are at a minimum since Arabic is not much used these days even in the coastal areas, except perhaps in Arabic or Islamic contexts. The Biblia Habari Njema merely followed this practice and unquestioningly employed such terminology as are current in the churches, which basically meant in practice the terminology already established in church usage and liturgy by the Taylor and Steere translations.

Julius Kambarage Nyerere, one of the architects of the current Swahili policy in Tanzania, translated the four gospels and the book of the Acts of the Apostles[73] in the style and genre of popular Swahili poetry, in the classical tradition of the nineteenth-century Swahili poets such as Muyaka of Mombasa. It is interesting that some of the most celebrated poets of this genre in the twentieth century were not ethnic Swahili but modern Swahili in the Tanzanian sense. Two of these stand out namely, Shaaban Robert of Tanga, Tanzania and Matthias Mnyampala of Dodoma, Tanzania. Shaaban was of Yao origin but thoroughly Swahilized and even Islamized. In one of his most memorable poems, "Kiswahili,"[74] Shaaban compares Swahili to mother's breast and as sweet as mother's breast, irreplaceable and indispensable (i.e. "Titi la mama litamu / lingine halishi tamu . . . Titi la mama litamu, hata likawa la mbwa"). Mnyampala was, on the other hand, a Christian and of Gogo ethnic origin. He attempted, among other things, a free translation of the Gospels and of the Psalms in the style and genre of the traditional Swahili poets of the Swahili Islamic settlement. To practice poetry in this genre and style one needs to be deeply steeped in traditional ethnic Swahili culture and literature. Poets of Shaaban Robert, Matthias Mnyampala, and Julius Kambarage Nyerere's caliber are providing the bridge that is grounding Swahili more deeply and firmly on the current realities of present-day East Africa societies.

How Does Postcolonial Translation Theory Fit in Here?

Postcolonial approaches to translation have only emerged in recent times. They are primarily concerned with the links between translation and empire

72. See Renju, "1 Cor 5.7 Culture-Context Sensitivities."

73. Published in 1996.

74. Robert, *Pambo la Lugha*, 27.

or translation and power, as well as the role of translation in processes of cultural domination and subordination, colonization and decolonization, indoctrination and control, and the problem of hybridization and creolization of cultures and languages. Postcolonial translation theory disputes the proposition that translation has to do mainly with questions of textual equivalences, or the faithfulness or fidelity of a target text to an original source text. On the contrary Postcolonial approaches to translation take it as an axiom that translation has much more to do with the 'macropolitics' of empire, and the promotion of the interests and well-being of empire. The periphery necessarily serves the interests of this imperial centre. Susan Bassnett and Harish Trivedi in their text *Postcolonial Translation*[75] remind us that "the act of translation always involves more than language. Translations are always embedded in cultural and political systems, and in history. For too long translation was seen as purely an aesthetic act, and ideological problems were disregarded. Yet the strategies employed by translators reflect the context in which texts are produced," as well as the hegemonic or power interests and values at stake. Translation from this perspective is supremely viewed as a tool of empire. Douglas Robinson[76] states that the study of 'translation and empire', or even of 'translation as empire', "was born in the mid-to late 1980s out of the realization that translation has always been an indispensable channel of imperial conquest and occupation. Not only must the imperial conquerors find some effective way of communicating with their new subjects; they must develop new ways of subjecting them, converting them into docile or 'cooperative' subjects." Maria Tymoczko's recent *Translation in a Postcolonial Context*[77] is a recent text that exemplifies the power and influence of this approach even within the corpus of western literature itself.

Postcolonial translation theory makes use of a number of leading ideas from the new polysystem theory usually associated with the work of a cluster of Dutch and Flemish translation scholars such as Theo Hermans, André Lefevere, José Lambert or Israeli translation scholars such as Gideon Toury and Itamar Even-Zohar. According to Edwin Gentzler[78] "The term 'polysystem' represents the aggregate of literary systems, including everything from 'high' forms such as innovative verse to 'low' forms such as romance novels and children's literature." For Even-Zohar within any literary polysystem, translations may play any of two basic functions, a primary function where-

75. Bassnett and Trivedi, *Postcolonial Translation*, 6.
76. Robinson, *Translation and Empire*, 10.
77. Tymoczko, *Translation in a Postcolonial Context*.
78. Gentzler, in Alvarez and Vidal, *Translation, Power, Subversion*, 117–18.

by they contribute to the creation of new genres and styles, new literary devices, practices, etc. or a secondary function whereby they legitimize and reinforce existing literary practices, discourses, genres and styles. Even-Zohar also speaks of two types of cultures—"weak" cultures and "strong" cultures and the place and role of translated literatures in each of these in the context of the corresponding literary polysystem. He suggests that "1) in cultures that are 'weak' translations tend to play a strong or primary role and located in the literary centre; and 2) in cultures that are 'strong' translations tend to play a secondary role and tend to be marginalized by the literary centres."[79] This suggestion has however been disputed, for example, by Gentzler[80] who expresses "concern over recent developments in the 'theory' branch of translation studies, i.e. the attempt to formulate 'laws' regarding translation phenomena based upon little supportive evidence." He correctly argues that the situation is not so simple or uni-directional, but that the opposite has also been documented.

This approach as developed for example by Even-Zohar, Toury, or Lefevere looks at translation as part of a cultural and literary system and the power dynamics underlying the process. It has proved fertile ground for new ideas on how translation functions in societies. This approach also, among other things, looks at the process of how the texts to be translated in a given culture are selected, the inter-relationship between a dominant and dominated, central and peripheral, major and minor, primary or secondary—literary and cultural systems in terms of transfer of norms, values, functions, poetics, aesthetics, etc. The poly-system school has yielded tools for the analysis of the relationship between a literary system and the politico-economic social systems operative in a given society. Edwin Gentzler is of the view that "Polysystem theory is entering a new phase in which extra literary factors such as patronage, social conditions, economics, and institutional manipulation are being correlated to the way translations are chosen and function in a literary system."[81]

There is no doubt that many of the insights of Postcolonial translation theory can be used to throw some light on the role of Arabic-Islamic language and culture in its encounter with the Swahili Bantu language and culture, and how this encounter led to the Islamization and Arabization of the Swahili to various degrees. The Islamized Swahili language and culture in turn exerted a certain influence and transformation in the languages and cultures it encountered. In effect the process of Swahilization was set

79. Ibid.
80. Ibid., 116.
81. Gentzler, *Contemporary Translation Theories*, 119.

off. Naturally Swahilization initially implied Islamization and to a certain extent Arabization. Such influence and transformation was certainly not uni-directional. It is safer to assume that it went both ways in the context of the dialectic of the power dynamics at play. Moreover this involved transformatory processes at several levels and in several areas—religious, linguistic, literary, cultural, economic, political, etc.

The arrival of Western Christianity and European civilization no doubt introduced new factors in this complex equation. The Western missionary translators in the East African region it should be borne in mind operated under cover of pax Britannica. This defined certain boundaries and co-ordinates, certain allegiances and ideological commitments, certain freedoms and opportunities, certain prejudices and biases, certain values and life-styles, etc. in the new communities where they served and laboured. It is tempting to see them merely as colonial agents, On Her Majesty's Service. However not all missionaries fully acquiesced in the demands and interests of the colonial power. Quite a number acted solely in response to the higher transcendent message and demands of the Christian message. This notwithstanding they did this as citizens of the Crown, and this had its own limitations and implications for their interaction and life in the communities where they lived.

Conclusion

The forces set in train by Islamization, Arabization, Westernization, Christianization, Swahilization, and now re-Bantuization are neither pure nor simple. Moreover, these forces are closely associated with power, hegemony, colonization and imperialism, and extend not just to matters of economics or politics but necessarily to the cultural and linguistic sphere, and in the present case directly to matters of religious belief and practice. In exploring the dynamics at play in the development of the Swahili Christian Bible we find a convergence of all the above forces. It is not always easy to disentangle them or to isolate them. While the missionary translators responsible for the coming of the Swahili Bible no doubt intended their translations of the Bible to be read in accordance with or consistent with the standard readings accepted in their church communities, possibilities for alternative non-standard readings could not be ruled out. After finishing their translations they had no control on how these texts were to be interpreted, on the multiple meanings that could be generated from the texts. They however set the stage for this process. This is where the church comes in, in the context of its institutional settings, its ideology, its economic relationships to other institutions, its political links and connections, its theology of mission and evangelism, its ecclesiology and theology, its rituals, liturgy and social practice. This is where, as they say, the rubber meets the road.

Bibliography

Abdalla Bin Ali Bin Nasir, Sayyid. *Al-Inkishafi—Catechism of a Soul.* Translated by James de Vere Allen. Nairobi: East African Literature Bureau, 1977.

Abdulaziz, Mohammed H. "Tanzania's National Language Police and the Rise of Swahili Political Culture." In *Language Use and Language Change—Problems of Multilingualism with Special Reference to Eastrn Africa,* edited by W. H. Whiteley, 160–78. London: Oxford University Press, 1971.

———. *Muyaka—19*[th] *Century Swahili Popular Poetry.* Nairobi: Kenya Literature Bureau, 1979.

Abungu, George H. O. "City States of the East African Coast and Their Maritime Contacts." In *Transformations in Africa—Essays on Africa's Later Past,* edited by Graham Connah, 204–18. London: Leicester University Press, 1998.

Allen, James de Vere. *Swahili Origins—Swahili Culture and the Shungwaya Phenomenon.* Nairobi: East African Educational, 1993.

Alvarez, Roman, and M. Carmen-Africa Vidal. *Translation, Power, Subversion.* Topics in Translation 8. Clevedon, UK: Multilingual Matters, 1996.

Anderson-Morshead, A. E. M. *The History of the Universities Mission to Central Africa.* Vol. 1, *1859-1909.* London: UMCA, 1955.

Angogo, Rachel Musimbi. "Standard Swahili—Its History and Development." MA thesis, University of Texas, Austin, 1978.

Bakari, Mohamed. *The Morpho-phonology of Kenyan Swahili Dialects.* Berlin: Reimer, 1985.

Bassnett, Susan and Harish Trivedi, eds. *Postcolonial Translation: Theory and Practice,* London: Routledge, 1999.

Bible in Swahili (Mombasa). London: British and Foreign Bible Society, 1914.

Bible in Swahili (Zanzibar). London: British and Foreign Bible Society, 1891.

Bible in Swahili (Roehl). Stuttgart: Württemberg Bible Society, 1937.

Bible in Swahili (Union/Standard). London: British and Foreign Bible Society, 1952.

Bible in Swahili (Common Language). Dodoma / Nairobi: Bible Society of Tanzania & Bible Society of Kenya, 1995.

Blood, A. G. *The History of the Universities Mission to Central Africa,* Vol. II, *1907–1932,* London: UMCA, 1957.

Bosha, I. *Taathira za Kiarabu katika Kiswahili pamoja na Kamusi Thulathiya (Kiswahili-Kiarabu-Kiingereza): The Influence of Arabic Language on Kiswahili With a Trilingual Dictionary (Swahili-Arabic-English).* Dar es Salaam: Dar es Salaam University Press, 1993.

Chimerah, Rocha. *Kiswahili: Past, Present and Future Horizons.* Nairobi: Nairobi University Press, 2000.

Connah, Graham, ed. *Transformations in Africa: Essays on Africa's Later Past.* London: Leicester University Press, 1998.

Frankl, P. J. L. "Siku ya Mwaka: New Year's Day in Swahili-land (with special reference to Mombasa)." *JRA* 23 (1993) 125–35.

————. "The Word for 'God' in Swahili: Further Considerations." *JRA* 25 (1995) 202–11.

Frankl, P. J. L., and Yahya Ali Omar. "The Idea of 'The Holy' in Swahili." *JRA* 29 (1999) 109–14.

Freeman-Grenville, G. S. P. *The East African Coast: Select Documents from the First Century to the Early Nineteenth Century.* London: Clarendon, 1962.

Gentzler, Edwin. *Contemporary Translation Theories.* Translation Studies. London: Routledge, 1993.

Ghaidan, Usam. *Lamu: A Study of the Swahili Town.* Nairobi: Kenya Literature Bureau, 1975.

Harries, Lyndon. *Some Swahili Poetry.* London: Clarendon, 1962.

Huntington, Samuel P. *The Clash of Civilizations and the Remaking of the World Order.* London: Touchstone, 1996.

Kanyoro, Rachel Angogo. *Unity in Diversity: A Linguistic Survey of the Abaluyia of Western Kenya.* Vienna: Institute für Afrikanistik und Ägyptologie der Universität Wien, 1983.

Knappert, Jan. *Four Centuries of Swahili Verse: A Literary History and Anthology.* London: Heinemann, 1979.

Madan, Arthur C. *Swahili-English Dictionary.* London: Oxford University Press, 1903.

Mazrui, Ali A., and Alamin M. Mazrui. *Swahili State & Society: The Political Economy of an African Language.* Nairobi: East African Educational, 1995.

Mazrui, Alamin M., and Ibrahim Noor Shariff. *The Swahili Idiom and Identity of an African People.* Trenton, NJ: Africa World, 1994.

Mazrui, Ali, and Pio Zirimu. "The Secularization of an Afro-Islamic Language: Church, State and Market Place in the Spread of Kiswahili." *JIS* 2 (1990) 25–53.

Mbaabu, Ireri. *Language Policy in East Africa—a Dependency Theory Perspective.* Nairobi: Educational Research, 1996.

————. *Historia ya Usanifishaji wa Kiswahili.* Nairobi: Longman Kenya, 1991.

Mlacha (mhariri), S. A. K. *Kiswahili Katika Kanda ya Africa Mashariki: Historia, Matumizi na Sera.* Dar es Salaam: Taasisi ya Uchunguzi wa Kiswahili, 1995.

Mnyampala, Matthias. *Utenzi wa Enjili Takatifu.* Peramiho, Tanzania: Benedictine Ndanda, 1963.

Mojola, Aloo Osotsi. *God Speaks in Our Own Languages: Bible Translation in East Africa, 1844–1998, A General Survey.* Nairobi: Bible Societies of Kenya, 2000.

Mojola, Aloo Osotsi. "The Chagga Scape-Goat Purification Ritual and Another Re-reading of the Goat of Azazel/Azazel in Leviticus 16: Some Preliminary Observations." *Melita Theologica* 1 (1999) 57–83.

————. "A Female God in East Africa: Or the Problem of Translating God's Name among the Iraqw of Mbulu, Tanzania." *Tyndale Commemorative Bulletin* 170–171 (1994) 87–93.

————. "Understanding Ancient Premonarchic Israelite Social Structure: Some Conceptual Confusions, A Bible Translator's Dilemma." *JSOT* 81 (1998) 15–29.

Msokile, Mbunda. *Historia na Matumizi ya* Kiswahili. Dar es Salaam: Educational Publishers & Distributors, 1992.

Mulokozi (mhariri), M. M. *Tenzi Tatu za Kale.* Dar es Salaam: Taasisi ya Uchunguzi wa Kiswahili, 1999.

Mulokozi, M. M., and T. Y. Sengo. *History of Kiswahili Poetry AD 1000–2000.* Dar es Salaam: Taasisi ya Uchunguzi wa Kiswahili, 1995,

Mutoro, Henry W. "Precolonial Trading Systems of the East African Interior." In *Transformations in Africa—Essays on Africa's Later Past,* edited by Graham M. Connar, 186–203. London: Leicester University Press, 1998.

Nida, Eugene A., and Charles R. Taber. *The Theory and Practice of Translation.* Helps for Translators 8. Leiden: Brill, 1969.

Nurse, Derek, and Thomas Spear. *The Swahili: Reconstructing the History and Language of An African Society,* 800–1500. Ethnohistory. Philadelphia: University of Pennsylvania Press, 1985.

Nyerere, Julius. *Utenzi wa Enjili Kadiri ya Utungo wa Matayo, Marko, Luka, Yohana na Matendo Ya Mitume (The Gospels and Acts in Classical Swahili Verse).* Peramiho, Tanzania: Benedictine Ndanda, 1996.

Polomé, Edgar C. *Swahili Language Handbook.* Washington, DC: Centre for Applied Linguistics, 1967.

Polomé, Edgar C., and C. P. Hill, eds. *Language in Tanzania.* Oxford: Oxford University Press, 1980.

Prior, Michael. *The Bible and Colonialism: A Moral Critique.* Biblical Seminar 48. Sheffield: Sheffield University Press, 1997.

Renju, Peter Masumbuko. "1 Cor 5.7 Culture-Context Sensitivities: A Basis for Interpretation and Translation of Scriptures." A paper presented at the UBS Triennial Translation Workshop, Malaga, Spain, June 16—July 25, 2000.

Robert, Shaaban. *Pambo la Lugha.* Nairobi: Oxford University Press, 1966.

Robinson, Douglas. *Translation and Empire: Postcolonial Theories Explained.* Manchester: St Jerome, 1997.

Romero, Patricia W. *Lamu: History, Society, and Family in an East African Port City.* Princeton: Wiener, 1997.

Sacleux, Charles. *Dictionnaire Swahili-Français.* Paris: Institut d'ethnologie, 1939.

———. *Grammaire des dialects Swahilis,* Paris: Institut d'ethnologie, 1909.

Said, Edward W. *Orientalism.* London: Penguin, 1978.

Salim, Ahmed I. *People of the Coast—Swahili.* Nairobi: Evans Brothers (Kenya), 1985.

———. *Swahili-speaking Peoples of Kenya's Coast.* Nairobi: East African, 1973.

Smart, Ninian. *Dimensions of the Sacred—An Anatomy of the World's Beliefs.* London: Fontana, 1996.

Smith, Linda Tuhiwai. *Decolonizing Methodologies: Research and Indigenous Peoples.* New York: Zed, 1999.

Steere, Edward. *A Handbook of the Swahili Language as Spoken in Zanzibar.* London: SPCK, 1870.

Stigand, C. H. *A Short Treatise on Dialectic Differences of Swahili.* London: Cambridge University Press, 1915.

Sugirtharajah, R. S. *Asian Biblical Hermeneutics and Postcolonialism: Contesting the Interpretations.* Biblical Seminar 64. Sheffield: Sheffield Academic Press, 1999.

———, ed. *The Postcolonial Bible.* Bible and Postcolonialism 1. Sheffield: Sheffield Academic, 1998.

Topan, Farouk. "Swahili as a Religious Language." *JRA* 22 (1992) 331–49.

TUKI. *Kamusi ya Kiswahili Sanifu (A Standard Swahili-Swahili Dictionary).* Dar es Salaam: Oxford University Press, 1981.

———. *English—Swahili Dictionary.* Dar es Salaam: Institute of Kiswahili Research, 1996.

Tuma, Tom, and Phares Mutibwa. *A Century of Christianity in Uganda.* Nairobi: Uzima, 1978.

Whiteley, W. H. *Swahili: The Rise of a National Language.* London: Methuen, 1969.

———. *Language Use and Social Change: Problems of Multilingualism with Special Reference to East Africa.* London: Oxford University Press, 1971.

3

A Postcolonial Analysis of Bible Translation and Its Effectiveness in Shaping and Enhancing the Discourse of Colonialism and the Discourse of Resistance

The Gĩkũyũ New Testament—A Case Study

Johnson Kiriaku Kinyua

Introduction

The primary objective in this essay is to highlight three main issues regarding Bible translation in Africa. In the first place, the essay seeks to show that Bible translation in colonial Africa, though in most cases defended as a neutral, legitimate, and benevolent act of redemption, disguises the colonial power situation.[1] To understand the process of Bible translation in Africa, I am of the opinion that one must address the question of the discourses of colonialism. By discourses of colonialism, I refer to the understanding of the representation and categorization of the African identities produced and reproduced by various colonial rules, systems, and procedures, in order to create and separate the Africans as "Other."

In the second place, this essay will show that even though Bible translators aimed at dominating and restructuring the colonized's view of reality, the translation process was not in itself immune to the restructuring power

---

1. Sugirtharajah, *Postcolonial Criticism and Biblical Interpretation*, 155–78; Barnstone, *The Poetics of Translation*, 135–216; Said, *Culture and Imperialism*, 230–40.

of decolonization. An analysis of colonial relationships reveals not just the individual or social groups but also a historical consciousness at work.[2] For this reason, the place of language, culture, and the individual within the political and economic realities have to remain at the forefront for a fuller comprehension of the evolution of Bible translation in Africa. One has to analyze words and images as they were used and applied in the historical transformation of the colonial society.

The third issue that this essay seeks to explore and understand is to what extent "ordinary African readers" are capable of participating in Bible translation. The term "ordinary readers" is used to refer specifically, in the first instance, to the literate African readers who remain poor and marginalized. In this category I include peasants and the unskilled laborers living both in the rural and urban areas of many African societies. Secondly, the term includes the illiterate and semi-literate African Bible readers.[3] Even though these categories of ordinary readers form the main bulk of the African Christian churches, they are usually assumed "passive" and their readings, translations, and interpretations not taken seriously. Set within a postcolonial framework, the concept of "ordinary African readers" helps me to look beyond the scholarly and official church based material to the way in which Bible translation may be carried out within a wide range of diverse contexts. This study will show that even though these African readers lack formal training in biblical scholarship, they have unique and logical ways of understanding biblical texts.

A Case Study Approach

I use the translation of the Gĩkũyũ New Testament as a case study to recover and reconstruct the historical encounters of the Africans with the Bible and to show that the semi-literate and illiterate do engage the Bible as capable translators and hermeneutists. There are some readers who may see the scope of this essay as narrow because of its focus on the Agĩkũyũ.[4] I need,

---

2. Ngũgĩ wa Thiong'o, *Writers in Politics*, 3–8.

3. West, *The Academy of the Poor*, 77.

4. In this study I use Agĩkũyũ (as opposed to the commonly used term Kikuyu) to refer to the community that lives in the central part of Kenya, stretching from Mt. Kenya in the north to Nairobi in the south, and Gĩkũyũ to refer to the land or country the community occupies as well as the language of the community. The term "Kikuyu" will only be used if included in citations and quotations. One of the missionaries whom we shall use in this regard, Rev. L. J. Beecher, concluded that the Agĩkũyũ was amongst the most discussed and least understood in Kenya. In fact, Europeans found it easier to acquire the Agĩkũyũ's land than the community's language; see Beecher, "The Kikuyu,"

however, to alert such readers to the fact that the essay, while taking a case study approach on Bible translation, goes beyond the limited boundaries of ethnology. Through this study I am able to make some general conclusions that are applicable in various African contexts.

Needless to say, Westerners and Africanists have succeeded in appropriating knowledge acquired through research or study on a particular African "tribe" and have successfully developed general theories on African people. It is my contention that it is appropriate for an African scholar to learn likewise from his own community as an entry into the larger field of knowledge. In addition, while every African ethnic community is unique, problems and questions about the right or appropriate translation and interpretation of religious texts are universally experienced. The case study is intended to make a case for a theory that accepts both scholarly readers and the "ordinary" readers as capable translators and hermeneutists. The case study captures the past occurrences not only to enable us to analyze words and images as they were used and applied in the historical transformation of a particular community, but also to prepare individuals and groups to make appropriate Bible translation decisions. Using postcolonial criticism, the case study approach has enabled me to draw insights of history and theory, apply the insights gained to actual situations, and make decision about theory and practice.

Postcolonial Criticism

While much research and writing have been done on the history of Christian mission and the development of Christianity and theology in many African countries, research literature in Bible translation, biblical studies, and hermeneutics pays little attention to the processes and consequences of colonization in Bible translation. In postcolonial Africa, where the Bible has widely been accepted as the supreme rule of faith, particularly in ethics and morality, few indigenous biblical scholars have engaged in critical biblical scholarship, which interrogates the relationship between the Bible and colonialism regarding the issues of language, class, gender, ideology, and human subjectivity. In addition, the postcolonial context, just as the colonial context, remains a site where the Bible has the potential of becoming both a solution and a problem, both an oppressor and a liberator.[5]

---

ii (Rev. L. J. Beecher, "The Kikuyu," (The Peoples of Kenya—no. 9), 14. In this booklet, Beecher argued religion in Africa was losing its functional role (as described by the anthropologists) with the coming of Western civilization.).

5. West, *Biblical Hermeneutics of Liberation*, 52.

In most African countries, the Bible is now widely accepted as an "African book" and a beloved text, however, its potency as a destructive force cannot be ignored. The Bible as literature remains a powerful tool in which a given ideology can be passed on and be received as the norm in daily practices. Moreover, the postcolonial context in which the Bible operates is still contestable and ambiguous.[6] The postcolonial situation in Africa demands a new critical tradition in biblical studies and hermeneutics that follow colonial resistant literature to affirm the right of people once again to seize the initiative of history. This study builds on the new methodological and theoretical approaches in African biblical studies, which have been laid out through the able minds of Gerald West, Musa Dube, Itumeleng J. Mosala, and Aloo O. Mojola, and in the work of other postcolonial biblical critics.

In my opinion, postcolonial criticism offers the best theoretical and methodological tool to help analyze and interpret archival materials and colonial texts. In biblical studies, postcolonial criticism is defined as: "scrutinizing and exposing colonial domination and power as they are embodied in biblical texts and in interpretations, and as searching for alternative hermeneutics while thus overturning and dismantling colonial perspectives."[7]

In addition, as Fernando Segovia shows, postcolonial studies take seriously the reality of the empire, of imperialism and colonization, as "an omnipresent, inescapable and overwhelming reality in the world."[8] Since colonization was not just about soldiers and cannons but also about forms, images, and imaginings, postcolonial inquiry is helpful in investigating the issues of empire, nation, ethnicity, migration, human subjectivity, race, and language.[9]

As a concept "postcolonialism," though problematic, helps bring together a number of issues, even conflicting ones.[10] First among these can be located in the term "colonialism." When using the term colonialism, I am aware of the fact that legacies of colonialism are varied and multiple even as they obviously share some important features. European colonialism was not a monolithic operation; rather, right from its inception, it deployed diverse strategies and methods of control and of representation. Nonetheless, whenever the term is invoked, it draws immediate reaction from both

---

6. Sugirtharajah, *The Postcolonial Bible*, 93; Loomba, *Colonialism/Postcolonialism*, 7–90; McLeod, *Beginning Postcolonialism*, 6–36.

7. Sugirtharajah, *Postcolonial Bible*, 16; Young, *Postcolonialism*, 16–18.

8. Sugirtharajah, *Postcolonial Biblical Reader*, 56.

9. Sugirtharajah, *Postcolonial Bible*, 16; Said, *Culture and Imperialism*, 6.

10. Ngũgĩ wa Thiong'o, *Writers in Politics*, xi.

sides of the aisle.[11] There are those from the former colonies who see today's indictment of colonialism as a brand of "cheap, demagogic and outmoded rhetoric."[12] The term conjures an image of people's inability to take responsibility for their problems. This group from the formerly colonized countries looks at the African inglorious past as paralleled to the modern day African failed state of affairs. In other words, rather than deal with their own failures, in self-defense, the formerly colonized people resort to apportioning blame to others for their problems. On their part, people from the former colonizing world see ingratitude. The group juxtaposes blessings of civilization that Europe brought to Africa against modern day African return of ingratitude. They are quick to remind us that the postmodern powers repudiate colonial missteps and in order to make up for these missteps, new relationships of equality between once-colonized and colonizers have been established.

Nevertheless, without merely apportioning blame and engaging in bouts of self-righteousness and indignation, there is a real need to investigate this rather complex relationship that developed with all of its totalizing discourses. The primacy and even the complete centrality of colonialism was so totalizing in its form, attitudes, and gestures that it virtually shut out any innovation or alternatives within the colony. Rather than accept colonialism as simply a divine project undertaken for the glory of God and an extension of the rule of law, through postcolonial inquiry we are able to understand that colonialism and all its manifestations, both in intentions and acts, was an integral part of capitalist development.[13] Colonialism, as wa Thiong'o and Aimé Césaire remind us, is a practice and not a theory. It is a historical process and not a metaphysical idea; a relationship of power at the economic, political, and cultural levels.[14]

Besides the domination of physical space, the other important aspect of colonialism is in its ability to persuade the colonized people to internalize colonial logic and speak its language. In the commonly known process of "colonizing the mind," the colonized succumbed by accepting the lower ranking in the colonial order while assimilating the values and assumptions of the colonizers.[15] Colonialism suggested certain ways of seeing reality and specific modes of understanding that reality. In the end it offered explanation as to the place of the colonized in the colonial world, which in

---

11. Loomba, *Colonialism/Postcolonialism*, 7–22.

12. Achebe, *Hopes and Impediments*, 46.

13. Memmi, *The Colonizer and the Colonized*, 1–18.

14. Ngũgĩ wa Thiong'o, *Writers in Politics*, 7; Césaire, *Discourse on Colonialism*, 32–33.

15. McLeod, *Postcolonialism*, 18.

almost all cases was a subservient position, while rendering the colonizer as superior in all ways.

It is in this subtle dynamic that led to the internalization of certain expectations about human relationships that colonialism was effectively devastating. Through language, colonialism took upon itself the power of describing, naming, defining, and representing the colonized. Since language, as wa Thiong'o has offered, is the carrier of culture and values by which we perceive ourselves and our place in the world, colonization by imposing upon the colonized a particular value-system, succeeded in denigrating the colonized's cultural values. Therefore, postcolonial inquiry, as wa Thiong'o articulates, brings to the fore the questions of language and their importance in answering the question of identity and being.[16]

Postcolonialism begins from the perspective that postcolonial reality is framed by active legacies of colonialism, by the institutional infrastructures inherited from colonial power by elite groups, or appropriated by later generations of elites.[17] In biblical studies' area of theory, the structure and culture of the colonial society are evident in the tendency to omit colonialism, racism, and ideologies of repression. Through postcolonial inquiry, we are not only able to challenge such tendencies, but also see colonialism and decolonization as not separate phases in history but as cultural processes in dialectical relationship with each other. Postcolonial criticism's ultimate goal is to offer an alternative intellectual inquiry and interpretation on the past and present encounters, with both the colonial and present global encounters of unequals.[18]

As an academic venture, postcolonial theory interrogates biblical texts as well as translation and interpretation of these texts for colonial intentions and tendencies. In a clearer way, it investigates and exposes the link between knowledge and power in textual production where the dialectical relationship between language and power is fundamental and far-reaching.[19] It is in this connection that I use the Agĩkũyũ of Kenya as a case study to recover and reconstruct the historical encounters of the Africans with the Bible, and to show that the semi-literate and illiterate do engage the Bible as capable translators and hermeneutists.

16. Ngũgĩ wa Thiong'o, *Writers in Politics*, xiii.

17. Said, *Culture and Imperialism*, 27.

18. Spivak, *A Critique of Postcolonial Reason*, 3.

19. Sugirtharajah, *Postcolonial Bible*, 92.

Unacknowledged Mutual Dependence
Inherent in Bible Translation

To the colonial Bible translators, nothing would serve as an important and an effective tool in the breaking dawn of the proselytizing mission project more than the vernacular translation of the Bible. J. N. Ogilvie, writing about Christian mission in colonial Kenya, suggested that the use of vernacular would serve several purposes.[20] First, the ability to read the simple Gospel was to precede "the opening of the mind, among people where it has been immemorially stunted and closed."[21] The act of reading was to serve as the key to the new order of knowledge and gnosis. Secondly, it was necessary to provide the written Word in the people's own tongue since "speech is at best a fleeting thing, while writing is permanent."[22] The written word reigned superior over the oral literature/spoken word. Third, the translated Word was to serve as a clear testimony to "peoples who through all the ages have sat in darkness" that light at long last had come, and "a new Earth as well as a new Heaven" stood revealed.[23]

Nonetheless, while the aims, nature, and reliability of Bible translation may never have been independent from the consciousness and will of the colonial discourse that assumed its own dominance and superiority, its development was not monolithic. The translation work carried out by the missionary-translators independent of the contributions of Africans fell short of the required standard of a good translation. At a practical level, as shall become clear in this essay, Bible translation in Africa relied heavily upon the natives for access to African language, knowledge, and culture. Such a dependence involved constant negotiation with or/and even incorporation of indigenous ideas. The incorporation of indigenous cultural and linguistic forms rendered a complete replication of the "original" impossible, thereby creating room for hybridity.[24]

Translation as a Complex Activity

Missionaries like J. N. Ogilvie understood Bible translation simply as the mediating agency between colonization and Christian conversion. However,

---

20. Ogilvie, *Our Empire's Debt to Missions*, 62–65. See also Ngũgĩ wa Thiong'o, *Writers in Politics*, 61.

21. Ibid., 63.

22. Ibid., 62.

23. Ibid., 65.

24. Bhabha, *The Location of Culture*, 121–31.

the act of translation was a complex activity and cannot be understood as a straightforward enterprise.[25] As this study will show, translation was not immune to the ambivalence and contradictions of the discourse of colonialism. Like any other colonial discourse, Bible translation betrays instability. By choosing to translate the Bible into the vernacular languages, the colonial church flung wide open the interrogatory interstices where biblical texts, hermeneutics, doctrines, culture, and power could be negotiated, contested, and hybridized. Since hybridity as understood in postcolonialism is never total or complete, it remains perpetually in motion, pursuing errant and unpredictable courses, and is open to change and inscription. There are several issues that add complexity in the Bible translation process.

Bible Translation and the Liminal Space

One of the issues that add complexity in the translation process is the translators' claim to fidelity to the source text(s) in order to authenticate the translated text.[26] The idea of true fidelity implies that translators can achieve perfect replication of the source text.[27] This assumption can be noticed as one reads, for example, the original translations of the Gĩkũyũ New Testament.[28] All of the translated versions have no introduction, editorial or translators' comments, margin notes, preface or foreword. The versions included reprints and re-editions, and left no hint about the translators, or about the translation process. The translator is completely invisible. The obvious implication of the translator's invisibility is that the text one is reading is an exact translation of the original.

One cannot, of course, ignore the explanation given for the decision to offer the translation without notes or comments. The original "Laws and Regulations" of the British and Foreign Bible Society (BFBS) founded in 1804 read in part that the "sole object" of the Society "shall be to encourage

25. Sugirtharajah, *Postcolonial Criticism*, 156; see also Rafael, *Contracting Colonialism*, xvii–xix.

26. See Arthur Ruffell Barlow's short account of the difficulties encountered in Bible translation. Barlow, "Language Report, 1943," 605.

27. Bible translators in Africa in most cases chose to use "The Revised Version" of the English Bible as their source text. Barlow, "Progress of Kikuyu Old Testament"; Mr. A. Ruffell Barlow to Rev. Dr. Kilgour editorial Superintendent, BSA/E3/3/253/2, Kikuyu 2, March 29 1919, BFBS Archives, University of Cambridge; Letter by Mr. A. Ruffell Barlow to the Editor Superintendent of BFBS, BSA/E3/3/253/2, Kikuyu 2, February 20 1919, BFBS Archives.

28. BFBS, *Kĩrĩkanĩro Kĩrĩa Kĩerũ Kĩa Jesu Kristo Ũrĩa Mwathani witũ o na Mũhonokia Witũ* (1926 ed. and 1936 ed.).

a wider circulation of the Holy Scriptures . . . without Note or Comment."[29] According to the BFBS, the rule sought to avoid hermeneutical conflicts that were likely to jeopardize the inter-confessional connections. However, besides the principle of maintaining inter-confessional links, the act of rendering the translators invisible also assumes that it is possible for translators to arrive objectively at a perfect replication of the original text. The corollary, therefore, is the belief that it is unnecessary for the translator to provide any comments or explanations as to why certain words or phrases in the translated text are chosen over the others.

Ideally, a translator must be completely anonymous from his or her work. However, the activity of translation, as Willis Barnstone observes, is not "a predictable, objective, and repeatable exercise but a venture into variations . . . an art of differences."[30] Just like with any other intellectual activity that involves a human element, Bible translators should not be oblivious to the subjective nature of any human translator. For instance, the way a translation handles an ambiguous verse (or where the meaning of the verse is uncertain) reveals the theological leanings of the translator. Besides, language is a human phenomenon and the Bible was written using human language. Translation involves human words that are used to translate biblical language which in itself is a human language. In addition, it is hardly possible to come to a perfect translation because no two languages or cultures are the same. The very existence of different languages is indicative of the fact that change is unavoidable in the act of translation.

Translation as a Second-Level Interpretation

While it is absolutely necessary to make a fine distinction between a translator and an interpreter of a written text, it is not possible for the translator to fully disengage him/herself from the role of an interpreter. Indeed, the notion of change as a key element in translation is alluded to in the Latin *translation*, which points to the activity of carrying meaning from one language across to another.[31] Robert J.C. Young has persuasively argued that translation takes "a kind of metaphorical displacement of a text from one language to another."[32] What this points to is that perfect replication can only be achieved if there is no change but mere repetition.[33]

29. As quoted in Smalley, *Translation as Mission*, 62, 64.
30. Barnstone, *Poetics of Translation*, 20.
31. Ibid., 15–17.
32. Young, *Postcolonialism*, 138.
33. Barnstone, *Poetics of Translation*, 16.

In translation of texts, however, there can be no identical transference because translation involves mental activity through reading of the written text. In the act of translating the Bible, the translator attempts to recreate in the mind of another that which was put in writing from someone else's mind, living many years in the past. That which existed at first orally was then transmitted through language, which had its simultaneous interrelated layers of sound, writing, style, grammar, and meaning. Consequently, what one has read is transformed into another written text making translation an act of interpretation.[34] Translation is for this reason, as Barnstone argues, an interpretive reading of the source text, "a hermeneutical process . . . performed in order to come up with the most complete understanding of the source text for the purpose of determining the target text."[35] After reading and understanding the source text, the translator embarks on a form of "second-level interpretation" to search for "equivalent target meanings"—an activity which takes place in the mind more than lingering on the pages of the source text.[36]

It is this "second-level interpretation" that appears in a translation as the translator's understanding of the source text. The second level of interpretation, as I shall demonstrate in the following pages, transforms the initial reading of the source text to more powerful and authoritative thought that finds its way as the translated text. Since it is never possible for a translation to be an exact one-to-one transference from one language to another, translation can only be seen, as William A. Smalley has pointed out, as "an approximation of the original."[37]

It follows, then, that the process of "approximation of the original" transforms the translator into an author who is both, to use Willis Barnstone's words, an "inventor and director of the text."[38] The "reader-author" not only creates meaning of the source text but also makes translational choices in an attempt to make the text accessible to the targeted readers. In the colonial situation, as shall be shown shortly, it is in the act of translation that the indigenous "original" (oral literature) is devalued as the colonial copy is overtly valued, becoming more powerful than the indigenous "original." Yet even in such a situation, some aspects of the indigenous culture remain untranslatable.[39] What all this means is that the technical activity

34. Johnson and Penner, *The Writings of the New Testament*, 77.

35. Barnstone, *Poetics of Translation*, 21.

36. Ibid.

37. Smalley, *Translation*, 3.

38. Barnstone, *Poetics of Translation*, 22.

39. Young, *Postcolonialism*, 138–39.

of translating a text from one language into another is always culturally
and historically specific.[40] A study of the process of translating the original
Gĩkũyũ New Testament reveals the translators' cultural and linguistic un-
dertones are closely linked to the colonial socio-political context in which
translation took place.[41]

A Summary of the Evolution of the Gĩkũyũ New Testament

For a better understanding of the translation of the Gĩkũyũ New Testament,
I will begin by laying out in a general way the early evolution of the Christian Bible in Kenya and how it relates to the Gĩkũyũ translation. Then, more
specifically, I will deal with the evolution of the Gĩkũyũ New Testament, its
objective, the process and issues in the translation process, and the overall
effects of the translation.

The Early Bible Translation in Kenya

Rev. Dr. J. Ludwig Krapf was the first European to carry out meaningful Bible translation in Kenya.[42] He became the first missionary to study Swahili
and to reduce the language into writing.[43] Three main factors influenced

40. Yorke and Renju, eds., *Bible Translation and African Languages*, i–iv.

41. For geo-political factors in translation, see Young, *Postcolonialism*, 138 as well as
wa Thiong'o's powerful analysis on the role of literature in subduing the emotions, the
imagination, and the consciousness of the colonized, as part of the economic exploitation and political oppression (Ngũgĩ wa Thiong'o, *Writers in Politics*, 8–11).

42. Dr. Ludwig Krapf was a young German who was enlisted by the Anglican
Church Mission Society to begin Mission exploration in East and Central Africa. His
first missionary journey was to Abyssinia in the company of Blumhardt in February
1837, having studied Latin, Greek, and Hebrew in grammar school; just before this
missionary journey he studied Ethiopic and Amharic. He first arrived in East Africa
in March 1844. His first work was a four-column dictionary which included English,
Swahili, Suaheli, "Kinika," and Kikamba, but finding this scope too comprehensive he
later dropped Kikamba. It is not known whether Mr. Wakefield, the missionary of the
Methodist Society at Ribe, to whom Dr. Krapf in 1860 had given a copy of his dictionary in four manuscript volumes, had enriched the work. J. Ludwig Krapf, *Travels,
Researches, and the Missionary Labours*, 132–34; see also CMS/C/A5/O/16/1–165, also
CMS/5/O/16/160/F, Special Collection, University of Birmingham.

43. While the British colonial administrator and historian Sir Harry H. Johnston failed to recognize Krapf's pioneering endeavors, Krapf's work received cred-
ible recognition from W. W. Greenough in his introductory remarks to Krapf's work
"Three Chapters of Genesis Translated into the Sooahelee Language" presented to the
American Oriental Society. Krapf's work as the first scientific study of Swahili received
endorsement eighty years later through K. Roehl. Krapf, "Three Chapters of Genesis

Krapf's translation work. First, he envisioned a "chain of missionary sta-tions" along the banks of the Nile from Alexandria to "Gondas," the capital of *Abessinia* (Ethiopia). In his estimation, such a chain of missionary activi-ties would be scriptural fulfillment to a promise in Psalm 68:31: "Ethiopia shall soon stretch out her hands unto God."[44] To enable Christian mission-aries to respond when the appeal came, Krapf translated the whole of the New Testament into Swahili, and compiled a grammar and dictionary of the language. In addition to translating Karl Barth's "Bible Stories," he also complied an English–Swahili dictionary.[45] Secondly, Krapf had heard of ru-mors about a "Galla" people who were said to be "Christian after the form of the Coptic Church in Egypt."[46] Although he had not met these people, Krapf considered them a nation "destined by Providence after their conversion to Christianity to attain importance and fulfil the mission which Heaven has pointed out to the Germans in Europe."[47] He feared that if "Gallas" were not gathered into the Christian Church, they would fall to Islam, forming a strong bulwark against the introduction of Christianity and "true morality" in Africa.[48] To this end, Krapf forecast the elevation of a Black bishop and Black clergy of the Protestant Church as a necessity in the civilization of Africa.[49]

Finally, according to Krapf, translation of the Bible would bring to the Africans the true knowledge of God through which material progress was guaranteed. In a conversation between Krapf and Senama, the mother of King Sahela Selassie, as they exchanged goods, Senama asked Krapf how the Europeans acquired knowledge "to invent and manufacture." In reply, Krapf said that God had promised in:

> His Word not only spiritual but temporal rewards to those who obeyed His commandments; that the English, Germans and Eu-ropeans in general, had once been as rude and ignorant as the Gallas, but after their acceptance of the Gospel God had given them with science and arts wondrous blessings of an earthly kind.[50]

Translated into the Sooahelee Language," 264; see also Roehl, "The Linguistic Situation in East Africa," 197

44. Johnston, *The Universities' Mission to Central Africa*, 13.

45. Krapf, *Travels*, 188.

46. Ibid., 36.

47. Ibid., 72.

48. Ibid., 123.

49. Ibid., 135.

50. Ibid., 89.

He predicted that completion of the Suez Canal would bring with it the weakening of Islam, the subjugation of East African heathenism by Christianity and its civilization, the end of the slave trade, and finally immigration of thousands of European emigrants "when America, Australia, and Tasmania cease to attract them."[51] It is the prospect of such material prosperity and evolution of new human relations that hastened Krapf's desire to complete the translation project.[52] All told, his translation became the basis of later translation work on the Swahili Bible and formed the watershed of Bible translation in Kenya, including work in Gĩkũyũ language, to which I now turn my attention.[53]

Translation as Hegemonic: Translation Work in Gĩkũyũ

The translation of Gĩkũyũ New Testament is a case in point where Bible translation was used simply as the mediating agency between colonization and Christian conversion. In its aims and nature, Bible translation remained entrenched in the consciousness and will of the colonial discourse that assumed its own dominance and superiority. The study of the translation of the Gĩkũyũ New Testament reveals a hierarchal process in which the missionary-translators ascribed to themselves the power to investigate, describe, name, define, and translate the source biblical texts to the Gĩkũyũ version of the New Testament. Following the Hegelian notion of Africa as moving slowly from nature to culture, missionaries desired a united front to tackle language problems before embarking on the translation process. Because of the hegemonic approach to the translation of the Bible, the African role in the process was relegated to the background or simply denied. It is no surprise, then, that even though mutual dependence inherent in Bible translation is apparent as one peruses missionaries' documents and journals, colonialism did not acknowledge this. Natives were only consulted on word meanings but not on how the translation was produced.

This work in the Gĩkũyũ language owes its origin to Dr. Karl Peter who was the first European to transverse the Gĩkũyũ country in 1883. Von Hohnel, who travelled with Count Teleki in 1887, noted half a dozen words

51. Ibid., 16.

52. Ibid., 193.

53. By 1935, about twenty-one languages in Kenya possessed some portion of Scripture. Two of these (Swahili and Giriyama) had the whole Bible, while Luo, Gĩkũyũ, Pokomo, Kamba, and Taita Sagalla had the New Testament. The Waswahili possessed a whole Bible since 1914. The first Giriyama scripture was Luke's Gospel translated by Rev. W. E. Taylor and published, with Mombasa Swahili version in parallel columns, in 1892.

and phrases in Gīkūyū.[54] However, it is the Rev. A.W. McGregor, the first Church Mission Society missionary, who started systematic work on the language at Kabete in 1900. His Gīkūyū translation of John was published by the British and Foreign Bible Society and served for several years as the only available Gospel in the mission field. His English–Gīkūyū vocabulary was published in 1904 by the Society for Promoting Christian Knowledge (SPCK).[55] Arthur Ruffell Barlow,[56] a Church of Scotland Mission layman, is the other important person in the process of translating the Gīkūyū Bible. "Bwana Barlow," as fondly remembered by his peers and African Christians, is said to have picked up the Gīkūyū language unaided by grammar or the support of a school teacher.[57] Barlow started noting words in 1903 and his first edition of Mark's Gospel in Gīkūyū was published by the National Bible Society of Scotland in 1909.[58]

Other translation works in Gīkūyū included Roman Catholic work which proceeded on separate lines.[59] The initial Roman Catholic publication was a handbook of Gīkūyū by the Rev. Father Hemery in 1902, pub-

54. "Kikuyu-English A to Ĩ, Dictionary Seminar on 13.1.58: Notes on the Kikuyu Dictionary," Barlow Papers, Gen 1785/1, Special Collection, University of Edinburgh.

55. Rev. McGregor's Vocabulary and *Grammar of the Gīkūyū Language* followed the orthography developed by the Royal Geographic Society of Great Britain. This was an orthography that had been adapted in regard to the spelling of African geographical names and transliteration of African dialects. McGregor, *English–Kikuyu Vocabulary*, 456–59.

56. A.R. Barlow's work is said to have begun in 1903 as a seventeen-year-old. His first contacts with Gīkūyū were through a farming venture to sell potatoes to the Transvaal under the workmanship of his uncle Dr. Ruffell Scott. After his uncle went on furlough in March 1906, Barlow (who now lived by himself fourteen miles 14 miles away from his uncle Dr. Scott in the Gīkūyū country) took his first service using the Gīkūyū language and in the same week took charge of the "school." By the time of the publication of his Grammar in 1914, Barlow had been a resident in the then British East Africa for ten years. In his desire to learn as much Gīkūyū as he could, Barlow on January 23, 1906 mistakenly entered the "closed District" of Nyeri which almost led to his deportation. Barlow's Papers, Gen. 1786/48; Rev. Dr. Arthur, "Arthur Ruffelle Barlow," 445–46.

57. Philp, "Bwana Barlow," 450; Arthur, "Arthur Ruffelle Barlow," 445.

58. By 1945, the dictionary had reached letter "m" and was later continued by A.R. Barlow as a compiler. The other major compilers included J. Ludwig Krapf, Rev. Arthur W. McGregor, Mūhoro wa Kareri among others) Work on the dictionary had to be postponed because of further work needed to the New Testament. Barlow Papers, Gen 1785/1; United Kikuyu Language Committee (UKLC) Minutes 6/4/1908–15/8/1933, Barlow papers, Gen. 1786/5 1a and 1b; UKLC Minutes of April 6, 1909 and October 3, 1910, Barlow papers, Gen. 1785/7.

59. Other Protestant mission works included that of Hildegarde Hinde, *Vocabularies of the Kamba and Gīkūyū Languages* (Cambridge University Press, 1904); and J. E. Henderson, *Easy Gikuyu Lessons* (Nairobi: The Times, n.d.).

lished by the Catholic Mission in Nairobi. The Italian Fathers at Nyeri also developed printing and a newspaper in a different script without diacritical marks.[60] Above all other translators it is Barlow and Rev. Harry Leakey[61] who did the bulk of translation. By the end of February 1941 Canon Leakey had done the lion's share of translation of the Old Testament in Gĩkũyũ.[62] Barlow is credited with the Gĩkũyũ New Testament and the Psalms.[63] To facilitate and consolidate translation of the Gĩkũyũ Bible,[64] the United Kikuyu Language Committee was formally constituted in 1912, representing various Protestant Missionary Societies in Gĩkũyũ country for the purpose of united action in translation.[65] Some efforts had started earlier under the guidance of Henry E. Scott to form a small Translation Committee which served as a form of consultancy for this work.[66]

60. One of the important works that came out of this printing press was Father C. Cagnolo, *Agĩkũyũ*.

61. Rev. Canon Harry Leakey served in Gĩkũyũ (Kabete) for 38 years. He retired from active service in 1933. He was joined by Barlow to form a partnership in the translation of the Bible and other literature. Canon Leakey spent most of his last seven years following his retirement in Limuru engaged in translation work.

62. Calderwood, "Extracts from the Annual Reports for 1940," 396.

63. By May 1907 Barlow had translated a school Primer, Book of Daily Services, 16 hymns, Shorter Catechism, Matthew's Gospel, a portion of John, the first 31 verses of Mark, 60 psalms, and the first chapter of "Peep of Day." Dr. Ruffell Scott, Report to the General Assembly, May 1907 p. 27, as collected by Dr. McMurtrie in Barlow Papers, Gen. 1786/46, Gen. 1786/48; Brown, "The New Grammar," 1233.

64. Rev. J. E. Hamshere in *Church Missionary Review* (January 1909), 30, noted that due to "the great population of the Gĩkũyũ tribe a complete Bible in their tongue might well be justified." BSA/E3/3/253/1, Kikuyu 1, March 1909—June 1915, BFBS Archives, University of Cambridge; see also letter by Editor Superintendent of BFBS to the Rev. Harry Leakey, BSA/E3/3/253/2, Kikuyu 2, July 24 1915, BFBS Archives.

65. Those appointed to represent their missions in the Committee included Rev. C. E. Hurlbut (director AIM: African Inland Mission), Rev. L. H. Downing (AIM), Rev. W.P. Knapp (AIM), Dr. J. E. Henderson (AIM), Mr. O. H. Scouten (AIM), Rev. H. Leakey (CMS: Church Mission Society), Dr. T. W. W. Crawford (CMS), Mr. A. W. McGregor (CMS), Rev. Dr. H. E. Scott (CSM: Church of Scotland Mission) and Mr. A. R. Barlow (CSM) with Rev. Leakey taking the chairmanship of the Committee. Letters to Rev. R. Kilgour (Editor Superintendent BFBS) by O. H. Scouten dated February 3, 1909 and April 28, 1909, BSA/E3/3/253/1, Kikuyu 1, March 1909—June 1915, BFBS Archives; see also Barlow, "Story of the Gĩkũyũ Bible," 1160.

66. Barlow papers, UKLC Minutes of January 28, 1909, Gen. 1785/7.

Translation as Hegemonic: The United Kikuyu Language Committee (UKLC); Formation of UKLC

The formation of UKLC is the other important factor in the translation process that saw the exclusion of the Africans in the important stages of translation work. The objectives of UKLC included, in the first place, the desire to secure as rapidly as possible a uniform translation of the Bible and other literature.[67] According to Marion Stevenson, the Committee's main work included the need to reduce the Gĩkũyũ language to writing and giving the Holy Scriptures to Gĩkũyũ people in their own language.[68] Besides promoting Bible translation, UKLC also offered a platform to discuss linguistic questions and difficulties. In order to secure an early translation and publication of the Scriptures, the New Testament first and later the Old Testament were assigned to various members of the Committee for translation.[69] UKLC chose to use "the Revised Version" as the source text in translation.[70] In addition, the Committee ruled that any book of the Bible for general publication was to be submitted to the Language Committee for criticism. No editorial approval by the BFBS would be received for any translation that did not go through the Translation Committee.[71] In like

67. Barlow papers, UKLC Minutes 6/4/1908–15/8/1933, Gen. 1786/5 1a and 1b.

68. Stevenson, "The Kikuyu Language Committee," BSA/E3/3/253/1, Kikuyu 1, March 1909–June 1915, BFBS Archives.

69. John's Gospel had been translated by Rev. A.W. Macgregor in 1903 and revised by Mr. Barlow; Mark by Mr. Barlow in 1909; Philippians by a member of African Inland Mission in 1912; the uniform renderings of the parallel passages in the Gospels was done in 1914 by Canon H. Leakey (CMS), Dr. Henderson (Gospel Mission), Mr. Barlow and Stefano (Rev. Leakey's Gĩkũyũ assessor). Matthew was completed in 1914 by Canon Leakey; Rev. Leakey also translated the Epistles of John; Luke in 1918 first by Dr. Henderson and Mr. O.H. Scouten, but completed by Canon Leakey. Rev. F.H. McKenrick asked to undertake the translation of the Acts of the Apostles. The first single volume of the four Gospels and Acts was published in 1920 with new translations of Mark and John by Mr. Barlow, and Acts translated by an AIM missionary but revised by Canon Leakey. Barlow papers, UKLC Minutes of June 7, 1909, Gen. 1785/7 and Minutes 6/4/1908–15/8/1933, Gen. 1786/5 1a and 1b; See also Barlow, "Story of the Kikuyu Bible," 1161.

70. Among the translators only Rev. Harry Leakey (CMS) and Rev. Lee H. Downing (AIM) had knowledge of the Greek language. Barlow used as reference the *Cambridge Bible for Schools and Colleges* commentaries (1886 and 1890 editions) which dealt with the particular books assigned to him to translate. The volume on Revelation by Simcox and "the Century Bible series" on the same were also recommended to him. Barlow, "Progress of Kikuyu Old Testament," 1053; Mr. A. Ruffell Barlow to Rev. Dr. Kilgour editorial Superintendent, BSA/E3/3/253/2, Kikuyu 2, March 29, 1919 and February 20, 1919, BFBS Archives.

71. Letters by Rev. A.W. McGregor to the Superintendent of BFBS on February 10, 1909 and the latter's reply to Rev. A.W. McGregor dated March 20, 1909, BSA/

manner, none could be accepted by any of the contributory societies until it had been passed by UKLC. All translations of the books of the Bible passed by UKLC had to bear the words, "This translation has been passed by the United Kikuyu Language Committee."[72]

In a great measure, as we shall see shortly, this by-law curtailed any African initiative to come up with an acceptable translation. Of course there were exceptions.[73] In addition, the Africans' role in the translation process, though crucial, was never given attention, and in most cases, was glossed over in the missionaries' reports.[74] Although the European translators claimed entitlement to the authorial power to translate, drawing benefits from and depending on the Africans' efforts, they refused the autonomy or independence of African translators. The by-laws of UKLC stated that all translations of the books of the Bible passed by UKLC had to bear the words, "This translation has been passed by the United Kikuyu Language Committee." The idea was to safeguard against any party apart from UKLC carrying out translation work.[75] Since only European missionaries appointed by their mission societies formed the membership of the Translation Committee, it goes without saying that Africans could only participate as observers, assessors, or assistants. Africans' opinions on translations were almost always relegated to a second place in the translation process. The individual missionary's decision on the subject matter was the one brought forward to the Language Committee for criticism and approval. Yet European translators remained handicapped without the help of their African "assessors."[76]

E3/3/253/1, BFBS Archives.

72. Barlow papers, UKLC Minutes 6/4/1908–15/8/1933, Gen. 1786/5 1a and 1b and minutes of June 15, 1912, Gen. 1785/7.

73. For example, in 1895 Johana Gona (an African catechist) made a version of Matthew's Gospel in Giriyama, which was revised by Rev. D.A. Hooper (C.MS) and Rev. Taylor, and published by the British and Foreign Bible Society. Another African to work as a translator was Abdullah who worked with Rev. F. Würtz of the Neukirchen Mission to translate Mark's Gospel in Galla which was published in 1894 by the British and Foreign Bible Society. John Otieno worked together with Mr. A. Morrison (a magistrate in Nairobi) to translate one of the Luo versions of Mark's Gospel. Philp, *A New Day in Kenya,* 176–81.

74. Individual missionaries used Africans as assessors or assistants. Missionaries had the liberty as translators to dismiss their assessors at will. For example, Barlow discharged Reuben who had been his assistant and "well of Gĩkũyũ, my critic, and research worker for more than eight years" in order to have the New Year's gift of "a fresh mind" to "irrigate the linguistic field" even though Reuben had been "trained so well as he had in his employer's ways and wants."

75. Barlow Papers, UKLC Minutes of June 15, 1912, Gen. 1785/7.

76. Authorities used by Barlow included Robinson Kimani on Proverbs; Kahahu wa Wang'ati on Gĩkũyũ; Muthũku wa Mwĩthiga (mbari-ya-Kĩnoo) on Songs; William

Invention of Gĩkũyũ Orthography

UKLC had also to deal with problems presented by the language at the local level. The first problem that UKLC had to confront was the deficiency of the English vowels[77] and alphabet in rendering the spoken Gĩkũyũ language into writing. The need for a new orthography became apparent, for example, when the missionaries learnt that they had been singing rather "lustily" "You are being strangled by Jesus, you are being strangled by Jesus" when using *ũgwitwo nĩ Jesu* (proper Gĩkũyũ *ũgũitwo*) under the impression they were singing, "You are called by Jesus" (*Ũgwĩtwo nĩ Jesu*).[78] Marion Stevenson recorded also a case where a Gĩkũyũ boy was astonished "over the fact that in Jerusalem there had been a great kettle with five eyes, into which, when it was boiling, sick people were put."[79] Apparently, this was in reference to an amazing translation rendering of the Pool of Bethesda in John 5:1–9. This rather comical discovery made it desirous for the missionaries to increase the number of vowels rather than stick to the English vowels.

To overcome this problem of orthography, the Language Committee unilaterally decided on a new spelling, adding additional vowels and augmenting their pronunciation.[80] UKLC adopted two elastic vowels ĩ and ũ

Waweru (Mahiga) on the killing of "Mũrogi"; Rev. Benjamen Githieya; Esau Karanja (Mahiga) on the inheritance of widows and a story on "Executing of Thief or Wizard"; Joshua Matenjwa of Kikuyu and a teacher in the mission together with Arthur Wang'ondu of Kikuyu; Stanely Kahahu (junior school teacher at Kikuyu); Paulo Kahehia (Kikuyu) on Sacrifice; Kahahu wa Wang'ati (Kikuyu) on "Ndahĩkanio"; Nathan Ngũgĩ (Kikuyu) on Songs (Mũthũngũcĩ, gĩcukia); Jakobo Kairianja, junior teacher in Kikuyu on *ũrigiti* and on "Recent History" (Kairianja also wrote about European military suppression, and about "the Ituika Ceremonies" with the assistance of Nathan Ngũgĩ); Douglas Mũchoki (Kikuyu) on Songs (Mũgoiyo, Ngũcũ); Simon Nguru; Tabitha N.; Asafu Mũigai on buying and selling. See Gĩkũyũ Various notes, etc., vol. I, Barlow Papers, Gen. 1785/6 and vol. II, Gen. 1785/7. Barlow, for example, relied heavily on the mission teachers and students as well as elders from various districts. These men and women would be asked to write on specific subjects and Barlow would later edit them. Harry Leakey likewise had in his employment Stefano, who accompanied him to England on furlough in order to "have someone who spoke Gĩkũyũ on his first furlough in England" to keep up his knowledge of the language. Leakey, *White African*, 14, 26; Crabtree, "The Systematic Study of African Languages," 185.

77. The Royal Geographical Society had adopted a system whose vowels had their German or Italian sounds, while in most parts the consonants followed English interpretation. For a full explanation of this system see McGregor, "The Orthography of African Names and Languages," 456–59.

78. Possible reference here may be to the Gĩkũyũ translation of the hymnal "Stand Up, Stand Up for Jesus" (Stevenson, "The Kikuyu Language Committee," 116; BSA/ E3/3/253/1, Kikuyu 1, March 1909–June 1915, BFBS Archives.

79. Ibid.

80. Ibid.

to be used as short and long, bringing the total of vowels accepted to seven: *a, e, i, ī, o, u, ū*.[81] The Committee also changed most of the vowel letters and some consonants; thus *chalia* became *caria* (seek); *ochio* became *ūciu* (that one—as in reference to a person), and further changes of that ilk.[82] The use of *ū* or *u*, or *w*, remained problematic and was left open.[83] In the case of combinations of vowels, when the phonetic spelling differed from that of derivation, the former was to be given preference in writing the language.[84] The Committee also agreed that two vowels should be written together where the sound required it as in *athiire* (he went) and *aathire* (he commanded).[85]

Homogenized Orthography

The other concern that UKLC had to deal with was the various dialects of the Gīkūyū language. The southern Gīkūyū spoke a slightly different dialect from their northern counterparts.[86] Because of the diverse dialects, several quite different orthographies had emerged with missionaries of various societies using different versions depending on their area of operation.[87] UKLC made it a matter of importance to reduce these dialects into a united orthography. Uniform orthography meant a given character or letter having one and the same value ascribed to it. It also signified that a given sound, which was common to all the dialects, was to be represented uniformly and universally by one and the same character in all said dialects. UKLC argued that "with the boon of a uniform version, natives from every district

81. Canon Harry Leakey (CMS) is said have been largely instrumental in introducing the form of Gīkūyū spelling with diacritical marks. Barlow papers, UKLC Minutes of May 27, 1908, Gen. 1785/7; John W. Arthur, "The Late Canon Harry Leakey," *KN* 152 (June 1940): 348.

82. Barlow papers, UKLC Minutes 6/4/1908–15/8/1933, Gen. 1786/5 1a and 1b.

83. Barlow papers, UKLC Minutes of August 13 and 14, 1913, Gen. 1785/7.

84. Barlow papers, UKLC Minutes of March 17–18 1909, Gen. 1785/7.

85. Barlow papers, UKLC Minutes of June 7, 1909, Gen. 1785/7.

86. The southern districts of Kīambu and Fort Hall comprised Kambūi mission under the American Gospel Mission Society (GMS); Kījabe mission under African Inland Mission, Kikuyu mission under Church of Scotland Mission (CSM); Kabete mission, Weithaga mission, and Kahuhia mission all under Church Mission Society (CMS). In the northern district of Nyeri, there was Tumutumu mission under CSM as well as Chuka and Chogoria in Meru. The Methodist mission was located in Imenti and in Embu, Kīrangari mission came under CMS. One of the serious mistakes made by missionaries was to assume Kīmerū and Embu languages were part of Gīkūyū dialects and thus placing them together under the Gīkūyū language.

87. Leakey, *Kenya*, 151.

could understand and take part in the worship of God."[88] Standardization of Gĩkũyũ orthography was duly approved and gazetted by the colonial government to be used not only in the Bible translation but also in translation of any other literature. In 1926, the first Gĩkũyũ New Testament was published by an inter-mission team of translators and on March 14, 1926 the first copy was laid on the communion table during the ordination service of the first five African ministers of the Church of Scotland Mission.[89] By 1935, the supply of Gĩkũyũ New Testaments had run out, and a reprint was decided upon.[90] This offered the opportunity to undertake the correction, alteration, and revision of the text, resulting in the second edition of the Gĩkũyũ New Testament, issued in 1936.[91] This edition had to go through yet another revision process, starting with "retranslation" of the Epistle to the Romans, resulting in the Gĩkũyũ New Testament and the Psalms.[92] The translation of the Gĩkũyũ New Testament reveals other issues in Bible translation that aimed at controlling influence on the Africans.

Common Language and Civilization

In the first instance, a common form of language was seen as the gateway to progress and civilization.[93] The idea was premised on the claim that it required a European to teach Africans the structure and idiomatic beauties of their own mother tongue, and how best to select and develop its finest features.[94] In order for the African mind and soul to reach their highest development, much fuller teaching in the best of their vernaculars was needed.[95] Therefore, a common policy in regard to the language problems would hasten unification of natives' dialects, make submission of the translations into one center possible, and afford a common method of spelling,

88. Scott, *A Saint in Kenya*, 137.

89. Barlow, "Language Work Notes," 19.

90. By end of 1945 Mr. Scott Dickson, one of the missionaries in Kenya, estimated that only over 100,000 copies of the Bible could satisfy the need. Barlow, "Note on Translation Work, 1948" 972; "Staff Notes," 707.

91. Ruffell Barlow and Canon Harry Leakey were assigned the revision with Barlow undertaking the final reading of all the proofs. Barlow, "Language Work Notes," 19; see also BFBS resolution under point 5. *Gĩkũyũ* E.S.C. minis. April 8, 1936 p. 3; BSA/E3/3/253/4, Kikuyu 4, BFBS Archives.

92. The "final" revision was done in 1944. Barlow, "Language Work, 1944," 693–94.

93. Sugirtharajah, *Postcolonial Criticism*, 158.

94. Rowling, "The Mother Tongue for African Readers," 133.

95. Ibid., 134.

and the same name for God, for Spirit, for Soul, among others.[96] This vision justified UKLC's action (as stated previously) to first order, harmonize, and standardize the Gĩkũyũ language through uniform orthography.

Unification of Language in East and Central Africa

The homogenization of native dialects as proposed by UKLC followed the broader colonial strategy of a fast forward in the linguistic evolution by merging all of the regional dialects into one common language. The strategic focus was to gradually introduce the African students to a "main" language chosen as most suitable. K.E. Roehl, having concluded that Swahili was the future lingua franca of East and Central Africa, proposed and recommended it as the ultimate language to which all translations in East Africa should aspire.[97] There was no need to spend much time on the small or medium-sized languages which had no prospect of exercising influence outside their own sphere. It was hoped that by targeting languages dominant in different areas, translation of the Bible would eventually quicken the assimilation of the smaller language groups in one common linguistic region.[98] But for purely scientific reasons the "small tribal languages" threatened by extinction and assimilation were to be thoroughly studied and recorded without delay. Such a study would be beneficial to the scientific world in that it would help correct some prevalent linguistic errors in this respect.[99] Although the Gĩkũyũ language, because of its considerable local importance, needed to have all of the kindred dialects united into one literary language, Roehl was pessimistic of its survival because of its exposure to the "assimilative power

96. Barlow Papers, "Report of United Conference of Missionary Society (no. 17): Printed Pamphlets on Kenya and Kikuyu and Gospel of St. Mark, 1906–63," Gen. 1786/12.

97. Roehl, "Linguistic Situation," 191.

98. Ibid., 192–93.

99. Such errors were thought to have led to the formation of pidgin or "trade" languages such as "coast English," "Creole French," and "Kitchen Kafir." Max Müller had earlier indicated that dialects which had "never produced any literature at all, the jargons of savage tribes, the clicks of the Hottentots, and the vocal modulations of the Indo-Chinese, are as important, nay, for the solutions of some of our problems, more important, than the poetry of Homer or the prose of Cicero" (as quoted in Werner, "The Languages of Africa," 120–21). A. Werner would years later add that "the unwritten . . . primitive languages . . . which the last generation, or the last but one, wont. No 'was' to look upon as barbarous jargons, not worth the attention of scholars" remained of great philological importance (Werner, "The Languages of Africa," 120–21; Crabtree, "The Systematic Study of African Languages"; American Mission Committee at Natal, "Plan for Effecting a Uniform Orthography of the South-African Dialects," 332.

of Swahili."[100] A united orthography in Gĩkũyũ country was to play a decisive role towards a projected unified language in East and Central Africa.[101]

Translation as a Colonial Strategy

The act of translation served yet another purpose. Barlow gave a very clear
view as to why learning Gĩkũyũ and translating the text was of paramount
importance. The "ability to converse with the people in their own tongue"
was in itself a great means of "inducing sympathy and mutual understanding between the native and his white master which it becomes more and
more necessary to foster as the tide of immigration of Europeans into the
British East Africa rises."[102] In essence, translation was to offer the linguistic
bridge needed in order to serve the larger colonial mission.[103] Barlow's idea
was not without precedent. It had already been debated and its importance
highlighted in South Africa in the quest for a united approach to the "Hottentots and Bushmen" languages of South Africa.[104] Colonization was not
going to follow the old ways of the Romans who were never troubled by difficulties which "barbarians" faced in understanding Latin or Greek. Modern
habits of thought, as evident in the invention of a new Gĩkũyũ orthography,
demanded that either the colonized learn the language of the colonizer or
the colonizers learn "alien speech" if "right rule" was to be possible.[105]

Translation as Cultural Imperialism

Translation of the Gĩkũyũ New Testament also assumed certain inalienable
cultural assumptions in the linguistic and literary activities associated with
the process. The translators had the power to choose and prescribe what they
thought good for the Africans and what to dismiss. By reducing the Gĩkũyũ
language into the written form, colonialism named and constituted this idiom into a linguistic system whose coherence came through the grammatical

---

100. Roehl, "Linguistic Situation," 194–95.

101. Rowling, "African Readers," 137–38; Roehl, "Linguistic Situation," 191–202.

102. Barlow, Preface to the 1946 edition of his *Tentative Studies in Kikuyu Grammar
and Idiom.*

103. The United Kikuyu Language Committee orthography was adopted by the
colonial government as the "official orthography for the Kikuyu Language." Barlow
Papers, Gen 1786/6 no. 71.

104. American Mission Committee at Natal, "Uniform Orthography," 330–34.

105. Werner, "Languages of Africa," 121.

grid of Western linguistics.[106] This process reduced the Gĩkũyũ language into a suave uniformity that the translators could control. In the process the translators would have the ability and authority to purge the language of any undesirable elements. Subsequently, UKLC categorized some Gĩkũyũ words as acceptable to use in the Christian context and others as having vastly different meaning from the intended purpose.[107] The best example is UKLC's adaptation of the Gĩkũyũ *Ngai*[108] as the best term for "God." The term still needed purging of its indigenous meaning in order to render the meaning of "our Father all powerful, all-holy, all-wise, all-loving."[109]

Barlow offered the best explanation as to why the term *Ngai* had to be adopted while at the same time exorcised its indigenous meaning. He stated that belief in God (*Ngai*) and *Ngai*'s existence compared to the biblical God in several ways. The term was universally admitted. *Ngai* possessed transcendent power as the Lord of nature and the source of life and increase. *Ngai*'s bounty and goodwill was also recognized. Not dissimilar to the Jewish worldview, *Ngai* was seen as a celestial being dwelling on mountain tops, invisible, immortal, and conceived of as glorious (*Mwene-nyaga*). *Ngai* existed prior to the beginnings of the "tribes" and was the disposer of events and the arbiter of fate. *Ngai* was admitted to overrule humans' actions, decide their fate, and decree the time of death. Like the Old Testament God, *Ngai* was a lawgiver, establishing customs and interested to some degree in human affairs. *Ngai* communicated through dreams and gave prophetic utterances and commands to the community through certain mediums. Invocation of *Ngai* and sacrifice to *Ngai* was believed to be an acknowledgment of God's pre-eminence and power.[110]

106. A good case in point is Barlow's *Tentative Studies in Gĩkũyũ Grammar and Idiom.*

107. Marion Stevenson is said to have collected some two hundred such words, and, after going over them with Mr. Barlow, wrote down what they would convey to the natives in their district. This list was typed and sent to the other missions, in order that they might add what the words meant in that part of the country. Scott, *A Saint in Kenya*, 606.

108. The following terms had been considered before finally agreeing on *Ngai* as the best translation for God. God = *Mũrungu*, Jehovah = *Yahua*; *baba* was adopted as being used as *father* in *our father* when addressing God (UKLC Minutes of May 22 and 27, 1908: Gen. 1785/7); Jehovah = taken as *Yehoba* (UKLC Minutes of June 17, 1908: Gen. 1785/7); God = *Ngai*, Jehovah = *Yehoba* (UKLC Minutes of June 7, 1909: Gen. 1785/7.

109. See also Barlow's notes on "Points of Comparison and Contrast between Kikuyu Religious Beliefs and Customs and Christianity" in "Conditions of Life and Religion in which the Missionary works in Africa Today," Barlow Papers, Gen. 1786/2/21; Stevenson, "The Kikuyu Language Committee," 117; Hobley, *Bantu Beliefs and Magic*, 36.

110. Barlow Papers, Gen. 1786/2/21.

However, on points of contrast, Barlow argued that there was general ignorance of the nature of God. *Ngai* was said to be unknown and remote and spoken of as though impersonal. Unlike the Old Testament God, *Ngai* was not a "jealous God," for *Ngai* permitted worship of other beings ("Ngoma") as well as *Ngai-self. Ngai* rarely concerned *Ngai-self* with human affairs. *Ngai* remained aloof and was an object of awe rather than of love and reverence. *Ngai's* presence was undesired for *Ngai* was feared to bring misfortune. *Ngai* was amoral and did not take cognizance of human conduct and was also indifferent to infringement of moral codes. Although the Agĩkũyũ acknowledged that they were the "children of *Ngai,*" they evinced a very inadequate conception of *Ngai* as their Father, who never offered any revelation. Above all, Agĩkũyũ religious beliefs and practices were dependent upon oral transmission of tradition and therefore undependable. Communications claimed to be received from *Ngai* by Agĩkũyũ prophets or mediums were of doubtful authenticity and lacking in religious purpose. The translators as such accepted the term *Ngai* on the condition that teachings and preaching would be intensified in order to draw the distinction between *Ngai* of the Bible and Gĩkũyũ's *Ngai.* Translators' choice to retain a Gĩkũyũ concept for God also constrained the universalizing assumptions and totalizing impulses in the translation process.

Another example of the overwhelming power of the European translators can been found in an African Christian language conference summoned by UKLC in Nairobi and held on January 8, 1910. The conference was intended to help the European translators test some of the words they had accumulated.[111] Barlow and Leakey were to be present and report their findings to UKLC.[112] The purpose of the conference was to have Gĩkũyũ words studied and discussed.[113] Most remarkably, it was brought to the

111. Unlike in the European meetings for the Language Committee where names of members present were entered and apologies included, the names of the Gĩkũyũ present in the African language conference were not given. Those in attendance were merely referred to as "natives present."

112. Lists of words decided upon by the Committee were first sent to all missions in Gĩkũyũ country asking them to go over them carefully at each station. Each station was also expected to send at least one or two African representatives to the conference. Barlow Papers, UKLC Minutes of January 8, 1910, Gen. 1785/7.

113. Some of the important words adopted as a result of the conference included *Ndumĩrĩri* and *Ũhoro mwega* to refer to "a succinct, specific message" as with John the Baptist, while *Ngumo* should be used to refer to "merely fame or reputation." It was also concluded that *Thimo* could be used as an explanation of the parable by Christ to his disciple. *Rĩathani* (singular), *Maathani* (plural) was unanimously decided upon as a word which could best translate "the Ten Commandments" as covering both the affirmative and negative commands.

attention of the conference, by some Africans that the word *Mūkohani*[114] (already introduced from the Kiswahili stem *-kuhani*) was objectionable in representing the concept of "priest" owing to the existence of the word *Mūkuuhani* (a fornicator) already in Gĩkũyũ. Considerable time was spent in examining other possible words to express the "sacrificial priest" of the Bible. Finally it was unanimously decided among the Africans that *Mūhakithia Ngai* was the best rendering for one whose main occupation was to officiate at sacrifices.[115] Nevertheless, Barlow and Leakey rejected the Africans' recommendation for "priest," *Mūhakithia Ngai*, arguing that it was not the accurate rendering of the term.[116] Eventually, UKLC, following the recommendation of the two European translators, unilaterally dropped *Mūkohani* and *Mūruti igongona*, replacing it with a new word introduced into the Gĩkũyũ lexicon, *Muthījīri Ngai* or *Muthījīri wa Ngai*, for priest. UKLC also opted to use *Munabii* (singular) and *A-nabii* (plural) for "prophet"—a Swahili word transliterated into Gĩkũyũ.[117]

What is apparent from the aforementioned issues such as the standardization and unification of the Gĩkũyũ language, is that translation was a hegemonic process that facilitated the domestication as well as homogenization of the idiom through the predetermined process of cooption and expansion of the linguistic tools. Since the Africans were not consulted or involved in the decision making process it was also an obvious act of imposition. However, even though the power of missionary-translators was always assumed, difference and hybridity, rather than perfect replication of the Bible into the targeted text, are the hallmarks of the Gĩkũyũ New Testament. When one considers the issues arising from the translation of the Gĩkũyũ New Testament as discussed previously, one cannot but agree with Barnstone who has observed that translation, "entails a complexity of ever-changing sense found in new signs with their own lexical code."[118] For example, the fact that the Gĩkũyũ New Testament had to be re-edited several times, as has been stated, within a span of ten years shows the tentative-

---

114. Words for the Priest, Prophet, Rabbi, and Preacher had be evaluated and vetted in different Committee meetings. Here are some of the words tested and evaluated: Preacher = *mūrutani, mūūmbūria, mūhubiri* (Swahili), *mūhunjia*; Priest = *Mūkohani* (Swahili); Prophet = *mūraguri, mūndū wa nyama ya mbūri* (these were considered in UKLC Minutes of June 17, 1908, Gen. 1785/7); Rabbi or teacher = *murutani*; Master = *mumenyeria, murutani, Mwene*; Preacher = *murutani, muumburia, muhubiri, muhunjia* (these were also addressed in UKLC Minutes of April 6, 1909, Gen. 1785/7).

115. Barlow Papers, UKLC Minutes of January 8, 1910, Gen. 1785/7.

116. Barlow Papers, UKLC Minutes of October 3, 1910: Gen. 1785/7.

117. Barlow Papers, UKLC Minutes of September 25, 1914, Gen. 1785/7.

118. Barnstone, *Poetics of Translation*, 18.

ness of the whole translation process. The same tentativeness would equally affect the publication of the Old Testament in its entirety due to "technical" delays.[119]

The indeterminate nature of the translated Gĩkũyũ New Testament also invokes an instability as well as an ambivalence that indicate not just internal contradictions but also the dynamics of resistance. In addition, study of the Gĩkũyũ New Testament shows that the act of translation offers an "in-between" space which, as elaborated by Homi Bhabha, provides "the terrain for elaborating strategies of selfhood—singular or communal—that initiate new signs of identity, and innovative sites of collaboration, and contestation, in the act of defining the idea of society itself."[120]

In the moment of historical transformation, an interrogatory interstice is opened between the act of representation and the presence of the community itself, where cultural values, community interests, and experiences are negotiated.

Discourse of Resistance: Translation as an "In-between" Space (Creolization)

Though colonial translation played a significant role in the domination of Africans, it could not gain absolute control either in language or culture. The process of Bible translation into African dialects, as Lamin Sanneh argues, afforded more than anything else the "indigenous discovery" of Christianity.[121] Sanneh posits that by translating the Bible into local languages and indigenous terminologies, the process opened the way for "indigenous innovation and motivation in the religious life."[122] On their part, the colonized translated themselves into the dominant culture by way of accommodation and mimicry.[123] Through such acts of appropriation, translation opened up the possibility of invoking equally forceful acts of questioning, resistance, and even reverse racism.[124]

---

119. The Old Testament was not published until 1951. Calderwood, "Extracts from Annual Reports for 1941," 468; Barlow, "Translation and Language Work, 1942," 529–30; Editor, "Report for 1936 as Presented to the General Assembly on 21st May 1937," 51–52; *KN* 176 (June 1946) 739–972.

120. Bhabha, *Location of Culture*, 2.

121. Sanneh, *Whose Religion is Christianity?*, 10.

122. Ibid.

123. Bhabha, *Location of Culture*, 132–44.

124. Ngũgĩ wa Thiong'o, *Writers in Politics*, 18–25.

When positively appropriated, translation took a new form: *Creolization*. Creolization used in the Caribbean context of the term "Creole" refers to translation as "displacement, the carrying over and transformation of the dominant culture into new identities that take on material elements from the culture of their new location."[125] The untranslatability of African religious terminologies opened an interstice that transformed the colonized from the passive victims of translation to active translators who recognized that they were in charge of their destiny. Translation became a performative act of decolonization.

Translation and the Untranslatability of Religious Terminologies

It has already been argued that translation is more than the simple transference of meaning from one language to another since it involves mental activities. Barnstone has convincingly argued that when a translator reads the source text, he or she commits into memory what has been read, to be recalled when the translator commits to writing what he or she read previously.[126] But before the writing happens, the translator will look for lexical equivalence of the source text in the targeted language. If the target language lacks convincing lexical equivalence, the translator will either borrow from elsewhere or create his or her own lexicon. Since all this happens simultaneously, the translator is in essence engaged in the hermeneutical process as an important act of translation. Once the new lexical equivalence is determined the translator resorts to writing his or her reading of the source texts. Gĩkũyũ translators, through the reader-author strategy described previously, argued that it was difficult finding words to express abstract ideas such as spirit, grace, eternity, and communion, which were said to be non-existent in the Gĩkũyũ language.[127]

The Gĩkũyũ equivalents for "spirit," for example, were dismissed as unintelligible.[128] This is in spite of the fact that there were some translators who believed that even though African languages may have been limited when it came to translating philosophical subjects, the Bantu vocabulary tended to be "larger than that of the average European language."[129] In order to overcome the difficulty in rendering religious terms not found in the Gĩkũyũ language, the Language Committee ruled that such words should be ad-

---

125. Young, *Postcolonialism*, 142.

126. Barnstone, *Poetics of Translation*, 20–24.

127. Scott, *A Saint in Kenya*, 244.

128. Stevenson, "The Kikuyu Language Committee," 117.

129. Doke, "The Basis of Bantu Literature," 285.

opted directly from Swahili. This rule was referred to as "Gikuyuization"[130] of the untranslatable words. As a rule all Biblical proper names had to be "Gikuyuized." Gikuyuizing of the untranslatable terms meant direct adaptation of Swahili words or phrases from the Swahili version of the New Testament into Gĩkũyũ to fill in the linguistic gap.[131] Since the translator believed that the Swahili Bible had closely followed the Greek version and that the use of Swahili Biblical proper names would induce a sense of familiarity to the reader,[132] "Gikuyuizing" would serve as preparation towards unification of British East Africa, bound together by a standardized Swahili.[133] The rule was revised later with emphasis that foreign words, including Swahili ones introduced into Gĩkũyũ, were to be transliterated.[134] As a result of this new revision, most of the words mentioned previously, plus a number of other terms, were all transliterated. A good case in point is "Satan," rendered in Swahili as *Cetani* and transliterated as *Shaitani*.[135]

Certain words retained their Hebraic or Greek forms because they were thought to have no exact equivalences in Gĩkũyũ. The translators argued that in order to retain the "purity" of the ideas that these words conveyed, it was imperative that they had to retain their original form.[136] Behind the view of untranslatability is the fact of difference within and between languages.[137] This notion helps reiterate the point that perfect translatability is impossible. It is this reality that frustrated the translators the most.[138]

At such moments of exasperation, biblical commentators offered little help because they were greatly at variance, both in their expert opinions as to the right reading of the Hebrew or Greek, and as to the sense it was originally intended to convey.[139] Barlow was at a loss when it came to such trans-

130. Barlow Papers, UKLC Minutes of April 6, 1909, Gen. 1785/7.

131. Marion Stevenson and others laboriously copied out and adapted some 750 of the proper names of the Bible to Kikuyu pronunciation and spelling. Scott, *A Saint in Kenya*, 245; see also Barlow Papers, UKLC Minutes of June 15, 1912, Gen. 1785/7.

132. Barlow Papers, UKLC Minutes of June 7, 1909, Gen. 1785/7; Letter by O. H. Scouten to Rev. R. Kilgour of BFBS on June 22, 1909. BSA/E3/3/253/1; See also Scott, *A Saint in Kenya*, 130.

133. Roehl, "The Linguistic Situation," 199; Scott, *A Saint in Kenya*, 130.

134. Barlow Papers, UKLC Minutes of January 27 and 28, 1914, Gen. 1785/7.

135. Barlow Papers, UKLC Minutes of June 17, 1908, Gen. 1785/7; See also Blakeslee, *Beyond the Kikuyu Curtain*, 41.

136. Barlow, "Language Report, 1943," 606.

137. Barnstone, *Poetics of Translation*, 42.

138. Barlow had been requested by the Bible Society's Translations Superintendent to give a short account of the difficulties encountered in Bible translation ("Language Report, 1943," 605).

139. Ibid.

lation as in 1 John 2, 12–14, "I write unto you" (present), "I have written unto you" (perfect) or "I wrote."[140] In the first instance, the present tense would be referring to the present Epistle, while in the perfect it would be referring to either the previous Epistle or John's Gospel. However, the perfect in English is considered non-committal and covered only hypotheses. On the other hand the perfect in Gĩkũyũ according to Barlow would "only refer to what precedes in the present." Because of perceived linguistic ambiguity of the text, as well as doctrinal interests, Barlow rendered the verse in question as "I wrote" in reference to or alluding to the Gospel. He argued that there was no suitable alternative in Gĩkũyũ.[141] To resolve the untranslatability problem the translators had to discover a "*via media*, avoiding with regret one or another attractively definite rendering, in order to preserve the indefiniteness of the original while yet making good sense."[142]

Translation as an Act of Resistance: African Ordinary Readers

Translation, as already pointed out, opened up the possibility of invoking equally forceful acts of questioning and resistance. In the postcolonial concept, translation as Creolization is viewed as "a space of re-empowerment."[143] It displaces, carries over, and transforms the dominant culture into new identities that take on material elements from the new milieu in which it is located. Such is the case of Charles Mũhoro Kareri, one of the Africans who played a pivotal role in the translation of the Bible to Gĩkũyũ language, despite the discriminatory by-law. Highly intelligent and well capable of carrying out translation work on his own, Kareri translated most of the *Psalms* by himself using Swahili and English Bibles.[144] In retrospect, Kareri wrote,

> I would translate about six or ten *Psalms*, then I would sit down and read them with Barlow to agree about how the words would follow one another. After reading and correcting the *Psalms* I had translated, I would be left to work on the others alone.[145]

140. Letter by Mr. A. Ruffell Barlow to the Editor Superintendent of BFBS as reply in a letter dated, February 20, 1919, BSA/E3/3/253/2.

141. February 20, 1919, BSA/E3/3/253/2.

142. Barlow, "Language Report, 1943," 605.

143. Young, *Postcolonialism*, 142.

144. Kareri, *The Life of Charles Muhoro Kareri*, 52.

145. Even though he was doing a similar task to that undertaken by missionaries like Barlow, Kareri saw himself as an assessor. Barlow on the other hand referred to him as his "African co-operator." Kareri, *Charles Muhoro Kareri*, 52; see also Barlow,

He traversed the Gĩkũyũ country collecting words and evaluating how such words were used in different Gĩkũyũ dialects. Kareri aimed at collecting and using "archaic words" which he feared would be lost if not preserved in written form.[146] In his opinion, though some of these words were difficult to most readers, he would rather people use a dictionary than lose the original Gĩkũyũ. Kareri felt strongly that it was his responsibility to preserve the words for the benefit of the community.[147] Kareri saw himself as a man with a mission. Nonetheless, without proper training in translation work and with no encouragement or further opportunities afforded him, Kareri found comfort in leaving the work to the man he highly exalted when he wrote: "In 1934, I realized that Barlow knew Gikuyu better than me."[148]

Another important figure is Bildad Kaggia,[149] who, unlike other African assessors and assistants, directly questioned and openly opposed the unilateral decisions missionaries took in translating certain words in the Gĩkũyũ New Testament. He was greatly surprised after reading the translated Gĩkũyũ version of the New Testament to discover a number of translation mistakes. The glaring translation errors prompted Kaggia to retranslate the Gĩkũyũ New Testament.[150] During his official military posting in Britain, Kaggia took his complete revision of the translated Gĩkũyũ version to the offices of the BFBS, which had published the Gĩkũyũ New Testament, and met with G. Cowan, the publishing superintendent. Kaggia wanted his revisions published (this was quite naïve but revolutionary). His visit to the London office coincided with John W. Arthur's furlough in Scotland.

"Language Work," 16.

146. Kareri, *Charles Muhoro Kareri*, 52.

147. Kareri also translated invectives for Mr. Barlow. Most of his work found its way not only into the Bible but also into Barlow's dictionary, and Benson's dictionary (See also letter to Rev. Leonard Beecher (then Bishop of Mombasa) by Mr. Benson dated May 18th, 1956, Barlow's Papers: Gen. 1785/1); Kareri, *Charles Muhoro Kareri*, 52.

148. Ibid.

149. Bildad Kaggia, born in 1922, was one of the founding fathers of the Nation of Kenya. He was one of the famous *Kapenguria Six* freedom fighters (himself, Jomo Kenyatta, Achieng Oneko, Kũng'ũ Karũmba, Paul Ngei, and Fred Kubai) who were detained by the colonial government during the struggle for independence in Kenya. He was known for his courage, radicalism, and adherence to truth. After finishing school in 1939, he worked in the District Commissioner's office in Fort Hall. He had been baptised and brought up an Anglican, in the Church Missionary Society. He also served as a World War II serviceman in the army and was quickly promoted to a Staff-Sergeant and finally Quartermaster-Sergeant. After his return to Kenya in 1946 from the war, he became a trade union activist, and rose rapidly to become leader of the Labour Trade Union of East Africa. He also started a newsletter, *Inooro ria Gikuyu* (Whetstone Of Gikuyu). Bildad Kaggia died on March 7, 2005.

150. Kaggia, *Roots of Freedom 1921–1963*, 37–39, 48.

At the time, Arthur was the chairman of UKLC. Cowan arranged for an appointment for Kaggia to meet with the chairman. Though John Arthur had not translated any of the New Testament books, to Kaggia's satisfaction, he spoke Gĩkũyũ, unlike G. Cowan who knew nothing about the language. After "two full days" of argument with Arthur, the missionary finally agreed that Kaggia's "amended New Testament" should be forwarded for consideration to UKLC.[151]

Some of the examples that Kaggia cited as having been wrongly translated included, first, the contentious rendering of the term "prophet," which had already been discussed in the African Language Conference, as mentioned previously. The Gĩkũyũ version now read *mũnabii*, a word which Kaggia said was borrowed from the Arabic, *nabii*. Kaggia was aware of the fact that loaning words from other languages enriches a language. He pointed out, "I was not against borrowing new words, as borrowing enriches a language, but I was very much against borrowing a word when there was a suitable Kikuyu word."[152] There was already in Gĩkũyũ a suitable word, *mũrathi*, for prophet. As such Kaggia argued there was no reason to use an Arabic word which the Agĩkũyũ would not understand.

Rev. Arthur's objection to Kaggia's proposal was on two fronts. First, the original meaning of *mũrathi* was "a heathen false prophet." Second, there was no difference between *mũrathi* and *mũndũ-mũgo* (medicine man or witchdoctor). Kaggia challenged Arthur's conclusion, arguing that in Israel there were both false and true prophets and the term prophet was used for both, only with the addition of an adjective. Logically, he postulated, Agĩkũyũ knew that there were two kinds of *mũrathi*, a true one who was accepted as speaking on behalf of *Ngai* and the pretender who if found out was immediately punished by death. Kaggia also categorically denied Rev. Arthur's sweeping generalization. The *mũrathi* was distinctively different from *mũndũ-mũgo*. *Mũrathi*, Kaggia argued, had free access to *Ngai* while *mũndũ-mũgo* used witchcraft and information gathered from the "client." Kaggia wondered why the Jews and the Arabs did not invent new words for God or prophet when they learnt of the "new" god but continued using the old ones. He pointed out that missionaries, in like manner, did not stop the use of the Gĩkũyũ *Ngai* despite the "heathen" origin of the term. He denounced as a double standard the missionaries' rejection of Gĩkũyũ words that were as valid as *Ngai*.[153]

151. Ibid., 50.
152. Ibid.
153. Ibid.

Kaggia also challenged the use of the word *ngoma* for "devil," which he saw as "a gross mistranslation," for the Agĩkũyũ term *ngoma* referred to ancestral spirits which Agĩkũyũ revered. *Ngoma* acted according to the behavior of the living community. If the living annoyed the spirits, evil was assured to befall, not only on the family that aggrieved such a spirit, but the community as well. But after appeasing the spirits, either by sprinkling beer or slaughtering livestock, normalcy was restored.

In using the term *Ngoma* for "devil," Kaggia postulated, the translation implied "evil spirits." In Arthur's opinion, the worship given to "*Ngoma*" went against the first of the Ten Commandments. "*Ngoma*" monopolized attention and took a more prominent place than God in the life of the people. Such worship (of "Ngoma"), therefore, was unnecessary, wrong, and insulting to God. Christianity taught direct access to God and the worship of God alone.[154] However, for Kaggia there was "nothing evil about the spirit of one's mother or father."[155]

Kaggia's observation is important because UKLC translated ᾅδης as used in its genitive form ᾅδου in Matt 16:18 to refer to "of Hades" as *kũndũ kwa Ngoma* (abode of Spirits).[156] However, in verse 23, where Peter is rebuked by Jesus and pointedly referred to as σατανᾶ, UKLC rendered that translation as *Shaitani* (a Gĩkũyũ transliteration of Swahili *Cetani*). This raises the question, since there was no Gĩkũyũ equivalence for "Devil" or "Satan" or "Demon" (as evident in the rendering of Matthew 16:18), of why the missionaries would liberally apply Gĩkũyũ terms when it came to the evil aspect of demonic or satanic manifestations. Is it not an example of the colonial ideological model that delighted in categorizing Africans' religious and cultural tenets in demonic terms, which are equivalent to modern day devil worship?

Kaggia also challenged the Gĩkũyũ rendering of Galatians 6:6. Kaggia's English rendition of the missionaries' Gĩkũyũ version given previously was *"let him that is taught the word of God give his teacher all his good things!"*[157] The problem with the translation, according to Kaggia, was that many

---

154. See also "Conditions of Life and Religion in which the Missionary works in Africa Today" in Gen. 1786/2/21 (Barlow Papers); Boyes. *King of the Wa-Kikuyu*, 156.

155. Kaggia, *Roots of Freedom*, 49.

156. See Matt 16:18 in *Kĩrĩkanĩro Kĩrĩa Kĩerũ Kĩa Jesu Kristo Ũrĩa Mwathani witũ o na Mũhonokia Witũ* (1926 ed.) as well as Barlow Papers, UKLC Minutes of September 25, 1914, Gen. 1785/7.

157. The italics are mine. The UKLC translation reads "Na rĩrĩ, nĩ wega mũndũ ũrĩa ũkũrutwo Ũhoro wa Ngai agayagĩre mũmũruti indo ciake ciothe njega" (*Kĩrĩkanĩro Kĩrĩa Kĩerũ kĩa Jesu Kristo*, 429. There was no change in the rev. ed. of 1936; see also Kaggia, *Roots of Freedom*, 48–49).

Gĩkũyũ Christians took it literally and had been encouraged to do so. They interpreted it to mean that they were expected to give all their good things to the Church because God had so commanded. The poor gave everything they had to the Church. Kaggia added that the Agĩkũyũ Christians would sometimes give everything away, including all their money, leaving themselves without sufficient resources for food or to pay school fees for their children. What made UKLC translation awkward, according to Kaggia, was that the Gĩkũyũ translation did not follow the Swahili version,[158] its English equivalent being "Let the student or disciple share or co-operate with the teacher in *all good things*."[159] A further difficulty was that "good things" in Swahili did not imply goats, cattle, sheep or money, but "good matters" whereas in Gĩkũyũ *indo* referred to material things. The hermeneutical danger of such a mistranslation is nowhere else better captured than in Kaggia's observation that such a translation always served the colonialists' larger mission.[160] Kaggia concluded that the African's greatest enemy was foreign religious beliefs from which he had to be liberated before the African could accept "new ideas about the injustices of British administration."[161] Liberation could not occur with God remaining on the side of the "colonialists as the whole church preached against the African way of life. God had to be brought to our side. The African had to understand that God supported our cause and the *mzungu* was in the wrong."[162]

It is not known whether Kaggia's translation was ever considered by UKLC but we know that his religious convictions and political consciousness led him into direct confrontation with the colonial government.[163]

---

158. The Swahili version read, "Mwanafunzi na amshirikishe Mfunzi *wake katika mema yote*." The italics are Kaggia's. Kaggia's translation follows BFBS, *Kitabu cha Agano Jipya la Bwana na Mwokozi wetu Yesu Kristo: Kimefasirika katika Maneno ya Kiyunani* (1921 ed.), Wagalatia 6:6. The verse in the Swahili version published 1913 reads "Aliyefundishwa ashiriki nae afundishae katika yote yaliyo mema," BFBS, *Kitabu cha Agano Jipya la Bwana na Mwokozi wetu Yesu Kristo: Kimefasirika katika Maneno ya Kiyunani* (1913 ed.), Wagalatia 6:6. But it reads "Lakini mwenyi kufundishwa lile neon na amgawie mfunzi mema yote, aliyo nayo!" in Würtemberg, *Agano Jipya la Bwana na Mwokozi wetu Yesu Kristo: Katika Msemo wa Kiswaheli cha Bara* (Stuttgart: Würtemberg, 1930), Wagalatia 6:6.

159. Kaggia, *Roots of Freedom*, 49.

160. Ibid., 56.

161. Ibid.

162. Ibid.

163. Ibid., 73.

Conclusion

The thrust of this essay has been to reveal the multifaceted nature of Bible translation and the relevance of the field of translation studies (Bible translation in particular) in revealing the complex nature of translation activity, often unearthing the socio-political issues involved in this process. The essay has sought to address the nature of Bible translation in relation to colonialism, as exemplified on the continent of Africa. Using the translation of the Gĩkũyũ New Testament in Kenya as a case study, the essay illustrates how the act and process of Bible translation can serve to advance the colonial agenda, while at the same time also help develop a resistant discourse among the target audience. More importantly, the essay shows that Bible translation is not a pure, value-free activity, but rather that translators have to make interpretative decisions when translating from one language to another. As a corollary, this means that theological and even ideological perspectives are given in the process, which are either sympathetic to the cultural context of the target language or speak against such indigenous factors.

This essay also demonstrates the complexity of the act of Bible translation, noting that there can be no exact translation of the source text, since no two languages and cultures are the same and since translation involves a mental activity through the reading of the written text. As such, the translators' influence on the way in which the Bible is translated into the target language is considerable, and from a cultural and linguistic point of view, their dominance is especially noteworthy. However, despite translators' claim to fidelity to the original-source text, as the hallmark that authenticates their translation, there are certain biblical concepts that are untranslatable. These, in turn, leave room for hybridity, and the negotiation of native words, terms, and concepts. The very act of translation reveals that colonialism was never able to fix African identities and representations into stable discourses because of its ambivalence and contractions.

The essay also highlights the important role of "ordinary readers" in the process of Bible translation. Even though ordinary readers form the bulk of the African Christian churches, they are usually assumed "passive" and their readings and interpretations are not taken seriously. Set within a postcolonial framework, this study shows that even though these African readers lack formal training in biblical scholarship and therefore approach the Bible pre-critically, they nevertheless have unique and logical ways of translating and even interpreting biblical texts. Translation, as we have seen, sometimes becomes "a space of re-empowerment," transforming ordinary readers from the passive victims of translation to active translators. Such is the case of the vigilant Kaggia who would use his knowledge to expose and challenge any claim to the innocence of the translated text. In an unequivocal fashion, he pointed to the hermeneutical danger of misappropriation and mistranslations of African terms and concepts.

In addition, this essay aims at provoking debate and challenging African scholars in biblical studies and hermeneutics to pay more attention to the processes and consequences of colonization in Bible translation and biblical interpretation. The essay seeks to encourage indigenous biblical scholars to engage in critical biblical scholarship, which interrogates the relationship between the Bible and colonialism regarding the issues of language, class, gender, ideology, and human subjectivity. The work reminds us that the postcolonial context, just as the colonial context, remains a site where the Bible has the potential of becoming both a solution and a problem, both an oppressor and liberator.

Therefore, the postcolonial situation in Africa demands a new critical tradition in biblical studies and hermeneutics that follows colonial resistant literature to affirm the right of people, once again, to seize the initiative of history. Biblical scholarship in Africa should be in a position to harness the true creative power of the African people. Since the impact of colonialism on culture was intimately related to economic processes, politics, and race, there is need to re-examine how the continuing realities affect the Africans' ongoing understanding of the Bible.

Bibliography

Achebe, Chinua. *Hopes and Impediments: Selected Essays 1965–1987.* New York: Heinemann, 1988.

American Mission Committee at Natal. "Plan for Effecting a Uniform Orthography of the South-African Dialects." *JAOS* 2 (1851) 330–34.

Barlow, Arthur Ruffell. "Language Report, 1943." *KN* 169 (September 1944) 605.

———. "Story of the Gĩkũyũ Bible." *KN* 196 (June 1951) 1160.

———. *Tentative Studies in Kikuyu Grammar and Idiom.* Edinburgh: SPCK & Foreign Mission Committee of the Church of Scotland, 1946.

———. "Progress of Kikuyu Old Testament." *KN* 190 (December 1949) 1053.

Barnstone, Willis. *The Poetics of Translation: History, Theory, Practice.* New Haven: Yale University Press, 1993.

Beecher (Rev.), Leonard J. "The Kikuyu," (The Peoples of Kenya—no. 9). No date.

———. "The Presentation of the Gospel Committed to Our Trust to Animists." University of Birmingham Libraries, Special Collections.

British and Foreign Bible Society. *Kĩrĩkanĩro Kĩrĩa Kĩerũ Kĩa Jesu Kristo Ũrĩa Mwathani witũ o na Mũhonokia Witũ.* London: British and Foreign Bible Socity, 1926 and 1936.

————. *Kitabu cha Agano Jipya la Bwana na Mwokozi wetu Yesu Kristo: Kimefasirika katika Maneno ya Kiyunani*. London: British and Foreign Bible Socity, 1913 and 1921.

Bhabha, Homi. *The Location of Culture*. London: Routledge, 2004.

Blakeslee, H. Virginia. *Beyond the Kikuyu Curtain*. Chicago: Moody, 1956.

Boyes, John. *King of the Wa-Kikuyu: A True Story of Travel and Adventure in Africa*. 4th ed. London: Methuen, 1912. Reprint, Frank Cass, 1968.

Cagnolo, Father C. *Agīkūyū: Their Customs, Traditions and Folklore*. English translation, Nyeri: Agīkūyū in the Mission Printing School, 1933.

Césaire, Aimé. *Discourse on Colonialism*. New York: New York University Press, 2000.

Crabtree, W. A. "The Systematic Study of African Languages." *JRAS* 12 46 (1913) 177–89.

Doke, C. M. "The Basis of Bantu Literature." *Africa* 18 4 (1948) 284–301.

Hinde, Hildegarde. *Vocabularies of the Kamba and Gīkūyū Languages*. Cambridge: Cambridge University Press, 1904.

Hobley, C. W. *Bantu Beliefs and Magic: With Particular Reference to the Kikuyu and Akamba Tribes of Kenya Colony; Together with Some Reflections on East Africa After War*. London: Witherby, 1922.

Johnson, Harry H. *The Universities' Mission to Central Africa: Atlas*. London: Office of the Universities' Mission to Central Africa, 1903.

Johnson, Luke Timothy, with Todd C. Penner. *The Writings of the New Testament: An Interpretation*. 2nd ed. Minneapolis: Fortress, 1999.

Kaggia, Bildad. *Roots of Freedom 1921–1963: The Autobiography of Bildad Kaggia*. Nairobi: East African, 1975.

Kareri, Charles Muhoro. *The Life of Charles Muhoro Kareri*. Edited with an introduction by Derek R. Peterson. Translated by Joseph Kariūki Mūriithi. Madison: University of Wisconsin–Madison African Studies Program, 2003.

Krapf, J. Ludwig. "Three Chapters of Genesis Translated into the Sooahelee Language." Introduction by W. W. Greenough. *JAOS* 1 (1847) 259–74.

————. *Travels, Researches, and the Missionary Labours, during an Eighteen Years' Residence in Eastern Africa: Together with Journeys to Jagga, Usambara, Ukambani, Shoa, Abessinia, and Khartum; and a Coasting Voyage from Mombaz to Cape Delgado*. London: Trubner, 1860.

Leakey, L. S. B. *Kenya: Contrasts and Problems*. London: Methuen and Company, 1936.

————. *White African*. London: Hodder & Stoughton, 1937.

Loomba, Ania. *Colonialism/Postcolonialism: The New Critical Idiom*. 2nd ed. London: Routledge, 2005.

McGregor, A. W. "The Orthography of African Names and Languages." *JRAS* 2/8 (1903) 456–59.

McLeod, John. *Beginning Postcolonialism*. Manchester: Manchester University Press, 2000.

Memmi, Albert. *The Colonizer and the Colonized*. Translated by Howard Greenfeld from *Portrait du Colonisé precede du Portrait du Colonisateur*, 1957. Boston: Beacon, 1967.

Ogilvie, J. N. *Our Empire's Debt to Missions: The Duff Missionary Lecture, 1923*. London: Hodder & Stoughton, 1923.

Philp, Horace R. A. *A New Day in Kenya*. London: World Dominion, 1936.

Rafael, Vicente L. *Contracting Colonialism: Translation and Christian Conversion in Tagalog Society under Early Spanish Rule.* Durham: Duke University Press, 1993.

Roehl, K. E. "The Linguistic Situation in East Africa." *JIAI* 3/2 (1930) 191–202.

Rowling, Canon F. "The Mother Tongue for African Readers." *JRAS* 38/150 (1939) 133–44.

Said, Edward. *Culture and Imperialism.* New York: Vintage, 1994.

Sanneh, Lamin. *Whose Religion is Christianity? The Gospel Beyond the West.* Grand Rapids: Eerdmans, 2003.

Scott, Henry E. *A Saint in Kenya: A Life of Marion Scott Stevenson.* London: Hodder & Stoughton, 1932.

Smalley, William A. *Translation as Mission: Bible Translation in the Modern Missionary Movement.* Macon, GA: Mercer University Press, 1991.

Spivak, Gayatri Chakravorty. *A Critique of Postcolonial Reason: Toward a History of the Vanishing Present.* Cambridge: Harvard University Press, 1999.

Sugirtharajah, R.S. *The Postcolonial Bible.* Bible and Postcolonialism 1. Sheffield: Sheffield Academic, 1998.

———. *Postcolonial Criticism and Biblical Interpretation.* Oxford: Oxford University Press, 2002.

———. *The Postcolonial Biblical Reader.* Oxford: Blackwell, 2006.

Ngũgĩ wa Thiong'o. *Decolonising the Mind: The Politics of Language in African Literature.* Oxford: Curry, 1986.

———. *Writers in Politics: A Re-engagement with Issues of Literature and Society.* Rev. ed. Oxford: Curry, 1997.

Werner, A. "The Languages of Africa." *JRAS* 12/46 (1913) 120–35.

West, Gerald. *Biblical Hermeneutics of Liberation: Modes of Reading the Bible in the South African Context.* 2nd edition. Maryknoll, NY: Orbis, 1995.

———. *The Academy of the Poor: Towards a Dialogical Reading of the Bible.* Pietermaritzburg: Cluster, 2003.

Yorke, Gosnell L. O. R., and Peter M. Renju. *Bible Translation and African Languages.* Nairobi: Acton, 2004.

Young, Robert J. C. *Postcolonialism: A Very Short Introduction.* Oxford: Oxford University Press, 2003.

PART II

Gender, Postcoloniality, and African Bible Translations

4

Translating the Divine

The Case of Modimo in the Setswana Bible[1]

Gomang Seratwa Ntloedibe-Kuswani

ntloegs@mopipi.ub.bw

> How do you translate the God of the Bible in terms of the "god" or "gods" of another culture? How do you change the categories and concepts of biblical religion to terms understood by those of native traditional religions? In general . . . the local gods, religious terminology, and categories are usually hijacked .and christianised, or infused with new biblical meaning. —Aloo Osotsi Mojola

> In many African cultures, for example, the name and concept of the deity are often female. It is also women who are responsible for the intervention between people and the deity. This concept was foreign to early missionary Bible translators, and most translations changed the word for God to adapt it to the Western, male God name. These kinds of translations, now accepted by churches, have helped to reverse the status of women in religious spheres, both in the church and in local cultures. —Musimbi R. A. Kanyoro

Long before the introduction of the Christian tradition in Africa, Africans had their own religious traditions, many of which have the concept of the Divine. For instance, Modimo of the Batswana, Unkulunkulu of the Zulu, Mwari of the Shona in Southern Africa, Olorun of the Yoruba in West

---

1. The word *Setswana* in the title refers to the language and culture of Botswana. *Motswana* refers to a person who comes from Botswana. The plural of *Motswana* is *Batswana*. Epigraphs are drawn from Mojola, "Bible Translation," 31; and Kanyoro, "Translation."

Africa, Ngai of the Kikuyu, Nyasaye of the Luo in East Africa, Nzambi of the Bankongo of the Congo in Central Africa and many other names in other parts of Africa. The colonial mission Christianity had first thought that Africans had no conscious of the Divine or "Something Other than the Ordinary." This was a colonial rhetoric of subjugation. The same missionaries later identified names of the Divine among African languages, which they used in biblical translations. African scholars' challenge to colonizing Christianity led to changed attitudes toward Africa and Africanity (African Spirituality). The changed attitudes are reflected in some later writings of some missionaries and theologians. However, the change remains minimal in the Book of God, the translated Setswana Bible.

This essay focuses on the Batswana concept of the divine, Modimo. The usage of Modimo in Christian Theology is different from its usage in African Batswana theology. The difference is articulated by John Hick's 1989 thesis; that modern awareness of religious plurality and conceptual relativity has brought about a new situation that sees religious thought and experience as a global continuum containing an immense variety of forms. Consequently, the discussions of religion have problems in defining concepts, precisely because each religious tradition has its own patterns. It is always a complex move, as this chapter demonstrates, to define the Divine that we mean by Allah of Islam, Brahman of Hinduism, Modimo of Batswana, Ngai of the Kikuyu, God of Christianity, Nyasayi of the Luo, Mwari of the Shona, YHWH of Judaism and Nzambi of the Bankongo. As the above quote from Aloo Osotsi Mojola indicates, this is precisely because we tend to try to understand various cultures' portraits of the Divine through the dominant form of the Divine—in this case, the biblical God.

The attempt to study religions as a "global continuum," in other words, consists of suppressing differences by attempting to present a general and global theory of religion that can be suitable for all religious traditions. As practiced in biblical translations, Mojola terms this suppression the hijacking and Christianizing of other cultures. It is, therefore, important for all religious traditions to acknowledge their differences before they celebrate their universality and think that they are coexisting in the so-called global village. Even where there are apparent similarities among concepts, one has to bear in mind that similar concepts may carry different meanings in different religious contexts. In the light of the global-continuum approach, it is important to grasp the uniqueness of each religion and its beliefs. In this essay, *the Divine* refers to the concepts of "God" listed above, as an attempt to underline the uniqueness of each concept and to avoid its suppression.

As the above quotes of Musimbi Kanyoro and Moja underline, part of the hijacking, Christianizing, westernizing, and gendering of African concepts of the Divine and of spiritual spaces—Africanity—was informed by the colonizing ideology that believed in the superiority of the Christian God and religion over others or the local religions. The Christian God was held to be the only saving God in the world, while African religions, or any other religion for that matter, were seen as *praeparatio evangelica*.[2] That is, they (other religious traditions) were regarded as lacking completeness and salvation on their own and seen as raw materials that prepared the ground for planting colonizing Christianity.[3] One cannot claim, however, that these colonizing subjugations ended with colonial times. They continue today, in the Postcolonial times, wrapped and girded in translation theory that holds that translation is a communication process that moves the message or meaning "from the source language to the receptor language."[4] According to this theory, the source text is the given and cannot be changed. In other words, the Bible is the source text that cannot be changed, while the languages and cultures into which the Bible is translated are "receptor languages" and cultures that must and can be changed to make room for the Bible.

In making the so-called receptor languages carry and communicate the biblical message, African and other non-biblical cultures are hijacked. Their identity and authority is sacrificed to make room for the source text. The relationship between source and receptor is not equal. In fact, it smacks of both gender and colonizing relationships, in which the man and the colonizer are regarded as the sources of knowledge, power, and leadership, while the woman and the colonized are the subjugated, the silenced, the ruled, and those guided to receive the colonizer's knowledge. Regardless of how these concepts are defined, whether the terms used are *source text* and *receptor languages* or *source text* and *targeted texts*, their relationship is grounded on inequality, on subjugation and domination of the targeted languages and cultures. Thus, within translation theory itself—still used in our day—there is an inherently colonizing and gendered ideology that renders the so-called receptor languages into servants of the "source text," namely, the Bible. As Mojola correctly points out, "Translation is never neutral. It is an instrument of ideological and theological *formation—within the limits of fidelity and faithfulness to the source text.*"[5] The source text is the power, the determinant. While Robert P. Carroll[6] argues persuasively that translation

2. Mbiti, *New Testament Eschatology in an African Background.*

3. Ntloedibe-Kuswani, "The Religious Life of an African."

4. Kanyoro, "Translation."

5. Mojola, "Bible Translation, 31; emphasis mine.

6. Carroll, "Cultural Encroachment and Bible Translation."

also does violence to the source text itself, the translator starts from the premise that they must be faithful to the Bible, the source text, which is held to be normative or authoritative.

But what of us and African cultures, which are equally normative to us? Who has the right to name us as "receptor languages" or "targeted texts," and to decide that our cultures must lose their authority and identity to the source text, the Bible? Why have translators not regarded both the source text and the receptor languages and cultures as equally authoritative and worthy of preservation? Given that proponents of translation theory cannot be separated easily, if at all, from the colonizer, these questions cannot be deferred any longer if the integrity and human rights of all are to be recognized. It is no longer enough to say that the translator's duty is to be faithful primary to the source text, nor is it enough to begin with the premise that the source text cannot be changed—unless one espoused the same commitment to the so-called receptor languages. The violence of biblical translations must be revisited and exposed, and alternative theories that respect both the receptor and source languages should be proposed and applied.

This essay pursues some of these concerns by focusing on the translation of *Modimo*, the divine figure of Batswana, and the ways in which *Modimo* was colonized and gendered in Setswana biblical translations. At issue is how these translations undermine the positions of women in the spirituality and social spaces. The exploration begins by tracing the earliest "written understanding" of *Modimo*, in an effort to illuminate the distinction between this concept and the biblical images and concepts of the divine. The gender neutrality of *Modimo* is illustrated by examining the contents of the Setswana divining set, *ditaola*, to show that, as a spiritual space, *Ditaola* espouses gender neutrality and resists giving *Modimo* human traits. This section is followed by an attempt, by briefly following the role of *Modimo* in Setswana biblical translations, to show how *Modimo* has been separated and taken away from its own people and tradition.

In conclusion, I underline the need for biblical translations that take the gender neutrality of Modimo into consideration, and that respect the difference between Modimo and the biblical concept of YHWH or the Christian God. The essay underlines the differences between YHWH-God and Modimo, even where they appear to be similar. This is a decolonizing strategy, necessary because the colonizing translations subjugated the so-called receptor languages or cultures by ignoring their differences, their uniqueness, and, indeed, by bending them to fit or to receive the so-called source text. It is, therefore, crucial to begin by acknowledging that the two views of the Divine, God and Modimo, are different, despite some discerning similarities. Above all, the differences must be respected.

Understanding Modimo of Batswana

J. Tom Brown, a London Missionary Society missionary who wrote the *Secwana–English Dictionary*, was puzzled by the Setswana verb *dima*. He consulted a Motswana old man versed in the traditions of his people. The old man demonstrated *go dima* to him by pouring a drop of ink on blotting paper. The ink penetrated, permeated, percolated, and spread, and the old man explained: "You see, that is *go dima;* and that is what Modimo does."[7] Then Tom Brown made this entry in his dictionary:

> *dima,* v.pft *dimile:* the true original meaning of the word is very obscure. Some say it is the verb from which *Modimo* comes or a verb formed from *Modimo*. It carries the force of a searching, penetrating insight into men and things (a kind of X-ray!). It may also mean to excel: *Moea o o dimang;* an excellent and searching spirit in understanding—to create.[8]

Modimo is not only the deity, but also all that pertains to the spirit world; hence, Modimo can neither be personified nor gendered. But other missionary writers of Setswana languages made the concept Modimo to mean man, ancestor, sky, and many other things that idolize Modimo. In spite of all attempts made to translate and define Modimo, "The fact is that there is much more to *Modimo* than the Christian missionaries dreamed of, rather than the much less which they came to think."[9]

There is an expression in Setswana, *Modimo ke Selo se se Boitshegang,* meaning that Modimo is "Something Mysterious or Awesome." First, the expression tells us that Modimo is not a being or a person but that it is "Something." Second, it tells us that this "Something" is "mysterious" and probably too big to be held captive in any one place, book, or tradition, or to be comprehended by human beings.[10] By *Selo—"Something"—the* expression does not mean something tangible, but something without form and that cannot be captivated through human gender. Modimo thus, in the Setswana understanding, forever remains in the neuter.

This expression helps to explain the Batswana understanding of and totality of the "Something Mysterious." That is, the characteristics of Modimo do not bear gender. The expression *Modimo ke Selo se Boitshegang* is further illustrated by an incident that occurred among the Bakgatla people of Botswana. Isaac Schapera has recorded the incident, which reflects the

---

7. Smith, *Towards a World Theology,* 51.

8. Setiloane, *The Image of God among the Sotho-Tswang,* 25.

9. Ibid., 78.

10. Smith, *Towards a World Theology;* Panikkar, *Myth, Faith, and Hermeneutics.*

Bakgatla's original understanding of the Divine and their early response toward Christian religion, especially their protests against what they understood as the Christian understanding of God. What follows is part of a *kgotla* (public meeting) that took place at the village of Mochudi during the early days of the colonial missionary era:

> It was "wrong" for God (Modimo) to have a house in the town; and they wanted him (the king) to pull it (the Church building) down and expel the Christians . . . At the meeting several speakers repeated the complaint that Christianity, and especially the Church building, was the cause of drought . . . There is no God (Modimo) for whom a house has to be built.[11]

This quotation is significant, for it highlights that Batswana, and most southern black Africans, never represented the Divine in physical forms, or even put up a physical abode for Modimo. Batswana neither believed nor worshipped idols; it is a new thing in their Africanity. Indeed, when colonizing missionaries first thought that the Batswana had no concept of God, they had partly misinterpreted the Batswana's refusal to represent the Divine in physical structures. Colonizing missionaries mistook Batswana's respect for the Divine for lack of knowledge of the Divine. The expression *Modimo ke Selo se Boitshegang,* supported by the Bakgatla's protest, indicates that Modimo is an awesome "Something" that is everywhere and that is larger than life. The word *something* underlines that Modimo is not human or gendered; Modimo is beyond such representation. Modimo cannot be given human or other specific characteristics (including gender) without distorting the Name Modimo's original meaning. It follows that Modimo cannot be contained or be fully captured by biblical traditions or by the language of the Divine without a serious hijacking or Christianizing of the Word or the Name.

Modimo, as "Something Mysterious," has hierophanies (representations). Modimo can be manifest in ways that are gender-inclusive, at different places and times. The "Something" is emphasized to underline that Modimo, above all, resists taking human form, let alone a particular gender, and that Modimo inhabits all space, in whatever form. This is why, for Batswana, the whole environment and other forms of life ("nature") are considered sacred, because Modimo inhabits them and is manifest through them. This further explains that Modimo is for all and in all of us, both in humanity and the rest of the natural order. Modimo is not for the chosen few or a favored gender. It is this understanding of Modimo that translators and theologians of the colonizing Christianity failed to grasp when

11. Schapera, *Rain-Making Rites of Tswana Tribes,* 19.

they translated the gendered Hebrew and Christian God as Modimo in the Setswana Bible.

Gabriel Setiloane has already argued in his book *The Image of God among the Sotho-Tswana* that the Batswana image of Modimo hardly fits with the biblical pattern of God; he proposed that we will better represent Modimo with the pronoun "It" than "He." In a response to an earlier version of this essay presented at the International SBL Meeting in Cape Town in 2000, Eric Hermanson supports my argument from a linguistic point of view:

> Grammatically the word *Modimo* is interesting. From its form, one would expect that it would belong to the Class 1 group of singular nouns, all of which are personal, and which have their plural in Class 2. However, *Badimo*, which is a personal plural in Class 2 and on surface looks as if it is the plural of *Modimo*, in fact is used only in plural. *Modimo*, like *moya*, is actually a Class 3, as can be seen from the pronoun used in the above-mentioned verses, viz. *ona*, instead of the Class 1 pronoun *yena*. So, *Modimo* is not placed on the same level as human.[12]

No doubt, many of the above-outlined characteristics of Modimo will sound familiar to a biblical reader or scholar, who may find many similar understandings of the Divine in both Testaments. For example, one may point to the commandment prohibiting "graven images" (Exod 20:4). The God of the Hebrew Bible is also represented as omnipresent, and in such gender-neutral images as a "small, still voice." In counteracting male images of God, Western feminists' strategy is to argue that this language should be taken metaphorically rather than literally.[13] They have argued that to equate God with the gendered male language would be idolatry—equating God with the image of a man, although this is strongly forbidden in the second commandment. Western feminists have also noted that God is sometimes referred to in feminine images such as midwife (Ps 22:9); mother (Jer 31:15–22; Isa 66:7–14); coin seeker (Luke 15:1–10); and baker woman (Matt 13:33).[14] Some have resurrected the Goddess as a spiritual figure that

12. Hermanson, "Response." Hermanson is a long-serving staff member of the Bible Society of South Africa, and he has overseen a number of their translations in the country and region. As a translator who fully subscribes to the theory of faithfulness to the "source text," he generally disagreed with my paper. Nonetheless, I found his linguistic comment instructive for my thesis.

13. See Johnson, "Images of God," for the strategies of resistance advanced by Western feminists.

14. Anderson and Moore, *Mark and Method*, 108–9.

empowers women.[15] Others have imagined God as friend, lover, or wisdom. Western feminists insist on searching "for a viable term for divine mystery, redemptive for women as well as men."[16] Their struggle with the naming of God comes with the realization that the dominant male gender associated with the Christian God has been and still is read literally, and it is used to marginalize women from positions of power in social and spiritual spaces.

While many of the divine traits highlighted by Western feminist readers indicate similarities with Modimo, it is important to respect the differences. It is important to resist collapsing Modimo into YHWH-God. To emphasize only the similarities easily legitimates the practice in translation of treating Setswana as a receptor language that has no right to exist on its own in front of the biblical source text. Differences include that YHWH is portrayed as having a physical place in which to dwell, namely the Holy of Holies, in which YHWH was served by male priests and other functionaries. One thus needs to be able to say that while YHWH-God is the creator of all (Gen 1–2), God still is said to have chosen some (Exod 19:4–5) and accepted others on the basis of faith (1 Pet 2:9–10). Similarly, YHWH-God is also a divine mystery, awesome, and omnipresent, beyond human characteristics and understanding, but "he" is more often than not cast in male garb. Modimo, however, never took any human gender, be it metaphorical or literal. According to Batswana religious traditions, Modimo never occupied a house or a tent constructed by humans; Modimo has never designated Batswana or any other as a chosen race, or favored a particular human gender. Modimo's characteristics operate differently from those of YHWH-God within this social context. Similarly, the impact on women's lives of these characterizations will be different.

While the Western feminist approach is to highlight the gender-neutral traits of YHWH-God against the predominantly male images in the Bible, we see male images imposed by the so-called source text, abetted by colonizing and patriarchal translation theories. Since those theories begin from the premise that source text should keep all its traits, the receptor languages and cultures lose their traits. Cultural and linguistic differences, however, need to be underlined and respected to counteract the colonizing ideology that legitimates the subjugation of non-biblical cultures and languages.[17]

---

15. Eller, *Goddess.*

16. Johnson, "God," 129.

17. Sugirthirajah, "Textual Cleansing."

The Divining Set—*Ditaola*, Modimo, and Gender Justice

When it comes to representation of Moditho in the Setswana spiritual space, the contents of the indigenous divining set, *ditaola*, further illustrate that the domination of one gender, male or female, was not characteristic (That divining set, which is used by *dingaka* (diviner-healers) in Batswana communities, reflects several aspects of Setswana life. The set is made out of the four major *ditaola* called *Kgadi* (female adult), *Moremogolo* (male adult), *Jaro* (young male adult), and *Kgatshana* (young female adult). These four *ditaola* indicate an inclusive gender representation in the Setswana spiritual ritual. In addition to the four, there is a *taola* called *Thakadu* (Ant-bear), represented as both female and male. *Thakadu* symbolizes Modimo as well as *Badimo* (ancestors), both of which reflect the Batswana's understanding of the Divine. *Badimo* are intermediaries between Modimo and the people. They include women and men and are always referred to in the plural.

The Batswana *dingaka* (diviner-healers) use the *Thakadu taola* as their symbol of the Divine because they say *Thakadu* is like Modimo and *Badimo* in many ways. For example, Thakadu (Ant-bear) cannot be seen easily except at night. Like Thakadu, Modimo and *Badimo* are hardly seen except through their deeds and at death or in dreams and visions. Thakadu digs big holes in the ground as it abode—the ground that the Batswana mythology teaches that it is from which people came to inhabit the world. The Thakadu-made holes were used traditionally as places of refuge during turmoil and wars. This gave people protection equivalent to that received from Modimo and *Badimo*, who enabled them to come out of the same holes to inhabit the world. The practice reminds us of the stories told about many Batswana men who escaped the British Colonizing Administration during the Second European War (1939–45) by hiding in *dithakadu*, "holes." This hiding concept had a theological significance for the Batswana, which was that they escaped being taken to the war by the colonizing administration because they hid themselves in Modimo. Thus they survived by divine protection.

It is also notable that the *ditaola* gives us the gender-balanced hierophany of Modimo or the Divine. There is no gendered *taola* without a male or female counterpart. Apart from the four main characters of *ditaola* and the two that represent *Badimo* and Modimo, other *ditaola* represent other peoples and different things, but in a compound way that does not reflect one gender. For instance, among the Bakwena group of Batswana, other *ditaola* represent groups like Basarwa, Bangwato, Bakgalagadi, and Makgowa without mentioning their gender. The *ditaola* presents a different picture of the Divine from the gendered Modimo of the colonizing Setswana Bible.

According to Batswana beliefs, Modimo cannot have exclusively male characteristics. Rather, Modimo includes both male and female and is above all genders. Modimo is a manifold reality that can act through ancestors, spirits, ghosts, gods, nature, and humanity, irrespective of gender. Thus, any act that relates to any manifestation of the Divine relates to Modimo. For Batswana to present Modimo in isolation from other divine powers or manifestations is ambiguous. The manifestations of the Divine remain part of the whole. Staugard has observed that, in Modimo, Batswana religious beliefs include the existence of an omnipotent transcendental principle.

When the Christian religion was translated into Setswana, the Modimo of the Batswana was divorced from its context of Batswana beliefs, myths, rituals, ethics, experience, and their general way of life. These elements were dismissed as diabolic and as a "masterpiece of hell's invention."[18] Modimo was taken into the Christian religion, which is highly male, leaving the Batswana traditions without a center. Further, the Modimo as preached in the Christian churches is a denouncer of the Batswana cultures. This strategy of translation became a masterpiece of the colonization of Batswana cultures and people. It left the Batswana religion without a divine spark of its own. Modimo, the Batswana divinity, was taken into the biblical cultures as a "receiver" of biblical beliefs and translated to fight against Batswana people and cultures. Setswana religions were also denied their own adherents, who were now colonized and christianized. They came to identify themselves with the translated Modimo of the Christian Bible and churches. The divinity appeared as a male parent, claimed as a God—not of all the Batswana—but of the chosen few who believe in Jesus Christ—the God's only son.

Reading from the Translated and Gendered Modimo

This colonization and gendering of Modimo, the hijacking of Setswana traditions, and the resulting marginalization of women can be observed by following the exiled Modimo in Setswana translations drawn from Wookey's Bible of 1908. An account of that process in both Testaments demonstrates how the translated Modimo now functions, how Modimo is heard by Batswana, and how, in fact, Modimo has been exiled from Batswana and their culture to function apart from and even against its people.

In the translated Setswana Hebrew Bible, the book of Genesis presents Modimo as the creator of the universe and humanity (Genesis 1–2). In Gen 1:26–27, we hear Modimo saying: "Me Modimo oa re: A re diheng motho

18. Gairdner, *Edinburgh, 1910*, 137.

mo setshwanon ea rona . . . kaha sechwanon sa rona. Me Modimo oa tlhola motho mo chwanon ea ona tota, oa mo tlhola mo chwanon ea Modimo; oa ba tlhola nona le tshadi" ("And God said, let us make humankind in our own image . . ."). In some English Bible translations, "humankind" is rendered with the generic "man." The verse strives to present both genders as created in God's image, but this is only one step away from likening God more with one gender than the other.[19] Indeed, in the following version of creation, Adam, a man, is created by God, while Eve is made from the rib of Adam and for Adam (Gen 2:15–25). As Batswana readers continue, they hear how a woman came to be blamed for the sin of humanity and to be subjected to harsh discipline and oppression. The creation story is perhaps the strongest link for casting God in human forms. First, it underlines that people were created in God's image or likeness (Gen 1:26–27). Then, it slants toward associating male gender rather than female gender with God's image (Gen 2:21–23). For a Motswana reader, in whose culture Modimo is distanced both from human forms and from gender-exclusive representations, both biblical creation stories are problematic.

As we continue in Genesis, we see Modimo calling and using mainly male figures like Noah, Abraham, Isaac, Jacob, Esau, and the twelve sons of Jacob, who later made up the tribes of Israel. The Setswana Hebrew Bible continues to underline the male gender in Exod 3:6, in which Modimo says, "I am the Modimo of your Father, the Modimo of Abraham, the Modimo of Isaac, and the Modimo of Jacob. And Moses hid his face; for he was afraid to look upon Modimo." Here Modimo is associated with the male line, to the exclusion of women and exclusion of its people -Batswana. Second, Modimo is revealing "himself" to another man. In this scene, it is also implied that if Moses had raised his face, he could have seen Modimo! Third, not only has Modimo been translated from a gender-neutral divinity to a male God, but Modimo works primarily through males. The male figures of Moses and his brother will set the children of Israel free from slavery in Egypt and settle in the Promised Land. God regularly sends the people prophets, most of whom are males, and eventually, in the Setswana Christian Testament, God sends a male messiah who is called "the only Son of Modimo." But above all, when a Motswana reader reads the translated Bible, they hear that Modimo belongs not to them, but to the Israelites—imagine *Modimo wa Iseraele* in Botswana!

In the New Testament of the Setswana Bible, one can go from the Gospels to the Acts of the Apostles, from the Epistles to Revelation, following

---

19. The Setswana creation myth holds that people came out of a hole in the ground when the rocks were still soft. The myth holds that women and men came out with their livestock and other property.

and highlighting the tragically translated, colonized, gendered, and exiled Modimo. For example, in Matt 10:8 in Wookey's Bible of 1908, Jesus is said to send out his disciples with the command *"kgoromeletsan badimo ntle"* (NRSV: "cast out demons"). In the Setswana translation, Jesus, whom that same Bible characterizes as the only son of Modimo, authorizes his disciples to go and cast out *Badimo*—Batswana ancestors. In Setswana religious thinking, *Badimo* are part and parcel of the Divine. They dwell and work with Modimo and represent the people before Modimo. In Wookey's translation, these same *Badimo* are to be "cast out." This command is given for several reasons. First, Jesus is now the only mediator between God and people. Second, the translation has equated *Badimo* with evil spirits and demons, recasting their role from divine to evil. The translation thus shows a Motswana that Jesus is presented as more powerful than *Badimo*, who tremble before the mighty Jesus. This result was achieved by separating Modimo from *Badimo* and from other aspects of the Setswana religious world. It was achieved by replacing the group- and gender-inclusive mediators of *Badimo* with the one and only Son of Modimo and God, Jesus Christ.

Undoubtedly, this form of translation christianizes, colonizes, and hijacks many African religious divinities, many of which do not share attributes with the biblical God. Such dis course has made it difficult to teach and learn African traditions without theologizing and christianizing them. For instance, the religious education curriculum in Botswana across all levels has a problem of freeing the African traditions from the Christian traditions. Setswana and many other African traditions are facing a great threat from the Christian biblical patterns. Since the beginning of colonial times, it has become an unquestionable right for Christians to define African concepts according to Christian understanding, without giving Setswana and other traditions the right to speak for themselves or to maintain their identity.

It is notable, however, that when reading from *Baebele e Boitshepo*, a revision of Wookey's Bible carried out by the Batswana under the coordination of Rev. Morolong of the United Congregational Church of Southern Africa in Botswana, a few changes have taken place. First, although Modimo retains gendered male characteristics, in Matt 10:8 and other cases where *Badimo* had been used to translate "demons," other words—mewa *ee maswe*—are now used for the casting out of "evil spirits." The revision has attempted to decolonize Wookey's translation, but it did not de-patriarchalize it. Modimo still remains *Rara* or *Rraetsho* ("Father" or "Our Father"), although the *Badimo* are no longer devils, demons, or evil spirits.[20] This is

---

20. Dube, "Consuming a Colonial Cultural Bomb."

instructive to Batswana and other African women, for it indicates that indigenous male translators bring their gender into biblical translation. Unless African women are involved in the translation process, the colonial gendering of their deities is likely to be maintained by indigenous male translators.

Implications of the Colonization and Gendering of Modimo

The gendering of Modimo has been used to support the exclusion of Batswana women in church and in other spheres of power. Many Batswana women are active members of the church, but as Sunday school teachers for young children, as caretakers of the church buildings, and sometimes as deacons. The United Congregational Church of Southern Africa (UCCSA) in Molepolole, for example - where I live and worship - is divided into "districts" (Dikgaolo), numbered, 1, 2, 3, . . . Each *kgaolo* is governed by a council of deacons (elders). Traditionally, every district (kgaolo) is chaired by a male deacon, regardless of whether there is a male deacon in the district or not. If there was none, the male deacon was borrowed from another district. Several times I asked my mother, a deacon in *Kgaolo 6*, why women from her Kgaolo could not be elected chairpersons. Her answer was obvious: The church does not allow it—He has to be a man.

We still see that, although many denominations in the postcolonial church recognize women for priesthood, the church in many other ways remains dominated by men. The impact of this male domination in the church, of course, is also found in society. Some women who used to have powerful roles, like healers, and who became church members, were forced, in many instances, to denounce these roles beforehand. Unlike men who received new power in the church, the women remain powerless. Ife Amadiume (1987) has studied her people, the Nnobi of Igboland, focusing on the position of women prior to colonialism and the impact of colonialism on their lives and social roles. She notes that while women had their own Goddess, Idemili, and their own crops, and while they ran the marketplace, Christianity, when it arrived, condemned indigenous religious beliefs and replaced them with Christian beliefs. The denunciation was enacted systematically through the church, the school, and the colonial job market, and it was taught in the first Christian lessons. In the end, more men could go to school and get hired in the school, church, or colonial offices. Women were marginalized from education, from their own indigenous religions, and from Christianity, which preferred male church leaders because of its male spiritual figures, such as God the Father and Jesus the Son. Like the Nnobi, the Batswana were turned against following their indigenous religious practices, which the colonizing Christianity interpreted negatively, as demonstrated by the equation of *Badimo* with demons and evils spirits. Batswana thus moved from largely gender-neutral religious space and symbols to male-centered substitutes. The Christian doctrine as presented claimed that God, who came to be translated as Modimo, was a "he" but not a "she."[21] Just as Amadiume closely studies the changes that followed the introduction of male-centered religion and its institutions, we cannot overlook how the colonial translation of Setswana spiritual space from gender-neutral to exclusively male has contributed to the marginalization of Batswana women in the society and the church.

Conclusion

The assumption that the Christian patterns of thought are universal has led many translators and writers to colonize other religions, particularly African religions. Although we celebrate Modimo and God as the Divine, the different understandings that the two terms convey help us to better understand the Christian and the Batswana traditions. Failure to recognize the uniqueness of African religions, or of the Batswana religion, has resulted in Africans and the Batswana losing their identity as well as their humanness (*botho*). For women, the situation has been worse; they have lost their place in the divine arena, in church leadership, and in social spaces. The Christian God has strong gender characteristics, which is not the case with the pre-colonial Modimo. The current study of African traditions and *"Modimology"* is problematic in the sense that time and again it identifies the Christian view of God with African divinities. The Christian theological assumption that Modimo and God are the same gives the impression that

- the Batswana have knowledge of the Divine, which in many ways exposes the colonizing missionary claim that Africans had no knowledge of the Divine as a colonizing rhetoric of subjugation;

- the unqualified equation of Modimo with YHWH-God justifies the religion of Batswana as the *praeparatio evangelica;* that is, it cannot be a religious tradition in its own right and for the salvation of its own adherents. Thus nullifying the existence of Batswana and their identities.

- the tradition of the Batswana is nothing other than the Christian tradition in another language; hence, many theologians present African Christian theology as the African theology, forgetting that Africa is

---

21. Amadiume, *Male Daughters, Female Husbands.*

rich in theologies—African, Jewish, Christian, Islamic, Hindu, Sikh, and many others—that need to be respected for their differences;

- religion can be defined in biblical Christian terms and thought of as belief in God, who is personified and highly gendered, thus hijacking the individual characteristics of Setswana and those of other religious faiths.

In short, I am inclined toward Raimundo Panikkar's (1979) thesis that considers the Divine as "the distinctive, not the uniting, factor of religion." That is, a similar concept in different religious traditions does not imply that those traditions understand the concept in the same way. The similarity in concepts does not call for one universal religious tradition. Religious traditions and concepts differ according to understanding, time, place, and people. Each set of terms is understood fully only at home, in its environment.[22] The Batswana understanding of the Divine was neither patriarchal nor gendered. Modimo was neither a man nor father, neither a woman nor mother. Rather, Modimo is above gender, above humans, above any other thing. Modimo is "Something." Modimo embraces both genders, as seen in the *ditaola* set, which contains a representation of Modimo (Divinity); *mosadi* (woman) and *manna* (man); animals (males and females); and *merafe* (other ethnic groups). The essay invites Bible translators of today to recognize the need to decolonize translation theory to embrace the equal authority of both the so-called source text and the receptor languages. In Botswana, we need to liberate Modimo from the gendered Christian coat that "he" wears today, for it legitimizes the marginalization of women in the church and society. For instance, the Lord's Prayer (Matt 6:9–13) can be retranslated using *Thakadu* (Antbear) instead of *Rara* (father), and *mosima* (earth hole or home) instead of "heaven," as follows:

> *Thakadu tsetsho tse di mo matsatseng* (Our Antbears in earth holes)
>
> *Leinala la gago a le itshepisiwe* (Let your name be sanctified)
>
> *Maatla a gaga a tle* (Let your power come)
>
> *Go rata ga gago a go dirwe gongwe le gongwe* (Let your will be done)
>
> *Re nee gompieno pabalelo ya rona ya letsatsi* (Give us our daily protection).

---

22. Hick, *An Interpretation of Religion.*

Mme o re rute go sa iphetlhele ba bangwe (Help us to treat others) *Jaaka le rona re sa rate ba re iphetlhela* (as we would like them to treat us)

Re heme mo thaelesegong (protect us from temptations)

Mme o re golole mo bosuleng (But deliver us from evil)

Go nne maatla a gago a magolo (For great is your power)

Le thata, le kgalalelo, ka bosenabokhutlo (The power and the glory forevermore)

Ditlhokwa di re robalele. Pula! (Let there be Peace and rain amongst us. Pula!)

Bibliography

Alverson, Hoyt. *Mind in the Heart of Darkness: Value and Self-Identity among the Tswana of Southern Africa.* New Haven: Yale University Press, 1978.

Amadiume, Ife. *Male Daughters, Female Husbands.* London: Zed, 1987.

Anderson, Janice Capel, and Stephen D. Moore. *Mark and Method: New Approaches to Biblical Studies.* Minneapolis: Fortress Press, 1992.

Baebeie e Boitshepo. Cape Town: Bible Society of South Africa.

Banana, Canaan S. "The Case for a New Bible." In *Voices from the Margin: Interpreting the Bible in the Third World*, edited by R. S. Surgirtharajah, 65–82. London: SPCK, 1991.

Brown, J. Tom. 1926. *Among the Bantu Nomads.* London: Seeley, Service, 1992, 1998.

Carroll, Robert P. "Cultural Encroachment and Bible Translation: Observations on Elements of Violence, Race, and Class in Production of Bibles in Translation." *Semeia* 76 (1996) 39–53.

Chidester, D. *Savage Systems: Colonialism and Comparative Religion in Southern Africa.* Cape Town: University of Cape Town, 1996.

Collins English Dictionary and Thesaurus. Glasgow: Harper Collins, 1993.

Comaroff, Jean, and John Comaroff. Of *Revelation and Revolution: Christianity, Colonialism, and Consciousness in South Africa.* Vol. 1. Chicago: University of Chicago Press, 1991.

Cox, James. *Ancestor Rational.* Cardiff: Cardiff Academic Express, 1998.

Dube, Musa W. "Consuming a Colonial Cultural Bomb: Translating *Badimo* into 'Demons' in the Setswana Bible (Matthew 8:28–34; 15:22; 10:8)." *JSNT* 73 (1999) 33–59.

Eller, Cynthia. "Goddess." In *Dictionary of Feminist Theologies,* edited by Letty M. Russell and J. Shannon Clarkson, 130–32. Louisville: Westminster John Knox Press, 1996.

Gairdner, W. H. T. *Edinburgh 1910: An Account and Interpretation of the World Missionary Conference.* London: Oliphant & Ferrier, 1910.

Hermanson, Eric A. "Response." Presented at the International Society of Biblical Literature Meeting, Capetown, South Africa, 2000.

Hick, John. *An Interpretation of Religion: Human Responses to the Transcendent*. London: Macmillan, 1989.

Johnson, Elizabeth A. "God." In *Dictionary of Feminist Theologies*, edited by Letty M. Russell and J. Shannon Clarkson, 128–30. Louisville: Westminster John Knox, 1996.

Johnson, Elizabeth A. "Images of God." In *Dictionary of Feminist Theologies*, edited by Letty M. Russell and J. Shannon Clarkson, 149–50. Louisville: Westminster John Knox Press, 1996.

Kanyoro, Musimbi R. "Translation." In *Dictionary of Feminist Theologies*. Edited by Letty M. Russell and J. Shannon Clarkson, 303. Louisville: Westminster John Knox Press, 1996.

Knitter, Paul F. *No Other Name: A Critical Survey of Christian Attitudes towards the World Religions*. American Society of Missiology Series 7. Maryknoll, NY: Orbis, 1985.

Maluleke, Tinyiko. S. "Denied, Discovered, and Still Denied: African Traditional Religions in the Christian and Religious Studies of Southern Africa." *URJ* 12 (1998) 1–14.

Marquard, L., and T. G. Standing. *The Southern Bantu*. London: Oxford University Press, 1939.

Mbiti, John S. *New Testament Eschatology in an African Background: A Study of the Encounter between New Testament Theology and African Traditional Concepts*. London: Oxford University Press, 1971.

Mogapi, Kgomotso. *Ngwao ya Setswana*. Mabopane, South Africa: L. Z. Sikwane, 1992.

Mojola, Aloo Osotsi. "Bible Translation." In *Dictionary of Third World Theologies*, edited by Virginia Fabella and R. S. Sugirtharajah, 30–31. Maryknoll; NY: Orbis, 2000.

Monnig, H. O. *The Pedi*. Pretoria: Van Schaik, 1967.

Monyaisi, Semakaleng D. P. *Go sa Baori*. Pretoria: van Schaik, 1979.

Ntloedibe-Kuswani, G.S. "The Religious Life of an African: A God Given Praeparatio Evangelica?" In *Talita cum! Theologies of African Women*, edited by N. J. Njoroge, and Musa W. Dube, 97–120. Pietermaritzburg, South Africa: Cluster, 2001.

Panikkar, Raimundo. *Myth, Faith, and Hermeneutics: Cross-Cultural Studies*. New York: Paulist, 1970.

Pauw, B. A. *Religion in a Tswana Chiefdom*. London: Oxford University Press, 1970.

Russell, Letty M., and J. Shannon Clarkson, eds., *Dictionary of Feminist Theologies*. Louisville: Westminster John Knox Press, 1996.

Schapera, Isaac. *Rain-Making Rites of Tswana Tribes*. Cambridge, England: African Studies Centre, 1971.

Schapera, Isaac, and J. L. Comaroff. *The Tswana*. Rev. ed. London: Kegan Paul International, 1991.

Setiloane, Gabriel. *The Image of God among the Sotho-Tswana*. Rotterdam: Balkema, 1976.

Setiloane, Gabriel. "How the Traditional World-View Persists in the Christianity of the Sotho-Tswana." In *Christianity in Independent Africa*, edited by Fashole Luke, 402–12. London: Rex Collins, 1978.

Setswana–English Dictionary. Tigerkloof, South Africa: LMS, 1923.

Smith, Wilfred Cantwell. *Towards a World Theology*. London: Macmillan, 1981.

Staugard, Frants. *Traditional Healers*. Gaborone, Botswana: Ipelegeng, 1985.

Sugirtharajah, R. S. "Textual Cleansing: A Move from the Colonial to the Postcolonial Version." *Semeia* 76 (1996) 7–20.

Westerlund, David. *African Religion in African Scholarship*. Stockholm: Almquist & Wiksell, 1985.

Young, T. C. *African Ways and Wisdom: A Contribution Towards Understanding*. London: Lutterworth, 1937.

5

How Local Divine Powers
Were Suppressed

A Case of Mwari of the Shona

Dora R. Mbuwayesango

Before the colonization of Zimbabwe by the British in 1890, the country comprised many different political entities that were united religiously by the belief in a Supreme Being. This Supreme Being was commonly known by the personal name "Mwari." The different political entities paid allegiance to Mwari in different ways. Zimbabwe can be divided into two major superficial regions, that is, Mashonaland and Matabeleland. In Mashonaland, the language is mainly Shona, although with different dialects. The language in Matabeleland is predominantly Ndebele. The Ndebele, to a limited extent, respected the Mwari cult that was centered in Matopo Hills in Matabeleland[1]. The Shona understand Mwari to be a genderless spirit, neither male nor female. The attributes of Mwari all have to do with Mwari's transcendence and creative activities.[2] Thus, these attributes include *Nyadenga* (of the sky), *Mutangakugara* (the first to exist), *Muumbi* (the one who forms), and *Musikavanhu* (the creator of humanity). Also, Mwari does not discriminate and can speak through women and even through objects, as well as through men.

Colonialism and Christianity came to Zimbabwe simultaneously. In fact, the two aided each other in "Christianizing" and dominating the

1. The limited allegiance of the Ndebele to Mwari can be demonstrated by the function of the Mwari cult during the first Ndebele-Shona uprising against the British settlers in 1896.

2. The claim that Mwari was divided into three—Father, Mother, and Son—is an attempt to make African religions compatible with the Christian concept of the trinity.

indigenous peoples of Zimbabwe. The partnership of colonialism and Christianity is well expressed in one of David Livingstone's letters, discussed by John Kirk:

> That you may have a clear idea of my objects, I may state that they have more in them than meets the eye. They are not merely exploratory, for I go with the intention of benefiting both the African and my own countrymen. I take a practical mining geologist to tell of the mineral resources of the country, an economic botanist to give full report of the vegetable productions, a naval officer to tell of the capacity of river communications, a moral agent to lay a Christian foundation for anything that mat follow. All this machinery has for its ostensible object the development of African trade and promotion of civilisation; but what I can tell none but such as you, in whom I have confidence, is this. *I hope it may result in an English colony in the healthy high lands of Central Africa.*[3]

Robert Moffat, one of the great missionary pioneers, also expressed the connections between missionary and colonial ventures in Africa:

> It is where the political organization is most perfect, and the social system still in its aboriginal vigour, that the missionary has the least success in making an impression. Where things have undergone a change and the feudal usages have lost their power, where there is a measure of disorganization, the new ideas which the gospel brings with it do not come into collision with any powerful political prejudice. The habits and modes of thinking have been broken up, and there is a preparation for the seed of the word.[4]

The European settler group that succeeded was the British South Africa Company (BSA Company) under Cecil Rhodes, after whom the country was later named Rhodesia. There were several European missionary organizations involved in Zimbabwe, although the initial missionary ventures had little success. The first missionary to operate in the country was Gançalo da Silveria, a Portuguese Jesuit, who was killed. The second phase of missionary activities in the country took place in the seventeenth century, when the Dominicans set up missions in the eastern part; by the end of that century, they had abandoned the missions. The next to attempt the evangelization of the Shona peoples were the Congregationalists, who worked among the eastern Shona in the 1870s. The Dutch Reformed Church, the Berlin Missionary Society,

---

3. Kirk, *Zambezi Journals and Letters,* 309; italics are mine.
4. Cited in Wallis, ed., *The Matabele Mission,* 70–71.

and the Anglicans also made tentative efforts in Mashonaland in the 1880s, but these missionary ventures were unsuccessful. It was only after Cecil John Rhodes had occupied Mashonaland that the missionaries started to experience success. Rhodes personally encouraged missionary work by allocating generous tracts of land to thirteen different societies during the 1890s. Later the Methodists and other missionary groups entered the country.

The missionaries found no need to explain the concept of God to the Shona people. In fact, they discovered that the Shona were a very spiritual and monotheistic people who believed in the Supreme Being by the name of Mwari, whose cult flourished in the Matopo Hills near Bulawayo. This cult seems to have been one of the strongest elements that united the different groups comprising the Shona. As Fortune notes,

> So many different clans are presented among the staff at each shrine as to make it likely that the location of the cult in the Matopos is to be regarded as an ancient structural feature. We find that priests, dancers, consecrated women and messengers are drawn from such diverse groups as the Karanga, Kalanga, Mbire, the Hera, Rozvi, and the Venda.[5]

The widespread belief in Mwari in the Matopo Hills is demonstrated by Daneel, who records finding a system of messengers and tribute in operation among Matonjeni and the districts of Chilimanzi, Gutu, Victoria, Melsetter, Bikita, Nadanga, Chibi, Chipinga, Belingwe, Gwanda, Plumtree, Nyamadlovu, and centers in Vendaland both north and south of the Limpopo.[6]

The Quest for a Shona Word for the Biblical Deity

One of the challenging tasks for the missionaries was to make the biblical deity relevant and acceptable to the Shona. While the missionaries eventually adopted the name Mwari to designate the biblical god (*Elohim* or *YHWH* in the Hebrew Bible, God, the Father in the New Testament), the history leading to that conclusion is reflected in the translations of the Bible, liturgical texts, and the catechisms of the different missionary organizations operating in Mashonaland.

Before the standardization of the Shona language, the missionary groups had different preferences for Shona terms for the biblical deity. The

---

5. Fortune, "Who was *Mwari?*," 5. Also J. M. Schoffeleers and R, Mwanza, "An Organizational Model of the Mwari Shrines," 308.

6. Daneel, *The God of the Matopo Hills*, 56–57.

first was *Modzimo or Mudzimu*, which was used in writings between 1899 and 1912 by Lutheran and Dutch Reformed churches operating among the Karangas.[7] The second term to refer to the biblical deity was *Wedenga*, "of the sky," found in the writings of the Dutch Reformed Church and the church of Sweden in 1909 and 1927, respectively.[8] The term *Wedenga* was also combined with the term *Mudzimu* as *Mudzimu Wedenga*, "the Ancestral Spirit of the Sky."[9]

In Shona, the term *Mudzimu* refers only to the ancestral spirit. Its early use among the Karanga seemed to have been influenced by the corresponding Sotho term *Molimo*, due to the missionary misunderstanding of the term. As Smith points out, the Tswana (the people of Botswana) were responding to a specific question posed by the missionaries: What is "the cause of all appearances in nature and the origin of all good and evil that happens to them without any act of their own?"[10] Attempts to correct this misunderstanding, as demonstrated by Louw's qualification with *Wedenga*, did not catch on.[11]

Other missionary organizations used the term *Mwari* exclusively from the beginning, especially the Anglicans, Methodists, and later, groups such as the Salvation Army, who operated among the Eastern Shona and the Zezuru.[12] The Roman Catholic Church was characterized by initial diversity in the terms used for the biblical deity before the general acceptance of *Mwari*. Some Catholics—in particular the Dominicans and Catholic translations at Waddilove—used *Mwari* from the outset.[13] Jesuit Catholic publications, however, used *Yave* from 1898.[14] The first edition of the Catholic Shona-English dictionary gives the following entries as translations of the English

7. *Buke eo ko Ravisa Tshekaranga* (The book for learning Karanga language) (Middleburg, South Africa:1899); Wederpohl, *Mashoko e Buke eo Modzimo*; Helm and Louw, *Evangeli ea Matthews* (Translation of Matthew's Gospel); *NziyodzechiKaranga dze "De. Ned. Ger. Kereke pa Mashonaland"* (Karanga hymns for the Mashonaland Church); *Vuzo dzeshoko ro Mudzimu* (Questions on the Word of God).

8. *Vuzo dxeshoko roWedenga* (Questions about the Word of God); *Mashoko e Bibele* (The Bible Stories).

9. Louw, *Manual of the Chikaranga Language*, 203

10. Smith, *African Ideas of God*, 116–17.

11. Louw, *Maual of the Chikaranga Language*, 203.

12. For example, for Anglicans: *Minamato neZwiyimbo Yamana weSangano*; Methodists: H. E. Springer, *A Handbook of Chikaranga*; Salvation Army, *Chizeruru and Chinynja Songs*.

13. *Testamente Itswa ya She Wedu Jesu Kristu no Rurimi rwe Chishona* (The New Testament of Our Lord Jesus Christ in Shona); Mayr, *Katekisima re MaKristo e Sangano reKatolike*.

14. Hartmann, *Rugwaro rgwo Kunamata*; Biehler, *Zwinamato Zwineitikwa*.

word God: *Yave* (a foreign word); *Mwea mukuru* (the great spirit); *Mwari* (the great spirit, according to native understanding); *Murenga* (the god of war, a word introduced from Matabeleland in the last rebellion: the cry was, *Murenga wamuka* [the God of war has risen].[15]

Although *Mwari* finally became the accepted Shona term for the biblical deity, the discussion that ensued between 1921 and 1924 in Catholic circles reveals the underlying distinctions between the Shona deity and the biblical deity. For example, Father Richartz argued that, although the Shona gods might be honored as gods or have godlike traits, their names were sullied by unworthy association, and, if used, they would confuse the simple. The term *Mwari*, he said, would be unsuitable because it did not connote the notion of judge—an essential ingredient of the Christian belief—nor the notion of creation in the strict sense. He also considered the views of those who went to the Mwari shrines as concerned only for material matters. Thus, the use of the term would be bound to being in many false notions.[16] Also, father Luobiere objected to the term *Mwari* for the Christian God on the grounds that it lacked moral connotations, in that both the good and the wicked are equally Mwari's offspring, and after death all would be treated alike.[17] Even non-Catholics such as Bullock weighed in on the debate, to express their reservation about the equation of Mwari and the Christian God: "I should be the last to advocate the translation of our word God by the Chishona word *Mwari*."[18] By the early 1960s, however, the Jesuits had joined the other Christian societies in using *Mwari* to refer to the Christian God. For example, one of the most influential persons in the standardization of the Shona language, Father Michael Hannan, used *Mwari* in his New Testament translation of 1966 and listed *Mwari* as one of the Shona terms for God, the Supreme Being, in his Shona dictionary.[19]

The missionary translation of the Bible was aimed at replacing the Shona Mwari with the biblical God in everything else but the name. If the missionaries had come to introduce a new God to the Shonas, they might have met much resistance, as happened in the earlier mission ventures. The adoption of Shona name Mwari for the biblical God was in reality the religious usurpation of the Shona. The missionaries took the Shona captive by colonizing the Shona Supreme Being. The results of this religious

---

15. *English–Chiswina Dictionary with an Outline Chiswina Grammar.*

16. Fortune, "Who Was *Mwari*?," 8.

17. Ibid., 9.

18. Bullock, *The Mashon,* 124; *The Mashona and the Matabele,* 147.

19. Hannan, *Chitendero Chitswa; Standard Shona Dictionary.*

colonization can be demonstrated by analyzing texts that were now taken to speak of Mwari, the Shona God.

The Effects of the Adoption of the Shona Term *Mwari*

Due to the similarities between the Shona culture and the culture depicted in the Hebrew Bible, the effects of the missionary adoption of the term *Mwari* will be considered from the Hebrew Bible context. There are several ways to refer to the deity in the Hebrew Bible. One of the ways is by personal names, such as Elohim as in Gen 1:1, or YHWH in Exod. 3:4, or a combination of the two, YHWH Elohim, in Gen 2:4. Another way is by a construct chain made up of Elohim with a proper name, such as Elohe-Abraham, Elohe-Isaac, and Elohe-Jacob (Exod 3:6). In other passages the name El may be juxtaposed to a place name, as El-Shadday or El Bethel.

The direct equation was made between Elohim and Mwari in Shona Bibles. Thus, for example, the first verse in Genesis reads, *Pakutanga Mwari vakasika denga nenyika . . .* (In the beginning Mwari created the heavens and earth . . .). The earlier Bible translation had *Tenzi* in place of YHWH, based on the English use of LORD to signify that divine name.[20] Tenzi means a variety of things depending on the context. It can mean 'master,' or 'owner,' or even 'employer.' The earliest and most translations use *Jehova*, based on the German transliteration and misunderstanding of the concept behind the vowel pointing.[21]

As a written record the Bible became the authentic voice on Mwari and Mwari's ways. The Shona believe that Mwari is the creator and the ultimate controller of the universe, the Supreme Being. However, the authentic way to describe Mwari's creative activity has come to be understood as that found in the Bible. The equation thus overruled the way the Shona spoke about and dealt with their deity. The missionaries designated the Shona as primitive and uncivilized in their understanding of God. While the Shona believed that Mwari had created everything, the missionaries granted no validity to the myths that describe the details of these creative activities. The equation of Mwari and Elohim resulted in the suppression of the Shona stories about Mwari's activities as creator. The Shona were basically an oral people, with no written documents. The Shona myths and folktales were not given the same status as the written material that the missionaries introduced to the Shona.

20. *Bhaibheri rine Apokirifa.*

21. *Bhaiberi Magwaro Matsvene Amwari Testamente Yekare Testament Itsva; Bhaibheri Magwaro Matsvene Amwari Namanyorero Anhasi.*

The biblical story of creation appears to be in line with the belief of the Shona that Mwari is the creator of the universe and of humanity. The details in the story, however, distort the details in Shona belief. The most evident distortion is found in Genesis 1:26–28, which depicts the creation of humanity. While to some feminists this account provides positive testimony for the equality of male and female before the biblical deity,[22] the depiction of the deity distorts the basic belief about the form of the Shona deity. In the Shona Bible translation, Mwari is given a human form. In Shona religious traditions, however, Mwari is truly holy, set apart from creation.[23] Mwari had no form or image. Mwari was truly a spirit without sexuality or gender,[24] but, in the Bible, Mwari is given human form (Gen 1:26–27). Although the story seems to portray Mwari as having both male and female attributes, by the time of the ancestral stories later in Genesis, Mwari has acquired male gender. In Genesis 18, when the deity by the name of YHWH appears to Abraham, there are three men with whom Abraham carries on a conversation and has a meal. Two of the men, identified as "messengers" leave Abraham and continue to Sodom. The implication is that the third "man" is actually the deity (Gen 18:22).

In the Hebrew Bible, the deity is presented as male in subtle ways. In languages that have grammatical gender, masculine forms are generally used. In the Prophetic books in general, and particularly in Hosea and Ezekiel, the metaphor that represents the relation between the deity and Israel is that of husband and wife, with God as the husband and Israel as the wife. The clearest reference to the deity as male in the Hebrew Bible is in Isaiah 63:16, in which the term *father* is used to address the deity.

The biblical stories of creation are products of the Jews in the exilic period whose basic aim was to preserve their beliefs in the face of the religious and cultural threat represented by the Babylonian environment. It is significant that these "priestly" writers did not replace Elohim with the Babylonian gods such as Marduk. *Elohim* is not a generic term for the deity but a specific name, just as *Mwari* is for the Shona. To take over the name Mwari is to rob the Shona of their traditions and to colonize Mwari. The Shona were a people whose traditions were passed orally from generation to generation. With no written records to concertize those traditions, the

22. For example, Trible, *God and the Rhetoric of Sexuality*, 18.

23. This understanding is contrary to Mbiti's assertion that the Ndebele and the Shona have a pantheon of God the father, God the Mother, and God the Son. This conclusion is actually a distortion that comes from the influence of Christianity. The Shona have never conceived of God in such human terms, which to their traditions would appear to limit the deity.

24. Shona languages lack the complication of grammatical gender.

missionaries replaced the unwritten records of the Shona with the Bible. As a result, the Bible now talks about Mwari, but *whose* Mwari?

In the stories of the Hebrew Bible, Mwari becomes the god of the Hebrews who had dealings with the Hebrews and not with the Shona peoples, and in the New Testament the only way to Mwari is through *his* son Jesus Christ. This pattern is made clear when *Mwari* functions as the term for God in the story of the rise of Israel as a nation. The call of Moses in Exodus 3 needs special attention, because it demonstrates clearly how the biblical god is tied to the nationhood of Israel. That crucial account, however, must be set in its narrative context.

The book of Genesis begins by considering the world in a broad spectrum and gradually narrows to focus on a specific family, the family of Abraham, who is promised a land and nationhood (Genesis 12). The story moves through the descendants of Abraham—Isaac and Jacob. The book of Genesis, however, closes with Abraham's descendants in Egypt, where they end up because of famine in the promised land (Genesis 50).

The book of Exodus opens with the *bene yisrael* (sons of Israel), at the death of Joseph, as a population of only seventy (1:1–5). When Joseph and his brothers died, the *bene yisrael* experienced a population surge—"they multiplied and grew exceedingly strong, so that the land was filled with them" (1:7). The Pharaoh, who did not know Joseph, saw the *bene yisrael* as a threat and devised measures to keep their population growth and strength in check (1:8–22). The story of the birth and survival of Moses, the founder of Israelite religion, relates to Pharaoh's attempts to suppress the growth of the Israelites. Moses is rescued by Pharaoh's daughter and subsequently grows up in the Egyptian environment (2:1–10). But Moses identified with the Hebrews. One day he saw an Egyptian mistreating a Hebrew man, and he killed the Egyptian and hid his body in the sand. When Pharaoh learned what Moses had done, he sought to kill him, and so Moses fled to Midian (2:11–22).

After a while, the Pharaoh who sought to kill Moses died, but the Hebrews continued to suffer in Egypt and groaned and cried; their cry for deliverance rose to Elohim. "Elohim heard their groaning, and Elohim remembered his covenant with Abraham, Isaac, and Jacob, Elohim looked upon the Israelites and Elohim took notice of them" (2:24–25). The name Elohim is repeated five times in 2:23–25. More significant, however, is the connection between Elohim and the ancestors of the Israelites. When in Shona Bibles, Elohim is replaced by the name Mwari, it becomes Mwari who remembers the covenant that Mwari made with the ancestors of Israel, not the ancestors of the Shona. For the Shona to relate to their deity, they have to adopt the traditions in the Bible. These traditions have no room for the ways in which various groups of the Shona deal with Mwari, such as through the epics or myths about how Mwari, through the leadership of a *mhondoro* (a spirit of founding ancestors), led each group to its current location.

Exodus 2 concludes by noting what was taking place in Egypt. Chapter 3, however, goes back to the scene in Midian, in which Moses is in exile. While in Midian, herding his father-in-law's flock, Moses has an encounter with the deity. The encounter takes place at a location identified as Horeb, the mountain of Elohim. The story is characterized by interchangeable use of biblical deity's two names, Elohim (*Mwari*) and YHWH (*Tenzi or Jehova*).[25] A messenger of YHWH appears to Moses in a flame, in a bush that is ablaze but not consumed. Moses investigates this unusual phenomenon, and when YHWH sees that Moses has turned aside to look, Elohim (Mwari) calls and Moses responds. The voice that calls identifies itself with the construct form of Elohim (*elohe*), juxtaposed with the names of Moses' ancestors, Abraham, Isaac, and Jacob (3:6). Once again the deity is identified in relationship to the ancestors of Israel—Abraham, Isaac, and Jacob. In Shona Bibles the text reads, "Mwari vaAbraham, Mwari vaIsaka, na Mwari vaJakobo." Thus, Mwari is identified exclusively with the Israelites, and the connection between Mwari and the Shona is disregarded. The Shona traditions about how different mediators, such as Chaminuka, Nehanda, and Kaguvi, serve as spokespersons of mwari are discredited and superseded by the biblical traditions. For example, the Mazezuru, a branch of the Shona, have a tradition about how Chaminuka became the link between Mwari and the people. Prior to Chaminuka's time, at a place called Maringari, was a special tree, *muti usinazita* (a tree without a name). According to Shona tradition, the tree fell and became a log from which shoots continued to sprout. The people would hear a voice, giving instructions and providing them with food. The voice was identified as Mwari's voice and later replaced by Chaminuka, such that Mwari now speaks through Chaminuka and the people speak to Mwari through Chaminuka.[26]

The biblical account of the encounter between Moses and the Israelite God continues with the deity's identification with a people: "I have observed the misery of my people who are in Egypt" (Exod 3:7). The Hebrew people belong to a specific deity, Elohim, who has come to deliver them from their suffering at the hands of their oppressors. The connection between the people and this deity is made even clearer. This deity has come down to bring

---

25. This interchangeable use of the two names has often been taken as evidence that the story results from the J and E sources, or traditions.

26. Gelfand, *Shona Ritual*, 13–14.

them "out of the land of Egypt to a good and broad land, a land flowing with milk and honey, to a country of the Canaanites, the Hittites . . . and the Jebusites" (3:8). This deity has a grand scheme for the Israelites—a scheme that involves replacing other peoples in the land. For Africans, this picture of the divine purpose is ironic in the face of the Shona peoples' displacement by the European settlers.

Moses' response to this grand scheme relates to his specific role. He is to go to Pharaoh and demand that Pharaoh give the Israelites freedom. Moses initially wants to know what qualifies him for this role: "Who am I that I should go to Pharaoh, and bring the Israelites out of Egypt?" (3:11). The deity's response is that Moses's qualifications are inconsequential to the grand scheme of deliverance. What is significant is that the deity will be with him.

Moses then wonders how to communicate the identity of the deity. The deity had identified itself as the God of the Israelite ancestors. Moses now says, "If I come to the Israelites and say to them, 'The God of your ancestors has sent me to you, and they ask me, 'What is his name?' what will I say to the?" (3:13). There are three parts to the deity's response. The first part seems to be the deity's refusal to respond and give its name: *Ehyeh asher ehyeh* (I am who I am).[27] The second part tells Moses how to respond to the Israelites' question: "Thus you shall say to the Israelites, '*Ehyeh* . . . has sent me to you'" (3:14b). The deity gives its name as *ehyeh,* which means "I am" in English and translates as *ndiri* in Shona. But that is not the final answer either. Moses is again told what to say to the Israelites: YHWH, the God of your ancestors, the God of Abraham, the God of Isaac, and the God of Jacob, has sent me to you" (3:15a). The God that Moses brings to the Israelites is none other than the God of their ancestors, who thus fulfill the promise made to the ancestors. Thus, in Shona Bibles, Tenzi becomes the name that stands for the new name revealed to Moses, and Mwari becomes the God of Abraham, of Isaac and of Jacob, the God of the Hebrews.

This adoption of the Shona God is a direct usurpation of the Shona deity by the biblical deity. Sanneh argues that the translation of the Scriptures into the vernacular languages assisted the Africans in preserving their names for the deity.[28] In fact, the translation of the Scriptures, at least as far as the Shona are concerned, resulted in the colonization of the Shona God. Mwari ceased to be the God of the Shona peoples and became the God of the Hebrews. Shona ways of relating to their deity are replaced by the news ways of relating to Mwari as YHWH. The missionaries, and the

27. Or "I am what I am," or "I will be what I will be."

28. Sanneh, *Translating the Message,* 181.

Bible as the missionaries interpreted it, thus had the final word on what is acceptable and not acceptable for Mwari's new identity; the ways of the Shona were deemed obsolete. The Mwari shrines became an abomination, the connection between the Mwari and the Shona ancestors invalid. The list of activities abhorrent to Mwari, according to Deuteronomy 18:9–13, includes most of the ways the Shona people communicated with their God, Mwari. The equation of *vadzimu* (the ancestors) with the "ghosts and spirits," with whom connection is prohibited in Deuteronomy 18:11, demonizes the Shona ancestors.

Unshackling *Mwari* from Colonial Chains

The Bible played a large role in the colonization of Zimbabwe. The religious colonization of the Shona began with the colonization of the Shona deity, Mwari. This colonization, as detailed above, occurred by equating the name of the Shona deity with the biblical god and by the consequent transformation of the Shona deity. For the Shona to relate to this god, they had to abandon their Shona identity and become Western. Their own religious traditions suddenly were deemed incompatible with Mwari.

There is no doubt that Christianity is now one of the major religions of Africa. Mainstream Christianity, however, is plagued by having remained a foreign religion. It continues to make Shona Christians feel inadequate for being Shona, because Shona understandings of Mwari are suppressed. There are several ways to deal with this problem. The Bible entered Zimbabwe as a propaganda tool. The writing of African languages was developed in order to translate the Scriptures, since the missionaries wanted Shona words to make their message less foreign and thus acceptable to the Shona; that is the basis on which the Shona name of the deity was appropriated and transferred to the biblical god. The Bible was also used as a text in schools, so that the adaptation of the deity was imprinted on those learning how to read and write. The power of the written word is demonstrated clearly by how the Bible suppressed oral traditions and led the biblical word to be seen as more authentic than the oral traditions it superseded. Shona values and beliefs had been transferred from generation to generation through folktales, but this process gradually ended and was replaced with the written word. Shona folktales were not accorded the same validity as the Bible, because they were said to be "myths" or unreal stories.

While the past cannot be undone, it is crucial now that the translation of the Shona Bibles be done independent of the evangelization of the Shona. In such a project, as Bird points out,

> The aim of the Bible translator . . . should be to enable a modern audience to *overhear* an ancient conversation, rather than to hear itself addressed directly . . . It is not the translator's duty to make her audience *accept* the author's message, or even [to] identify themselves with the ancient audience.[29]

This idea also calls for a move from translating the Bible through European languages such as English, and instead to working directly from the Hebrew and Greek texts. There should be a Hebrew–Shona dictionary and Greek–Shona dictionary to allow the Shona to meet the Bible, not on English terms, but on the terms of the Shona and of the original languages.

The inadequacy of the Bible to the Shona people's experience is expressed well by Canaan Banana, a Zimbabwean theologian, who argues not only for a translation from the original languages, but even for a rewriting of the Bible:

> This would include revision and editing to what is already there, but would also involve adding that which is not included. . . . I see that a re-written Bible, one that is more universal, embracing the rich plurality of the human experience in response to God, would be a more authentic and relevant document in today's world.[30]

The assumption behind Banana's proposal is that the Christian deity and the Shona deity are one and the same. This assumption still falls into the trap of making Mwari compatible with the Christian concepts. In my judgment, the two should be kept separate and distinct. There should be separate documents containing the Shona stories and traditions about their deity. The Shona traditions should have authenticity apart from the Bible.

In the project I propose, the Hebrew names of God would be maintained in order to maintain the differences between Mwari and YHWH Elohim. The pen should rescue the Shona deity. Writing merged Mwari with the biblical god, and it is through writing that the identification of Mwari with the genderless Shona deity will be reclaimed.

Bibliography

Banana, Canaan. "The Case for a New Bible." In *Rewriting the Bible: The Real Issues Perspectives from within Biblical and Religious Studies in Zimbabwe*, edited by Isabel Mukonyora, et al., 17–32. Gweru, Zimbabwe: Mambo, 1993.

29. Bird, *Missing Persons and Mistaken Identities*, 243.
30. Banana, "The Case for a New Bible," 81

Bhaibheri Magwaro Matsvene Amwari Testamente Yekare Testamente Itsva. London: British Foreign Bible Society, 1949.

Bhaibheri Magwaro Matsvene Amwari Namanyorero Anhasi. Harare: Bible Society of Zimbabwe, 1995.

Bhaibheri rine Apokirifa. Harare: Bible Society of Zimbabwe, 1979.

Biehler, E., *Zwinamato Zwineitikwa*. Roermond, Netherlands: Romen, 1906.

Buke eo ko Ravisa Tshekaranga (The Book for Learning Karanga language). Middleburg, South Africa, 1899.

Bird, Phyllis A. *Missing Persons and Mistaken Identities: Women and Gender in Ancient Israel*. OBT. Minneapolis: Fortress, 1997.

Bullock, Charles. *The Mashona*. Cape Town: Juta, 1928.

———. *The Mashona and Matabele*. Capetown: Juta, 1950.

Chizezuru and Chinyanja Songs. Capetown: Salvation Army, 1920.

Daneel, M. L. *The Gods of the Matopos*. London: Mouton, 1970.

English–Chiswina Dictionary with an Outline Chiswina Grammar. Chishawasha: Jesuit Mission, 1906.

Fortune G. "Who Was Mwari?" *Rhodesian History: Journal of the Central African Historical Association* 4 (1973) 1–20.

Gelfand, Michael. *Shona Ritual with Special Reference to the Chaminuka Cult*. Capetown, South Africa: Juta, 1959.

Hannan, M. *Chitendero Chitsva*. Gwelo, Rhodesia: Mambo, 1966.

———. *Standard Shona Dictionary*. Rhodesia: Rhodesia Literature Bureau, 1959, 1974.

Hartman, A. M. *Rugwaro rgwo Kunamata*. Chishawasha, Rhodesia: Jesuit Mission, 1898.

Helm, J. T., and A. A. Louw. *Evangeli ea Mattheus* (Translation of Matthew's Gospel). London: British Foreign Bible Society, 1904.

Kirk, John. *Zambezi Journals and Letters*. Vol. 1. Edited by Reginald Foskett. Edinburgh: Oliver & Boyd, 1965.

Louw, C. S. *Manual of the Chikaranga Language*. Bulawayo, Rhodesia: Philpot & Collins, 1915.

Mayr, F. *Katekisima re Makristo e Sangano re Katolike*. Pinetown, South Africa: Miriannhill, 1910.

Mashoko e Bibele (The Bible Stories). Belingwe, Rhodesia: Southern Rhodesia Church of Sweden Mission, 1927.

Minamato neZwiyimbo Yamana weSangano. London: SPCK, 1900.

Nziyo dzechiKaranga dze. "De Ned. Ger. Kereke pa Mashonaland" (Karanga hymns for the Mashonaland Church). Cape Town: Citadel, 1910.

Sanneh, Lamin. *Translating the Message: The Missionary Impact on Culture*. American Society of Missiology Series 13. Maryknoll, NY: Orbis, 1989.

Schoffeleers, J. M., and R. Mwanza. "An Organizational Model of the Mwari Shrines." In *Guardians of the Land: Essays on Central African Territorial Cults*, edited by J. M. Schoffeleers, 279–315. Gwelo: Mambo, 1978.

Smith, Edwin W., ed. *African Ideas of God: A Symposium*. London: Edinburgh House, 1950.

Springer, H. E. *A Handbook of Chikaranga or, The language of Mashonaland*. Cincinnati: Jennings & Graham, 1905.

Testamente Itswa ya She Wedu Jesu Kristu no Rurimi rwe Chishona. London: British & Foreign Bible Society, 1907.

Trible, Phyllis. *God and the Rhetoric of Sexuality.* OBT. Philadelphia: Fortress, 1978.

Vunzo dzeshoko roWedenga (Questions about the Word of God). Fort Victoria, Rhodesia: Morgenster Mission, 1909.

Vunzo dzeshoko ro Mudzimu (Questions on the Word of God). Fort Victoria, Rhodesia: Morgenster Mision, 1912.

Wallis, J. P. R., ed. *The Matabele Mission.* Rhodesia, Southern. Central African Archives. Oppenheimer Series 2. London: Chatto & Windus, 1945.

Wedenpohl, Rev. *Mashoko e Buke eo Modzimo: nga Tshekaranga.* (Compiled Bible stories). Berlin: Berliner Evangelischer Missionsgesellschaft, 1902.

6

(Con)figuring Gender in Bible Translation

Cultural, Translational, and Gender Critical Intersections

Jeremy Punt

Introduction

Translation studies are caught up in a culture war raging in and beyond classical studies, a confrontation which mostly manifests in epistemology and theory. Those called literary theorists hold that the world is constructed of words and that truth is elusive. They are sceptical about science, and therefore see culture as independent of non-cultural forces. For so-called social scientists, however, the world is composed of physical elements, which they explore through models derived from economics, political science, and demography. The two positions do not seem to share any common ground. Literary theorists condemn social scientific lists and rubrics of information and their attempts to account for real life through numbers and generalisations, and suspect political bias as mainstay of social scientific work as of the scientific enterprise as a whole. Social scientists on their part deride literary theorists' perplexity regarding the rich diversity of human life, and the postmodern impulse to reject and relegate science, facts and truth to "scare-quote status." A third group, the historical positivists has been around for longer and in their very specific focus on particularities from surviving fragmentary evidence, continues to privilege authorial intent and frown upon both literary and social-science theory.[1]

---

1. Holleran and Pudsey, *Demography and the Graeco-Roman World.*

One should admit of course to the stereotyped and simplistic nature of such categories, which can be further differentiated and added to.[2] But what such configurations demonstrate are crucial dividing lines to consider when engaging ancient texts, whether in interpretation, translation, or other investigations. Literary, social, historical and other configurations are committed to the quest for scholarly excellence, the promotion of (their) academic ideals and even the pursuit of intellectual converts. There is little indication that differences will be resolved and no synthesis is anticipated. These culture wars have no peace, truce or even diminishing in hostilities in sight. What follows will take these theoretical positions as starting point for illustrating the relevance of cultural studies for translation studies amidst the culture wars. In fact, it is on such uneven and contested terrain of theory that one needs to plot, trace and evaluate translation studies, which means neither to pick sides nor to insist on facile conjunctures. Methodological— not to mention epistemological—accord in translation theory and work is acknowledged as a distant dream. Scholars increasingly admit that translation and interpretation cannot be separated from one another and that neither of these pursuits can be considered outside of culture and ideology.[3] Or to put it differently, translation studies (also) are simultaneously impacting on and being impacted upon by contested and contesting theoretical positions and practices serving vested interests (of power). In this vein my contribution is an ideological-critical investigation of the intersection of translation and cultural studies, from a gender-critical perspective, with a further purpose to demonstrate how gender is (con)figured in NT translations.[4] Initial brief theoretical considerations are followed by an investiga-

2. For more elaborate discussions of theories of interpretation, see, e.g., Bernstein *Beyond Objectivism and Relativism*; Bible and Culture Collective, *The Postmodern Bible*; and, Lundin, *The Culture of Interpretation*. Some scholars find the use of "culture wars" ubiquitous to the extent of losing explanatory power, or even contest the culture war thesis in favour of social groups distinctions (e.g., Evans, "Worldviews or Social Groups").

3. Elliot and Boer, "Introduction," 2. Other issues relevant to the cultural and translation studies intersection, e.g., culture as translation; translation as boundary crossing; and, translational practices broadly (beyond interlingual practices) conceived, cannot be addressed here.

4. Ideology criticism is not limited to attempts at addressing the biased nature of texts and interpretations, but also challenges the notion of "fixed meaning" and "correct interpretation" as, e.g., Aichele, *The Control of Biblical Meaning*, 61–83, suggests. Ideology refers "to the ways in which meanings serve, in particular circumstances, to establish and sustain relations of power which are systematically asymmetrical" (Thompson, *Ideology and Modern Culture*, 7). Our ideological focus here is on exploring how sex and gender is constructed in translations of the Pauline documents, rather than on their construction in these documents themselves, i.e. how certain ideologies

tion of the interplay between gender, sexuality and translation issues in a few biblical (Pauline) texts.

Cultural Studies and Translation Work

The recent work on the role of bible translations in colonial settings, on missionaries and their goals and on indigenous people and bible reception as well as the considerable developments that took place since the days of vociferous debates on literal or formal versus dynamic or functional equivalence, all feed into my argument.[5] On the margins of biblical studies, we have seen work of scholars and theorists such as Nord, Gutt and others making important inroads in translation work.[6] To take one example pertinent to my argument, the functionalist translation model of Christiane Nord has been mooted as part of a "cultural turn" in translation studies.[7]

Nord's work moves away from rigid guidelines for establishing equivalence at several linguistic levels between source and target texts, as she opts for descriptive oriented investigations into culture-embedded translational acts. Some cracks start to show however when Nord's focus on a translation's *skopos*, i.e. the target-text's purpose or the pragmatic content of the translator initiator's instructions, is interrupted by her claims regarding the

---

have become normalised (Pérez, "Introduction," 5); and while not denying that ideology often is interwoven into theology and various other spheres, our attention will remain on the translation, culture and gender intersections. A plea such as Werner's for an ethical code in translation (Werner, "Toward an Ethical Code in Bible Translation Consulting") falls outside our scope.

5. Recent work on colonialism, missionaries and Bible translation includes, e.g., Boer, *Last Stop*; Dube, "What I Have Written"; Petterson, "Configuring the Language"; Stine *Bible Translation*. Cf. Punt ("Translating the Bible in South Africa" and "Whose Bible") for the South(ern) African context. Cf. Porter ("Assessing Translation Theory"; cf. Bailey and Pippin, "Race, Class, and the Politics of Bible Translation") for a recent take on the literal(ist)/formal versus the dynamic/functional distinction, and for apprehension about the contribution of ideological awareness to translation practice, if not also to theory.

6. Closer to home, the translation project of the new direct Afrikaans Bible translation in SA is largely built on the theories of Christiane Nord (especially her functionalist approach) and Ernst-August Gutt (with his focus on relevance) (cf. Van der Merwe, "The Bible in Afrikaans")—space does not allow extensive discussion of these theorists or their work.

7. Nord is selected from many translation theories and theorists, because of our focus on the translation and cultural studies-intersection and given the current attention for Nord's work in SA (e.g., through the preparation of the new Afrikaans Bible; cf. Van der Merwe, "The Bible in Afrikaans," 3).

importance of source text analysis.[8] Serious consideration of the cultural and translation studies intersection appears to require a still broader cultural scope, moving beyond the study of translation's "function-in-culture."[9] In fact, while her text analysis appears culturally attuned,[10] at times it amounts to an application of prevailing norms. The alignment of norms of "our culture"[11] or "our culture-specific concept"[12] with "average Western cultures"[13] shows the dominance of and preference for a specific "culture," and accompanying ideological concerns. Also, her aversion for subjectivity and indeterminism is backed up by her insistence on control in translation, which is effected theoretically, at least, through her dominating *skopos*-theory.[14] In short, Nord's work interacts with cultural concerns probably more than earlier translation studies, but the question is whether it introduces a cultural turn or rather a refined functionalist position?

On Cultural and Other Turns

Turn-talk in scholarly discourse follows on the heels of the late twentieth-century linguistic turn, and is part of the scholarly culture wars. The linguistic turn marked the beginning of a new consciousness about hermeneutics and even epistemology in New Testament studies and introduced new practices. Traditional, long-held beliefs in historical objectivity and the ability to describe a past as it actually happened were replaced with the

---

8. The importance of source-text claims is underwritten by Nord's insistence on "compatibility between source-text intention and target-text functions if translation is to be possible at all" (*Text Analysis in Translation*, 32); that "the translator must not act contrary to the sender's intention" (ibid., 54); and that the translation *skopos* requires "equivalence of effect" (ibid., 201).

9. Nord, *Text Analysis in Translation*, 24.

10. E.g., "[t]he meaning or function of a text is not something inherent in the linguistic signs; it cannot simply be extracted by anyone who knows the code. A text is made meaningful by its receiver and for its receiver" ("Dealing with Purposes," 152).

11. *Text Analysis in Translation*, 32, 73.

12. Ibid., 73.

13. Ibid., 201.

14. Since this is not primarily or in essence a discussion of Nord's work, two final comments must suffice: one, Nord's use of auctorial intention both with reference to source texts and translations does not sit well with either more functionalist or more subjectivist approaches; two, her use of categories such as "space," "time," "culture," and "text functions" (e.g., ibid., 43–83) may create the untenable situation of four disjointed, categorically separate spheres (her claims about the interdependence of extra-textual factors do not resolve the problem of disjointedness altogether, cf. ibid., 83–87). Cf. also the critical review of Nord's 1991 publication by Pym, "Review," 184–90.

acknowledgement that the past does not exist outside its literary presentation.[15] As cultural sensitive elements were picked up and translated into biblical studies practices, the notion of a cultural turn (also) became more popular. Literary texts increasingly were seen as part of a larger "inseparable, relational web of residues and artifacts that hang together in ways that are not always easily comprehensible."[16] Such interconnectedness is seen as embedded further in various power constellations and gives rise to claims about a "political turn"[17] in New Testament studies.

With lingering linguistic and incipient political turns, and a growing interest in cultural studies among scholars, a "cultural turn" is discernible in biblical studies.[18] For some the cultural turn may imply the employment of various poststructural methods to show how language shaped the sociocultural setting of the early Christian world. For others it may entail the use of cultural anthropology as analytical method. What in any case has become clear is the implication of scholarly movement beyond the universalisms of the Enlightenment and nineteenth- and twentieth-century liberalism. The result is that scholars more and more "have come to view human beings as historical creatures located within the complex matrices of particular cultures and social worlds," and increasingly deal with the "located, particular, pluralistic, and thoroughly historical nature of human existence, experience, and knowledge."[19] In fact, since the latter part of the twentieth century, social history is replacing institutional or intellectual history,[20] and investigations are shifting towards the ways in which the socio-cultural settings of antiquity influenced rhetorical strategies found in the ancient texts.

Cultural and Biblical Studies

When culture is understood as "the dynamic and contentious process by which meaning, and with it, power is produced, circulated, and negotiated by all who reside within a particular cultural milieu,"[21] it follows that cul-

15. With the acknowledgement that the past exists only in its literary representation came the realisation that such representations are always imbued with ideologies.

16. Lopez, "Visualizing Significant Otherness," 80.

17. Stanley, "Paul the Ethnic Hybrid?," 111.

18. The originating moments and location of cultural studies are commonly disputed, yet broadly connected to movements as early as the 1950's to study also popular or mass culture (Easthope, "Cultural Studies in the United Kingdom, 176) yet variously described (Vanhoozer, et al., *Everyday Theology*, 248).

19. Davaney, "Theology and the Turn to Cultural Analysis," 5.

20. Martin, "Introduction," 5.

21. Davaney, "Theology and the Turn to Cultural Analysis," 5.

tural studies can be described as an interdisciplinary "theoretical-political project." Culture is not a synonym for ideology, not even in the Mannheim sense of ideology as more or less worldview. But the overlaps between culture and ideology are quite evident: ideology is more connected to normalised frameworks of thought, while culture refers to learnt behaviour patterns.[22] Cultural studies incorporates these sentiments. Cultural studies has academic and political dimensions that holds to the democratization of culture and is interested in all cultural productions such as cultural practices, operations, and formations. "At its best, the movement deploys a convergence of research methodologies (not a single or unified methodological prism) to interrogate the valorization of culture, to demystify the politics of representation, to foster practices of self-reflexive inquiry, and to promote actively a radical progressive cultural politics."[23]

In biblical scholarship the once lauded ideals of objectivity and neutrality are increasingly recognised as impossible to achieve, and also berated for obscuring cultural imperialism and ideology. The modernist theory of an ideal observer and narrator is being replaced by the alternative, postmodernist construct of a narrator and observer who is always situated and engaged.[24] As much as the Genesis story about the tower of Babel concerns the inevitable need for translation, in a powerful way it also presents the collapse of empire in the sense of showing the impossibility of attaining the complete, the ultimate and the total. It is Babel that shows how every reading is a rewriting, every reading is a translation—it upsets the notion of the original by pointing out its lack, and its constant desire to be translated.[25] Moving away from understanding translation as the objective rendering of an original, and viewing translation rather as crafting an intertextual co-

22. Perez, "Introduction," 5–6.

23. Smith, "Cultural Studies." This is a worthwhile description of cultural studies which like the term culture also suffers from a wide range of definitions. At the same time, using this understanding of cultural studies is of course not meant to deny other, divergent notions and certainly not to conceive of cultural studies as homogenous.

24. The reigning master paradigm of interpretive neutrality and hermeneutic objectivity is "a historical experience and cultural reality as particularized and contextualized as any other [and] is bracketed and universalized as normative human experience and reality—the reality and experience of center—with the rest unable to transcend their social locations—the realities and experiences of the margins" (Segovia, *Decolonizing Biblical Studies*, 173). Translation work can feed into such a paradigm, as Aichele argues: "Christian sacrifice of the physical text of the scriptures has had important repercussions for Christian attitudes towards Jews, Muslims, and those of other religions and belief systems, including atheists, for according to the Christian ideology of the canon, the Bible must be brimming with clear, coherent meaning" (Aichele, *The Control of Biblical Meaning*, 83).

25. Derrida, "Des Tours des Babel," 104–11.

text, requires sensitivity for and concern about the situated persons and positions of translators.

Proceeding from a cultural studies position is not without danger, particularly in idiosyncratic or even exotic garb. However, a normalising approach is equally dangerous. Describing cultural hermeneutics as "approaches to interpretation in which the social and cultural location of the interpreter (e.g., feminist, African-American) serves as a principle of interpretation"[26] does not show self-awareness about the discrepancy it introduces. Quite simply, interpretation is *never* devoid of social or cultural influence, regardless of the extent of its acknowledgement. Interpretation is in and of itself social and cultural. Interpretation like translation can never be aloof of interpreters and is mostly not without consuming listeners. Of course, in both instances (even if in various ways) interpreters as well as users of the interpretation simultaneously are connected to and constitutive of their social locations.[27] In short, no methodological prisms—neither in biblical interpretation nor in Bible translation—are free from wider cultural currents, as all methods are "culturally contextualized."[28]

Cultural Studies, Biblical Studies, and Translation

While the cultural turn in biblical studies can be explained variously, the understanding and emphasis upon certain antecedents—unsurprisingly— also are likely to vary between social locations. In biblical studies, it is on the one hand the impending demise of the once all-vanquishing historical critical approach that raises questions about various aspects of biblical studies work. At the same time, increased attention is given to the nature of historical work,[29] to linguistic and textual concerns and to readers and their interpretative communities and histories. On the other hand, the rise of a more culturally or socially attuned historiography and consideration for the social location of scholars and scholarship begs the question about the modes of including historical consciousness in scholarship, taking the

26. Vanhoozer, *Everyday Theology*, 248.

27. "'The people' are not just passive consumers of meaning, values, and practices devised by the powerful. They are the producers of culture on multiple levels, including through resistance to elites" (Davaney "Theology and the Turn to Cultural Analysis," 6).

28. Segovia, *Decolonizing Biblical Studies*, 24.

29. In cultural studies, "[t]he goal of the historian becomes not the conscious or even unconscious intentions of the author, but the larger matrix of symbol systems provided by the author's society from which he must have drawn whatever resources he used to 'speak his mind'" (Martin, "Introduction," 17).

social embeddedness of biblical studies as point of departure and frame of understanding.[30]

This starting point implies a rejection of a logocentric approach to translation work, which in simple terms assumes the placement of retrievable meaning in a text by an author. And beyond logocentrism the distinction between textual means and semantic message is no longer evident or useful.[31] The interpretative interests at play in translation as much as in hermeneutics are now also more in focus, interests which can fruitfully be explored through ideological criticism. In a cultural studies approach both the value and authenticity of popular readings are acknowledged, but without necessarily assuming the legitimacy or condoning the effects of any particular reading. Popular translations and interpretations can be "an uneven mix of insights, prejudices, contradictions, and images imposed by hegemonic discourse,"[32] and are not necessarily innovative and liberatory.[33] Ideological concerns are not the preserve of the publicly powerful only!

Moreover, ideological concerns characterise "turn-talk." It has been suggested that the combination of rhetorical emphasis and feminist theory will enable the "full-turn" of biblical studies.[34] And that a paradigm shift in biblical studies has so far stayed out due to the inability of rhetoric to link up with feminist, liberationist and postcolonial studies. But what would an identity politics-focused approach such as feminism entail? From a cul-

30. Cultural studies do not seek to exclude, or take scholarly terrain hostage, as it "seeks to integrate, in different ways, the historical, formalist, and sociocultural questions and concerns of other paradigms," but it does seek to do so "on a different key, with a situated and interested reader and interpreter always at its core" (Segovia, *Decolonizing Biblical Studies*, 30, 41). And translation is always closely connected to ideology: "any translation is ideological since the choice of a source texts and the use to which the subsequent source texts is pit is determined by the interests, aims, and objectives of social agents. But ideological elements can also be determined within a text itself" (Schäffner, "Third Ways and New Centres," 23).

31. Aichele, *The Control of Biblical Meaning*, 61–62, blames both the "Christian confidence in the reliability of translation" and "Christian willingness to resolve or overlook the dilemma of a double canon" on a logocentric or "Greek" approach to language, which separates thought and language. "The signifier is simply a dispensable transmitting mechanism." The end results are disastrous: "Christianity has been unable to tolerate diversity," and "[i]n freeing the meaning of the canonical texts from their physical embodiments and allowing the unlimited translation of the scriptures, Christianity set itself on that course of intolerance and even fanaticism from which it has not yet freed itself" (Aichele, *The Control of Biblical Meaning*, 82–83).

32. Glancy, "House Reading and Field Readings," 476.

33. In fact, scholarly readings can serve a useful purpose in conjunction with popular readings, for example in addressing the needs of the poor (cf. Rowland, "Open Thy Mouth for the Dumb," 239, 241).

34. Schüssler Fiorenza, *Rhetoric and Ethic*, 13.

tural studies perspective identity politics defined by the Free Dictionary as "political attitudes or positions that focus on the concerns of social groups identified mainly on the basis of gender, race, ethnicity, or sexual orientation"[35] conjure up concern about the imposition of another regulating regime with which to replace the former. Without suggesting some impossible neutrality in interpretation and translation, a predefined one-sided and biased approach is clearly not the most profitable alternative course of action. Cultural studies, however, may offer an alternative to bland detachment or partisan activism when it, in concert with gender studies, holds that gender is neither a natural nor fixed identification category. Gender is not primarily derivative from biological differences but is "a culturally constructed script, role, or set of regulatory practices that helps to identify a given society's hegemonic norms about material bodies. Examining gender in cultures then exposes the submerged histories of those who do not fit such norms."[36]

A focus on gender concerns informed by cultural studies is wary of identity politics, while appreciative of the gains and importance of feminist work. But a broader and non-binary optic may fit better with the constructed nature, the performativity of gender. Of the many mechanisms operative in the discourse of gender the particular influence of biblical texts in many parts of the world should not be overlooked. The intersection of cultural and gender studies allows for an ideology-adept approach to translating biblical texts.

Translating NT Gender Identities and Roles: The Gender Colour Chart

Gender is constructed in NT translations, that is figured or scripted but potentially in a conniving or disingenuous way, and done deliberately or inadvertently—thus (con)structed or (con)figured.[37] Since gender is

---

35. Cf. Free Dictionary 2014. And, "[t]he laden phrase 'identity politics' has come to signify a wide range of political activity and theorizing founded in the shared experiences of injustice of members of certain social groups. Rather than organizing solely around belief systems, programmatic manifestos, or party affiliation, identity political formations typically aim to secure the political freedom of a specific constituency marginalized within its larger context. Members of that constituency assert or reclaim ways of understanding their distinctiveness that challenge dominant oppressive characterizations, with the goal of greater self-determination" (Heyes, "Identity Politics").

36. Smith, "Cultural Studies."

37. Along similar lines, Bailey and Pippin's, "Race, Class, and the Politics of Bible Translation," 1–2. promotes the corrupting of translation in the deconstruction sense

performativity (Butler), it is scripted according to norms of the societies in which translators live, (con)figuring gender of and for the first century through modern-day lenses. And unless such translated gender figurations are acknowledged as such, they are rather con-figurations, deceptive portrayals of gender that with reference to the first century mislead. While self-respecting academics do not view translations as innocent representations of some original truth, various culturally ordered social arrangements are at times left unaccounted. Social conventions—and here our focus is on those regarding gender—both ancient and modern, impact in numerous but often neither in visible nor acknowledged ways on translation work. This impact can generate a double-bind. On the one hand, attempts to make gender more visible in translated biblical texts (e.g., inclusive language)[38] generally only reinforce current conventions and render past gender patterns virtually undetectable in translations. On the other hand, acknowledgement of the effect of past gender constructions on biblical texts as much as the impact of reception history with its earlier and current gender conventions, cannot always be accommodated in bible translations. In this way, a safe course is frequently plotted in assuming a sort of neutral translation, or defaulting to—still the darling of theologians—a (so-called) "literal" translation.[39] Both the attempts to make gender constructions visible and, ironically, also those endeavours to acknowledge their impact on bible texts and translations ensure that the double bind stays firmly in place.[40] A longer example demonstrates a broader trend.

---

of the word, "exposing and undoing racism and classicism that have been part of Eurocentric-controlled translations."

38. Nord, "Function and Loyalty in Bible Translation," 110–11.

39. The remark by Aichele, *The Control of Biblical Meaning*, 70, is appropriate: "Even the most literal of translations inevitably changes the signifiers of the source texts in many ways." And theologians all too often use "literal translation" as neutral, middle of the road option in which the message of the text is evident, which is in any case not like Aichele: "Literal translation forces the reader back to the materiality of the source text, not in order to receive a message that is contained there, but rather to uncover the 'primal elements' in which pure language [a la Benjamin, JP] rustles" (Aichele, *The Control of Biblical Meaning*, 74).

40. The role of a gender chart in determining translation decisions has the effect of potentially blinding translators to patriarchal and heteronormative positions encapsulated in the reception history of the Bible, while at the same time reinforcing such positions. Here the tricky issue of inclusive language in translations of ancient texts also needs further attention.

Phoebe as διάκονος in Romans

Gendered assumptions and their effects are evident in translations of Romans where Paul introduced Phoebe, one of ten other women in the chapter, as τὴν ἀδελφὴν ἡμῶν, οὖσαν [καὶ] διάκονον τῆς ἐκκλησίας τῆς ἐν Κεγχρεαῖς . . . καὶ γὰρ αὐτὴ προστάτις πολλῶν ἐγενήθη καὶ ἐμοῦ αὐτοῦ (Rom 16:1–2, emphasis added). Phoebe's role is couched in terms that Paul used also for male counterparts and trusted co-workers such as Timothy (cf. 1 Th 3:2). However, when Phoebe is introduced in Romans 16 as διάκονος she often ends up in translations as "deacon" or even—over against the Greek male form—as "deaconess."[41, 42] Translating with deacon/ess in Rom 16:1 goes against the scope of use of διάκονος in the NT, and is probably indicative of gender bias and (con)figuration more than anything else.[43]

The range of meanings for διάκονος in the NT is broad and includes "assistant," "servant," "helper," "attendant," or "agent." The lemma has a varied prevalence in different parts of speech in the NT; except for Phm 13, the verb διακονέω is not used in any of the other authentic Pauline letters.[44] It is especially the personal noun, the term διάκονος, that is important here, and particularly its rendering in different translations. Both the personal noun (διάκονος) and the abstract noun (διακονία), however, are used with greater frequency in the Pauline letters, respectively 12 and 18 times.[45] Paul

41. The masculine form of the noun should not be taken to indicate a masculine identity imposed on Phoebe, but rather using an established term for a particular woman. Translating "deacon" changes Phoebe "from a leader and minister to the churches of Cenchrae into a second-level functionary," and begs the question why she would have been entrusted with this letter (Castelli, "Paul on Women and Gender," 224). MacDonald, "Reading Real Women through the Undisputed Letters of Paul," 207, however, rates the diaconate as rather important within the early Christian church, and sees the participation of women in it as development leading to it being gendered female, including the coining of a female terms, deaconess. She does admit that this is a later development of the third and fourth centuries (see also Whelan, "Amica Pauli," 68).

42. Castelli, "Paul on Women and Gender," 224–25; Whelan, "Amica Pauli," 67–85.

43. A more blatant example is of course where "malestream" (cf. Schüssler Fiorenza) interpretation turned the name of Junia into a masculine version, Junias, regardless of the fact that the latter name never appears in contemporaneous writings (Castelli, "Paul on Women and Gender," 225). From ascribing the change of Junia into a masculine version, to transcription of the Greek accusative (Myers, "Romans," 829), simply begs the question why transcription is deemed appropriate only here and not with any of the other names mentioned in Rom 16? Cf. also Du Toit, "The Ecclesiastical Situation of the First Generation Roman Christians," 509–10.

44. Even in the deutero-Pauline letters the use of διακονέω is limited to 1 Tim 3:10, 13.

45. The texts are respectively Rom 13:4 [2]; 15:8; 16:1; 1 Cor 3:5; 2 Cor 3:6; 6:4; 11:15 [2], 25; Gal 2:17; Phil 1:1; and Rom 11:13; 12:7 [2]; 15:31; 1 Cor 12:5; 16:15; 2

often applied the term to himself and his co-workers, particularly where the preaching of the gospel was central, e.g., 1 Cor 3:5; 2 Cor 3:6; 11:23; cf. Rom 11:13; 1 Cor 16:15; 2 Cor 5:18; 6:3.[46] In Phil 1:1 where Paul used διακόνοις in conjunction with ἐπισκόποι it is more likely that he indicated general terms, "helpers" or "assistants" or "co-workers" as well as "overseers" rather than instances of official roles such as "deacons" and "bishops."[47] When Paul lists "officers" of the church in 1 Cor 12:28 (cf. Eph 4:11) he only mentioned apostles, prophets, teachers, evangelists but made no mention of "overseers" or "deacons."[48]

In the later parts of the NT διάκονος is used as a technical term in a few instances. Before διάκονος acquired a more technical meaning, that of an official position in church leadership ("deacon") as may be the case in rare instances such as 1 Tim 3:8, 12, it was used in the New Testament with both sacred and secular connotations. Epaphras who was associated with the church in Colossae and called a διάκονος in Col 1:7, is correctly indicated in contemporary translations not as a deacon but as "minister" (e.g., ESV, RSV, NIV, NRSV). Similarly, when 1 Tim 4:6 still later refers to Timothy, associated with the Ephesus church, as a διάκονος it is obvious that he was not a deacon but a "minister" (RSV, NIV) or "servant" (ESV, NRSV). In Matt 20:26–28 Jesus is reported as using the term to describe those who followed in his footsteps and in John 12:26 to describe the relationship between him and his followers. Similarly in Col 1:23 Paul is identified as διάκονος in the sense of a messenger of the gospel about Jesus Christ. The term was not reserved for positive descriptions only. Earlier, in Rom 13:4, Paul himself referred to state authorities, switching to the singular, as θεοῦ . . . διάκονος and in 2 Cor 11:13–15 to false apostles as οἱ διάκονοι of Satan.

When Paul introduces Phoebe as διάκονος in Romans 16:1–2, her role is best translated as a minister or co-worker of Paul and not as deacon/ess

---

Cor 3:7, 8, 9 [2]; 4:1; 5:18; 6:3; 8:4; 9:1, 12, 13; 11:8). At a statistical level, the words are better represented among the Pauline letters than the NT taken as a whole, where διάκονος and διακονία are use a total of 29 and 34 times respectively; of which 21 and 23 times in the Pauline corpus. in the deutero-Pauline letters they are used 9 times (Eph 3:7; 6:21; Col 1:7, 23, 25; 4:7; 1 Tim 3:8, 12; 4:6) and 5 (Eph 4:12; Col 4:17; 2 Tim 1:12; 4:5, 11) times respectively.

46. MacDonald, "Reading Real Women," 208.

47. "Translators, however, differ considerably on how to render ἐπισκόποις καὶ διακόνοις in Phil 1:1: 'bishops and deacons' (AV, ASV, RSV, NEB, NRSV), 'overseers and deacons' (NIV, NASB), 'church leaders and helpers' (GNB), 'overseers and assistants' (Williams), 'ministers of the Church and their assistants' (Weymouth), 'superintendents and assistants' (Goodspeed), 'overseers and ministers' (Darby), or 'presidents and assistant officers' (TCNT)" (Hawthorne, *Philippians*, 12).

48. Hawthorne, *Philippians*, 8–9.

as borne out by her further portrayal as both προστάτις and ἀδελφή. Even if the debate on clergy chronology remains open, ascribing a technical meaning to διάκονος when used for Phoebe but not when used for others such as Timothy, is due probably more to gender construction and ideology than church organisation.

Phoebe as προστάτις in Romans

Translating διάκονος as deacon/ess when used of Phoebe in Rom 16 does not take the use of the word in the NT into consideration, does not consider the more common meaning of the word, and appears to rely on a stance dating back to later developments when the exclusion of women from positions of leadership in the early Jesus follower communities apparently was promoted. The importance of translating διάκονος with a term such as minister or servant is highlighted by the social status of Phoebe expressed in προστάτις.[49] The loaded term προστάτις is often rendered as "helper" in translations with seeming disregard for first-century patronage systems,[50] and little acknowledgement that Paul used προστάτις as NT *hapax legomenon* for Phoebe only.

In the first century, patronage informed social structures more than most other socio-political systems with the Emperor as the supreme patron of the Roman Empire, with direct access to the gods.[51] Closeness to the Emperor ensured social power, and officials and local elites were able to act as brokers and clients of the Emperor. Social relations were governed in a sophisticated reciprocal relationship[52] where honour, prestige and power dynamics governed behaviour.[53] Patronage was often covered in a "kinship

49. Paul used the feminine form of προστάτης, which hints at her financial support of the Jesus follower-communities, which would have implied significant economic means and social independence (cf. Castelli, "Paul on Women and Gender," 224).

50. Ibid., 224–25.

51. The importance of family metaphors in Roman society, and the father and son metaphor in particular, has also been ascribed to the portrayal of the emperor as *pater patriae*. Cf., e.g., Carter, *John and Empire*, 235–55; Lassen, "The Roman Family," 103–20; White, *The Apostle of God*, 139–72. For the relation between Empire's notion of order and family relations, cf. Johnson, "Empire and Order," 161–73.

52. Reciprocity in patronal relations is often depicted as "generalised" (interest of others as primary), "balanced" (mutual interests as important) or "negative" (dominant self-interest) (cf. Osiek, "The Politics of Patronage and the Politics of Kinship," 144.)

53. The effect of patronage was particularly evident in the relationship between freed persons and their former masters, often compared to the relationship between son and father. The patron retained power over the freed person who was reminded of owing his or her "new life" to the patron. Honouring of the patron was expected, and

glaze" so as to soften the harshness of the client's position. Folded into fatherliness or siblinghood, and even more often, friendship terminology[54] kinship language did not hide the uneven power relationships which ruled out equality in the sense of equity or even mutuality.[55]

Paul's identification of Phoebe both as minister and as patron undergirds her respected position and bestows on her a coveted social status, a public role of patronage, protection and authority, all of which would have been acknowledged publicly. "Phoebe's role crossed the divide between public and private in Greco-Roman society" (MacDonald 1999:209). According to Paul she became (ἐγενήθη) the patron of many (πολλῶν), and, in fact, also of Paul himself (καὶ ἐμοῦ αὐτοῦ), which suggest a strong bond between her and Paul, which did not necessarily privilege Paul. Describing Phoebe as patron also fits right in with how Paul invoked fictive kinship in his communities, and his reference to her as sister.

Phoebe as ἀδελφή in Romans

References to brothers and sisters in Paul's letters can simply imply membership as co-believers in Jesus, but they sometimes indicated a wider semantic reach. In 1 Cor 7 the differentiated use of the general ἄνθρωπος (e.g., 1 Cor 7:1) and particular ἀδελφός (e.g., 1 Cor 7:12) is a good example of the latter reserved for a fellow believer in Christ but also illustrates the varied use of sibling terms. While Paul used similar terminology to distinguish between a fellow believer (ἀδελφός) and his non-believing wife (γυναῖκα ἄπιστον) in 1 Cor 7:12, he did not use cognate terms to make a similar contrast between a married believing woman (only γυνὴ, not ἀδελφή) and her non-believing husband (ἄνδρα ἄπιστον) in 1 Cor 7:13. Although describing

---

practices such as legal recourse in court for injustice suffered by the freed person, forbidden. A freed person was under the power of the patron, just as the son was under the power of the father. This unequal power relationship was managed through legislation in conjunction with honour and shame values and manifested the practical outworking of a dyadic contract, beyond manumission (cf. Chow, "Patronage in Roman Corinth," 121).

54. Other elements of patronage can be summarised as follows: asymmetrical relationships; simultaneous exchange of resources; interpersonal obligations; relational favouritism; reciprocity; exchange of honour; and, the "kinship glaze" (Osiek, "The Politics of Patronage and the Politics of Kinship," 144; cf. Neyrey, "God, Benefactor and Patron," 467–68).

55. Cf. also Aasgaard, My Beloved Brothers and Sisters, 20–21. In a sense, κοινωνοί, as business terminology, rather than ἀδελφοί (as kinship term), would have come closer to notions such as equity (equality in the contemporary context was not a socio-cultural possibility).

a parallel situation, a siblinghood term is used for the man only, not for the woman—in contrast with 1 Cor 7:15 where both ἀδελφός and ἀδελφή are used. Such inconsistent usage begs interpretive and translation caution.

In Rom 16:1 Phoebe is in the first place introduced as τὴν ἀδελφὴν ἡμῶν (our sister), not unlike how Paul used sibling terminology in communities of Jesus followers. But in Rom 16:1 he used the sibling term in neither a collective nor a generic sense. Paul did not often use the title for individuals, and there is little doubt that great respect was garnered by its use, particularly in conjunction with διάκονος and προστάτις. Paul used the masculine counterpart ἀδελφός for Timothy who was probably the most important collaborator in his mission (cf. Phlm 1; 2 Cor 1:1; 1 Thess 3:2). Paul's identification of Phoebe as sister measures up with her otherwise positive description, as her assessment on par with those of his closest associates.[56] Phoebe's description fits in with the fact that she is one of three women introduced without reference to a specific partner. Some of the nine other women mentioned in Rom 16 were involved in missionary partnerships, including women (Tryphaena and Tryphosa, 16:12), male-female pairs (e.g., Prisca and Aquila, 16:3), and Rufus and his mother (16:13). But Phoebe, and maybe Mary and Persis (16:6, 12), are mentioned individually, with no missionary partner.

In sum, translating διάκονος with a technical term such as *deacon/ess* and προστάτις with a general notion of *helper* are not helpful and rest heavily upon gender constructions, or better, are gendered constructions. In the first instance these translations relegate the importance of Phoebe's role by attaching a restricted scope to it in the one case, and in the other a too casual connotation of assistance greatly diminishes what was an important socio-cultural position and role. Translation choices about Phoebe appear to be dependent on her gender. Translating διάκονος incongruously as technical term and προστάτις equally inappropriately as generalisation has a wider negative impact, affecting the translation of the remaining part of the text. (Con)figuring gender in translation also warps the socio-historical image of the community, as is the case in (con)figured sexuality—as another example shows.

---

56. Only in one other instance, Apphia in Phlm 2, did Paul identify an individual woman as ἀδελφή in terms of fictive kinship. In the reference to the sister of Nereus (Rom 16:5) it is not clear whether Nereus' sibling or his missionary companion should be inferred. The 1 Tim 5:2 exhortation παρακάλει . . . νεωτέρας ὡς ἀδελφάς probably expects that young women should be treated as siblings or sisters—as much as older men and older women should be treated as father and mothers respectively (1 Tim 5:1–2).

Broadening the Agenda: (Con)figuring Sex and Sexuality

In the *ABD*, Myers[57] self-confidently writes that "Rom 1:27 is the clearest statement in the NT regarding the issue of homosexual behavior between consenting adult males, and Rom 1:26 is the only biblical text that addresses the particular issue of homosexual behavior between consenting females."[58] Myers rightly concludes that Paul's theological argument puts "homosexuality" as consequence of sin rather than its cause or embodiment, and also that this augurs against singling out "homosexuality" in Rom 1.[59] However, choosing the modern term "homosexuality" to express homoerotic actions and relations in antiquity demonstrates a hermeneutical bind similar to the translation of terms with which Pauline woman co-workers are described:[60] how to translate without obliterating a socio-culturally different informed notion of same-sex intercourse, or without banalising or obscuring the source texts?[61]

Terminology used to refer to same-sex relations in the NT, in the three texts often cited in this regard, pose a particular challenge for bible translation.[62] The challenge is impacted by a dissimilar socio-historical context, by the often less than clear language of the NT, and also by contemporary

---

57. Myers, "Romans, Epistle to the Romans," 827.

58. Ibid.; he also claims: "Apparently, homosexual behavior among consenting males was quite rare among Israelites" and "[a]lthough homosexual love (usually in the form of pederasty, the love of an older man for a younger) enjoyed a relatively prominent place in ancient Greek social life beginning in the sixth century BC, homosexuality was viewed differently in the world of the first century AD. To be sure, it was still practiced among some segments of society, but moral philosophers were beginning to question its merit. Homosexuality was viewed as grossly self-indulgent, essentially exploitative, and an expression of absolutely insatiable lust".

59. A bolder position is taken by Townsley, who claims that "[t]here is little reason to believe that Paul's intent in this passage is anything but an exhortation against the worship of other gods, and even less basis to infer the general content of Paul's beliefs about sexual orientations, specifically the use of this passage as a condemnation of contemporary queer relationships" (Townsley, "Paul, the Goddess Religions, and Queer Sects," 728).

60. For homoeroticism, cf. especially Nissinen (*Homoeroticism in the Biblical World*). Also to avoid illegitimately transferring modern connotations onto ancient texts which shows no evidence of a modern sexuality binary of homosexuality and heterosexuality, Townsley ("Paul, the Goddess Religions, and Queer Sects") uses heterogenital and homogenital.

61. For more detailed arguments, cf. earlier work done on Rom 1 in Punt ("Rom 1:18–32 amidst the Gay Debate"; and "Sin as Sex or Sex as Sin?").

62. Rom 1:26–27, especially εἰς τὴν παρὰ φύσιν and τὴν φυσικὲν χρῆσιν; 1 Cor 6:9 μαλακοὶ and ἀρσενοκοῖται; 1 Tm 1:10 ἀρσενοκοίταις; cf. also my earlier arguments in Punt (2008).

debates regarding human sexuality. The stakes are raised further if one admits that Rom 1 does not deal with modern categories such as homosexual orientation; that at the time sexuality was not conceptualised along the lines modern people do;[63] that sex was described most often as a medium of power in the first century CE; and, that homoerotic, like other sexual activities, took place in relationships characterised by inequalities of power.[64] In addition, the translation of terms often connected to and translated as "homosexual" or "homosexuality" is further impacted upon when cognisance is given to modern-day debates on essentialism versus constructivism, when moving from identity politics biased towards a bipolar gender system to where gender is subverted, and even in some quarters already experienced as subverted—issues central (also) in cultural studies.

Φύσις and φυσικός in Rom 1:24–27

Embedded in Rom 1:21–28 (32) or more properly Rom 1:1—3:20, is Paul's strong argument of Rom 1:24–27. In these verses Paul uses homoeroticism as an example of what happens when God is not duly acknowledged. As part of his reasoning, homoerotic activities are portrayed as unnatural and participants as consumed by uncontrollable passion.[65]

A widespread first-century assumption held that men could have moderate or passionless sex with women, but that male homoerotic sex was akin to *passions* out of control and associated dangers.[66] Although the

63. Balch, "Paul, Families, and Households," 266–68, briefly surveys a wide spectrum of first-century CE Greco-Roman medical (Epicurus, Celsus, Soranus and Galen) and theological and philosophical (including ascetics like the Therapeutae, Philo, Chaeremon) opinions about "sexuality" and appropriate sexual behaviour. A general uneasiness with sex is palpable, given the possibility that men might succumb to sex rather than exercising power over it in their relations with women and subordinates.

64. Biblical discussions of homoerotic activity cannot simplistically be "cut and pasted" into today's debate; regardless of the Bible's status as authoritative text it does not directly address the issues involved (cf. Elliott, *Liberating Paul*, 181–230). Moreover, the consistent goal of early Christian ethics was the "limitation of desire for things, experiences, and pleasures, 'thou shall not desire'" (Stowers, "Paul and Self-Mastery," 546).

65. Homoerotic activities were typically aligned in the first century with excessive passion: "the ancient moralist, and here we must include Paul, considered homosexual behaviour to be 'the most extreme expression of heterosexual lust'" (Martin, "Heterosexism and the Interpretation of Romans 1:18–32," 342).

66. Giving oneself over to one's passions and relishing pleasure were thought to make men soft and weak, which did not have homoerotic overtones as much as an uncontrollable desire for sex with women (Stowers, "Paul and Self-Mastery," 544–45). Deeds of softness typically included vices caused by excess, greed or lack of self-control

example may have been extended to homoerotic activities between women (1:26),[67] the passionate nature of male homoeroticism (1:27) required a longer explanation.[68] Probably influenced by Stoicism, Paul's argument in Rom 1 is biased towards self-mastery, implying constancy based on acting in a way that appears reasonable.[69] Passion and not the modern day homosexual-heterosexual binary was a great challenge for most first-century philosophers in the Greek and Roman world, partly because passion always threatened reason and self-mastery, but also because uncontrollable passion was equated with disaster.[70] While his contemporaries emphasised moderation of passion and desire and even affirmed their importance for procreative copulation, Paul is never positive about passion or desire[71][72] Much emphasis is put on impassioned bodily and sexual terms such as desires

---

(Frederickson, "Natural and Unnatural Use in Romans 1:24–27," 219.

67. The gender of these women's sex partners is not identified. The words ἐν αὐτοῖς ("among themselves," 1:24) suggests it was people, and not, e.g., animals or angels (Swancutt, "Sexy Stoics and the Rereading of Romans," 63). But Rom 1:26 might not refer to homoerotic acts but to women who assumed a more active and hence unnatural role with men (cf. Balch, "Pauls, Families, and Households," 277–78; Hanks, *The Subversive Gospel*, 90; Miller, "The Practices of Romans 1:26," 4–8, 10; also the majority of early Christian commentators on Romans, according to Martin, "Heterosexism and the Interpretation of Romans," 348 n40; Townsley, "Paul, the Goddess Religions, and Queer Sects," 708). Frederickson, "Natural and Unnatural Use in Romans," 201, claims that he did not find any examples of the term "use" in descriptions of homoerotic activities between women. Brooten, *Love between Women*, 189–302), however, believes that 1:26 refers to homoerotic acts between women, which she backs up with numerous references to such acts in Greco-Roman authors: "In sum, early Christianity was born into a world in which people from various walks of life acknowledged that women could have sexual contact with other women" (ibid., 190).

68. Martin, "Heterosexism and the Interpretation of Romans 1:18–32," 343–47; Stowers, "Paul and Self-Mastery," 544.

69. Stowers, "Paul and Self-Mastery," 529.

70. Paul's harsh words of pronouncing divine judgement on idolatry rest on the assumption of maintaining proper social structures, and the failure of which will mean disorder. "[I]n failing to respect the proper boundaries, they themselves fall into disarray" (Berger, *Identity and Experience in the New Testament*, 146).

71. Paul used ἐπιθυμία in a positive sense (cf. Phil 1:23; 1 Th 2:17) but not in a sexual context (Martin, "Heterosexism and the Interpretations of Romans," 347). Platonist and Stoic thinking went further and prescibed ἀπάθεια (passionlessness or restraint), or "freedom from emotions" according to Liddell, Scott, and Jones (*A Greek English Lexicon*, 174). Paul did combine "use" with "natural" in describing the curtailing (or even absence) of passion, as one of the three forms of "natural" sex: procreative sex, sex preserving male superiority and sex devoid of passion (Fredrickson, "Natural and Unnatural Use in Romans," 205–6).

72. Martin, "Heterosexism and the Interpretation of Romans 1:18–32," 347. Swancutt, "The Disease of Effemination," 197–205.

(ἐπιθυμίαις, 1:24),[73] passions (πάθη, 1:26) and infatuation (ὀρέξει, 1:27), and being inflamed (ἐξεκαύθησαν, 1:27): "[v]erses 24–27 scream this language of passion."[74] Paul's disquiet about desire as such—neither a distinction between homosexual and heterosexual desire nor privileging heterosexual desire—is at issue in Rom 1.

Paul shared with his contemporaries a concern for "natural use" of sex. Natural sex partly entailed measures to ensure that passions are kept in check and under control; unnatural did not imply "disoriented desire" but "inordinate desire."[75] In Paul's argument in Rom 1 homoeroticism becomes the example of corruption wrought by desire. Homoeroticism represented excess and loss of control and subverted the conventional male-female hierarchy rather than representing a different form of desire.[76] In Paul's thinking, sex was primarily troublesome where it could no longer be controlled, or when it was not regulated and limited by satisfaction.[77]

Natural was defined in the first century not by reference to a scientific-biological model typical of the twenty-first century. "Unnatural" referred to unconventional practices, actions out of the ordinary or contrary to accepted social practices.[78] In contemporary literature, φύσις or φυσικός was generally

73. The plural may indicate a deviation from the Stoic notion of desire as root cause of the human predicament, but rather the biblical notions of desires and passions, i e "the complex and devious crosscurrents of human motivation involving the entire person" (Jewett, "The Social Context and Implications of Homoerotic Refrences in Romans," 225).

74. Cf. Swancutt, "The Disease of Effemination, 202, on the danger of overindulgence in sex. Bodily vices are altogether absent from the long vice list in Rom 1:29–31, in contrast to antisocial behaviour (Jewett, "The Social Context and Implications of Homoerotic References in Romans," 226). The list focuses on social rather than individual vices. The first item in the vice list (ἀδικία, 1:29) *injustice*—a relational concept—confirms the recognised paradigm of social, relational vices in the ancient ethical tradition (Engberg-Pedersen, *Paul and the Stoics*, 211; cf. Swancutt, "Sexy Stoics and the Rereading of Romans," 66). Individual and social vices were seen connected by what philosophers saw as the underlying motif of social vices: self-directedness, or the individual's concerns for his or her own body, to the exclusion of others

75. Martin, "Heterosexism and the Interpretation of Romas," 293, 342, n56) argues that it was a minority of Greco-Roman authors who contemplated the complete absence of desire in marriage. Frederickson puts more emphasis on the ancients' concern to control desire (2000).

76. Martin, "Heterosexism and the Interpretation of Romans," 348.

77. Engberg-Pedersen, *Paul and the Stoics*, 210–11.

78. Nature in the first century and in the twentieth century presupposes different cultural assumptions, worldviews and symbolic universes (Szesnat, "In Fear of Androgyny," 40). Invoking the notion of "divine creation" to conclude towards a supra-cultural design of God in Pauline thought (cf. Wright, "Homosexuality," 413) is untenable at least since Paul's argument is perched on Hellenistic Jewish thought and custom where

used for two categories of meaning: origin or constitution, and secondly, in medical-technical and vulgar language with reference to the genitals. The reference to genitals is not picked up by the translation "natural *relations*"[79] (τὴν φυσικὲν χρῆσιν, 1:26, 27) which rather should be rendered as "natural *uses/acts*," i.e. acts that are in accordance with the social hierarchy of society, the conventional way of acting.[80] Paul's use of "unnatural" with reference to *actions* is borne out also by his reference to desire.[81] "[χ]ρῆσις does not refer to a relation carried out in the medium of sexual pleasure but the activity of the desiring subject, usually male, performed on the desired object, female or male."[82] To translate "contrary to nature" as though Romans' reference is to the wrong object choice will be anachronistic (Martin 1995: 332–55).

Finally, the general appeal to φύσις (*nature*) as decisive argument is not helpful. In other instances where Paul used the same rationale in his argument (e.g., 1 Cor 11:13–15, regarding hairstyles; Rom 11:17–24 especially 24, on the unnaturalness of the inclusion of Gentiles among believers), biblical interpreters generally agree on its contextually determined nature and relevance.[83] The natural use of sexual desire was often treated

---

homoerotic activity was not tolerated, within a Greco-Roman world with varying opinions amidst an apparent decreasing prevalence of homoeroticsm.

79. Or, natural sexual intercourse for which τὴν φυσικὲν χρῆσιν is a euphemism (cf. also Szesnat, "In Fear of Androgyny," 39 n8). The expression in the singular is mostly translated in the plural.

80. The nature argument heard so often in the New Testament rested on a gendered cosmology, which in terms of sexually prescribed active and passive roles, determining roles regarding penetration and, conversely, the particular penetration role determined gender. With reference to today's context Countryman, "New Testament Sexual Ethics and Today's World," 522, argues, "To deny an entire class of human beings the right peaceably and without harming others to pursue the kind of sexuality that corresponds to their nature is a perversion of the gospel".

81. Martin, "Heterosexism and the Interpretation of Romans," 341.

82. Frederickson, "Natural and Unnatural Use in Romans," 199. The gender of the sexual partner is hardly important as his/er social status and the sexual act have to conform to the "social status hierarchy" of the participants. Philo of Alexandria laments that "gender-bending" will result in "men appearing as women," which might be reflected in the "shameless acts" or Rom 1:27. Ἄρσενες ἐν ἄρσενιν τὴν ἀσχημοσύνην κατεργαζόμενοι can also be translated "men effecting shamelessness in men," or "men working genitals in men"—in the LXX ἀσχημοσύνη is a euphemism for genitals (e.g., Lev 18) (Szesnat, "In Fear of Androgyny," 39 n9; 43), as well as for genital nakedness and intercourse (Exod 20:26; cf. Rev 16:15) Swancutt, "Sexy Stoics and the Rereading of Romans," 64.

83. The various terms for illicit sexual activity, expressed in different ways in the NT including various technical terms such as μοιχεία (adultery), ἀσέλγεια (sexual immorality, 2 Cor 2:21; Gal 5:19; Rom 13:13) or, in particular, πορνεία (sexual immorality), do not appear in Rom 1. However, Paul did use the word ἀκαθαρσία (Rom 1:24) to describe what he believed God delivered those who refused to acknowledge him,

in the Greco-Roman world as analogous to the natural use of hunger, since both were to be limited by satisfaction: pleasure of sex and a full stomach were of a kind![84] Gluttony was unnatural not because of perverted desire but because of indulging in excess which resulted in loss of control. In short, when serving variety through such cravings, uncontrolled eating was also seen to lead to brutality and disorder.[85] Using words such as "homosexuality" or "unnatural relations" in translations of Rom 1 do not do justice to the text but rather indicates a modern worldview.

Ἀρσενοκοῖται and μαλακοὶ (1 Cor 6:9/1 Tim 1:10)

Brief reference can also be made to two terms, ἀρσενοκοῖται and μαλακοὶ which Paul included in the vice list of 1 Cor 6:9–10; the first term also forms part of the list of deutero-Pauline 1 Tim 1:10. Given their placement in these lists, both terms are used in pejorative and stereotyped rather than descriptive sense, and pose a challenge to translators. But again translations often reflect current day concerns rather than the words' entrenchment in a first-century context. The translation of ἀρσενοκοῖται (1 Corinthians 6 / 1 Timothy 1), probably a Pauline neologism for active males in a homoerotic context, is sometimes translated as "behaving like a homosexual" (cf. CEV) or as "sodomites" (NRSV). Μαλακοὶ (1 Corinthians 6), "effeminates" may have referred to a passive male in a homoerotic context or a (male) prostitute and is often translated as "(sexual) pervert" (cf. CEV, GNB, RSV). Such translations, again, are informed by modern and heteronormative understandings of sexuality with its homosexual-heterosexual dividing line, rather than a sexual boundary that was constituted through social status and determined by activity as opposed to passivity.[86]

---

into: "uncleanness" or "impurity." It is a Pauline word for impurity in settings of sexual immorality, e.g., 1 Th 4:7; 2 Cor 12:21; Gal 5:19; Rom 1:24; 6:19 (cf. Eph 4:19; 5:3; Col 3:5)—elsewhere in the NT, ἀκαθαρσία appears only in Matt 23:27. But impurity is used as part of the broader argument of Rom 1:18–32 which describes the results of and not the reason for idolatry (Punt "Sin as Sex or Sex as Sin?").

84. At the time, sexual activity was no more but also no less dangerous than having a meal, and eating habits were as much regulated as sexual activity. The relationship between texts in the Hebrew Bible on food and those on sex, and in particular texts comparing food and sex, makes it important to consider food and sex in relation to one another (Stone, *Practicing Safer Texts*), also in NT texts.

85. Frederickson, "Natural and Unnatural Use in Romans," 199; Martin, "Heterosexism and the Interpretation of Romans," 344; Punt, "Translating the Bible in South Africa"; Swancutt, "Sexy Stoics and the Rereading of Romans, 62, 64–65.

86. Stegemann, "Paul and the Sexual Mentality of His World," 164. Martin (38–43; cf. Johnson, "Empire and Order," 167) argues that ἀρσενοκοῖται was used in contexts

To retain the stigmatizing of ἀρσενοκοῖται and μαλακοὶ it would therefore be important to translate with derisive terms but whose derision reflects first and not twenty-first century thinking and practices. It is possible to use for ἀρσενοκοῖται a term such as "men-sleepers" and for μαλακοὶ "softies" or "pansies" may carry the appropriate connotations of availability, lack of control, and susceptibility to desire.[87] A chauvinist approach to human sexuality complete with sanctioned male prerogative and regulated female submission ties in with a literalist appropriation of Romans 1.[88] Paul's argument that homoerotic acts are unnatural because it subverts the natural order of male-female hierarchy[89] would not allow the modern reader to escape the accompanying gender ideology of the inferiority of the woman, the seducible seductress, whose dangerous sexual ability should be controlled by male sexual power.

Conclusion

Cultural studies' attention to both first-century sexual norms and practices and a long history of interpretation is neither a guarantee for proper translation, nor for addressing the latent link between misogynist and homophobic impulses,[90] but provides a more responsible and accountable point of departure for translation and interpretation. Mine is not an argument for a specific translation approach as though a proper choice of theory would either eliminate or set aside cultural, ideological and other considerations, but for cultural studies awareness in translation theory and practice. Culture wars are fought not only in classical studies but on a broader front, with pressure also on translation work to consider its varied intersections with cultural studies. If the relationship between text and translator is as strong as

---

reflecting economic injustice.

87. Space does not allow attention for the translations used for texts in 2 Pet and Jude re Sodom.

88. Davies, "New Testament Ethics and Ours," 315–32.

89. Discussions on homoerotic acts in the NT should consider as serious the pervasiveness of patriarchal ideology and practice at the time, as well as the serious concerns about biological productivity (Van Wijk-Bos, "How to Read What We Read," 70). "Injustice toward the vulnerable neighbour, on the basis of human-made, time-bound, patriarchal rules, constitutes a practice of idolatry in elevating cultural norms to the status of divine commandment" (ibid., 73.)

90. Heteronormativity goes beyond "compulsory heterosexuality" (Plaskow, "Authority, Resistance, and Transformation," 49ff; cf. Loughlin, "Biblical Bodies," 24–25) and is maintained by and therefore biased towards patriarchy (cf. Punt, "Translating the Bible in South Africa").

expressed in the axiom that in translation we create the texts that create us,[91] gender considerations in translation studies are neither inconsequential nor of mere academic interest. It is not a question whether translation work and cultural studies intersect, but rather to what degree, in which ways, to what effect and how such intersections are acknowledged and handled.[92]

Opting for cultural studies is not about expressing a normative claim but privileging an epistemology which engages culture seriously. One should not turn a blind eye to the cultural turn's tendency towards the balkanisation of knowledge, especially when conservative or traditional scholars withdraw to their "bounded communities" away from the public realm. Nor should liberal scholars' uncritical engagement with popular culture be celebrated, or social location and identity be allowed to replace reason giving as the source of legitimation and legitimization for our positions.[93] However, acknowledgement of the intersections between cultural and translation studies allows for the required attention to be given to central concerns such as gender-appropriate translations of NT texts.

Bibliography

Aasgaard, Reidar. *My Beloved Brothers and Sisters: Christian Siblingship in Paul.* Studies of the New Testament and Its World. London: T. & T. Clark, 2004.

Aichele, George. *The Control of Biblical Meaning: Canon as Semiotic Mechanism.* Harrisburg, PA: Trinity, 2001.

Bailey, Randall C., and Tina Pippin. "Race, Class, and the Politics of Bible Translation: Introduction." *Semeia* 76 (1996) 1–6.

Balch, David L. "Paul, Families, and Households." In *Paul in the Greco-Roman World: A Handbook*, edited by J. Paul Sampley, 258–92. Harrisburg, PA: Trinity, 2003.

Berger, Klaus. *Identity and Experience in the New Testament.* Translated by Charles Muenchow. Minneapolis: Fortress, 2003.

Bernstein, Richard J. *Beyond Objectivism and Relativism: Science, Hermeneutics and Practice.* Oxford: Blackwell, 1983.

Boer, Roland. *Last Stop before Antarctica: The Bible and Postcolonialism in Australia.* 2nd ed. Semeia Studies 64. Atlanta: Society of Biblical Literature, 2008.

91. Elliott and Boer, "Introduction," 1.

92. Since translations are often interfaces between competing cultural and ideological positions, the danger of bending a translation because of prevailing target norms is real (cf. Harvey, "Events and Horizons," 43–69).

93. Davaney, "Theology and the Turn to Cultural Analysis," 10. Another danger is obscure language: "Too often . . . the cultural turn seems to involve a linguistic turn . . . towards a gestural use of language that seems designed to cloak any meaning with wispy veils of unclarity" (Louth, "Review," 215).

Brooten, Bernadette J. *Love Between Women: Early Christian Responses to Female Homoeroticism*. Chicago Series on Sexuality, History, and Society. Chicago: University of Chicago Press, 1996.

Carter, Warren. *John and Empire: Initial Explorations*. New York: T. & T. Clark, 2008.

Castelli, Elizabeth. "Paul on Women and Gender." In *Women and Christian Origins*, edited by Ross S. Kraemer and Mary Rose D'Angelo, 221–35. Oxford: Oxford University Press, 1999.

Chow, John K. "Patronage in Roman Corinth." In *Paul and Empire: Religion and Power in Roman Imperial Society*, edited by Richard A. Horsley, 104–25. Harrisville, PA: Trinity, 1997.

Countryman, L. William. "New Testament Sexual Ethics and Today's World." In *Sexuality: A Reader*, edited by Karen Lebacqz and David Sinacore-Guinn, 515–43. Cleveland: Pilgrim, 1999.

Bible and Culture Collective. *The Postmodern Bible*. New Haven: Yale University Press, 1995.

Davaney, Sheila G. "Theology and the Turn to Cultural Analysis." In *Converging on Culture: Theologians in Dialogue with Cultural Analysis and Criticism*, edited by Delvin Brown, et al., 3–16. New York: Oxford University Press, 2001.

Davies, Margaret. "New Testament Ethics and Ours: Homosexuality and Sexuality in Romans 1:26–27." *BibInt* 3 (1995) 315–31.

Derrida, Jacques. "Des Tours des Babel." In *Acts of Religion*, edited by Gil Anidjar, 102–34. New York: Routledge, 2002.

Holleran, Claire, and April Pudsey eds. *Demography and the Graeco-Roman World: New Insights and Approaches*. Cambridge: Cambridge University Press, 2011.

Dube, Musa W. "'What I Have Written, I Have Written' (John 19:22)?" In *Interpreting the New Testament in Africa*, edited by Mary N. Getui, et al., 145–63. Nairobi: Acton, 2001.

Du Toit, Andrie B. "The Ecclesiastical Situation of the First Generation Roman Christians." *Teologiese Studies/Theological Studies* 53 (1997) 498–512.

Easthope, Alan. "Cultural Studies in the United Kingdom." In *The Johns Hopkins Guide to Literary Theory & Criticism*, edited by Michael Groden and Martin Kreiswirth, 176–79. Baltimore: Johns Hopkins University Press, 1994.

Elliott, Neil. *Liberating Paul: The Justice of God and the Politics of the Apostle*. Bible & Liberation. 1994. Reprint, Minneapolis: Fortress, 2005.

Elliott, Scott S., and Roland Boer. "Introduction." In *Ideology, Culture and Translation*, edited by Scott S. Elliott and Roland Boer, 1–10. Semeia Studies 69. Atlanta: Society of Biblical Literature, 2012.

Engberg-Pedersen, Troels. *Paul and the Stoics*. Louisville: Westminster John Knox, 2000.

Evans, John H. "Worldviews or Social Groups As the Source of Moral Value Attributes: Implications for the Culture Wars Thesis." *Sociological Forum* 12 (1997) 371–404.

Frederickson, David E. "Natural and Unnatural Use in Romans 1:24–27: Paul and the Philosophic Critique of Eros." In *Homosexuality, Science and the "Plain Sense" of Scripture*, edited by David L. Balch, 197–222. 2000. Reprint, Eugene, OR: Wipf & Stock, 2007.

Free Dictionary. "Identity Politics." No pages. Cited 15 January 2014. http://www.thefreedictionary.com/identity+politics.

Glancy, Jennifer A. "House Reading and Field Readings: The Discourse of Slavery and Biblical/Cultural Studies." In *Biblical Studies/Cultural Studies. The Third Sheffield Colloquium*, edited by J. Cheryl Exum and Stephen D. Moore, 460–77. Journal for the Study of the Old Testament Supplements 266. Sheffield: Sheffield Academic, 1998.

Hanks, Tom. *The Subversive Gospel: A New Testament Commentary on Liberation.* Translated by John P. Doner. Cleveland: Pilgrim, 2000.

Harvey, Keith. "'Events' and 'Horizons': 'Reading Ideology in the 'Bindings' of 'Translations.'" In *Apropos of Ideology: Translation Studies on Ideology-Ideologies in Translation Studies*, edited by Maria C. Pérez, 43–69. Manchester: St Jerome. 2003.

Hawthorne, Gerald F. *Philippians.* Word Biblical Commentary 43. Dallas: Word, 2004.

Heyes, Cressida. "Identity Politics." In *The Stanford Encyclopedia of Philosophy* (Spring 2012 Edition). No pages. Online: http://plato.stanford.edu/archives/spr2012/entries/identity-politics/.

Jewett, Robert. "The Social Context and Implications of Homoerotic References in Romans 1:24–27." In *Homosexuality, Science and the "Plain Sense" of Scripture*, edited by David L. Balch, 223–41. 2000. Reprint, Eugene, OR: Wipf & Stock, 2007.

Johnson, W Stacey. "Empire and Order: The Gospel and Same-Gender Relationships." *BTB* 37 (2007) 161–73.

Lassen, Eva Marie. "The Roman Family: Ideal and Metaphor." In *Constructing Early Christian Families: Family as Social Reality and Metaphor*, edited by Halvor Moxnes, 103–20. New York: Routledge, 1997.

Liddell, Henry G., et al. *A Greek-English Lexicon.* 9th ed. Oxford: Clarendon, 1983.

Lopez, Davina. "Visualizing Significant Otherness. Reimagining Paul(ine Studies) through Hybrid Lenses." In *The Colonized Apostle: Paul through Postcolonial Eyes*, edited by Christopher D. Stanley, 74–94. Minneapolis: Fortress, 2011.

Loughlin, Gerard. "Biblical Bodies." *T&S* 12 (2005) 9–27.

Louth, Andrew. "Review." *T&S* 13 (2007) 214–15.

Lundin, Robert. *The Culture of Interpretation: Christian Faith and the Modern World.* Grand Rapids: Eerdmans, 1993.

MacDonald, Margaret Y. "Reading Real Women through the Undisputed Letters of Paul." In *Women and Christian Origins*, edited by Ross S. Kraemer and Mary Rose D'Angelo, 199–220. Oxford: Oxford University Press, 1999.

Martin, Dale B. "Heterosexism and the Interpretation of Romans 1:18–32." *BibInt* 3 (1995) 332–55.

———. "Introduction." In *The Cultural Turn in Late Ancient Studies: Gender, Asceticism, and Historiography*, edited by Dale B. Martin and Patricia Cox Miller, 1–21. Durham: Duke University Press, 2005.

———. *Sex and the Single Savior: Gender and Sexuality in Biblical Interpretation.* Louisville: Westminster John Knox, 2006.

Miller, James E. "The Practices of Romans 1:26: Homosexual or Heterosexual?" *Novum Testamentum* 37 (1995) 1–11.

Myers, Charles D., Jr. "Romans, Epistle to the Romans." In *The Anchor Bible Dictionary*, edited by David Noel Freedman, 5:816–29. New York: Doubleday, 1992.

Neyrey, Jerome H. "God, Benefactor and Patron: The Major Cultural Model for Interpreting the Deity in Greco-Roman Antiquity." *JSNT* 27 (2005) 465–92.

Nissinen, Martti. *Homoeroticism in the Biblical World: A Historical Perspective.* Translated by Kirsi Stjerna. Minneapolis: Fortress, 1998.

Nord, Christiane. "Dealing with Purposes in Intercultural Communication: Some Methodological Considerations." *Revista Alicantina de Estudios Ingleses* 14 (2001) 151–66.

———. "Function and Loyalty in Bible Translation." In *Apropos of Ideology: Translation Studies on Ideology-Ideologies in Translation Studies,* edited by Marie C. Pérez, 89–112. Manchester: St Jerome, 2003.

———. *Text Analysis in Translation: Theory, Method, and Didactic Application of a Model for Translation-Oriented Text Analysis.* 2nd ed. Translated by Christiane Nord and Penelope Sparrow. Amsterdammer Publikationen zur Sprache und Literatur 94. Amsterdam: Rodopi, 2005.

Osiek, Carolyn. "The Politics of Patronage and the Politics of Kinship: The Meeting of the Ways." *BTB* 39 3 (2009) 143–52.

Pérez, Marie C. "Introduction." In *Apropos of Ideology. Translation Studies on Ideology-Ideologies in Translation Studies.* Edited by Marie C. Pérez, 1–22. Manchester: St Jerome, 2003.

Petterson, Christina. "Configuring the Language to Convert the People: Translating the Bible in Greenland." In *Ideology, Culture and Translation,* edited by Scott S. Elliott and Roland Boer, 139–50. Semeia Studies 69. Atlanta: Society of Biblical Literature, 2012.

Plaskow, Judith. "Authority, Resistance, and Transformation. Jewish Feminist Reflections on Good Sex." In *Body and Soul: Rethinking Sexuality as Justice-Love,* edited by Marvin M. Ellison and Sylvia Thorson-Smith, 45–60. Cleveland: Pilgrim, 2003.

Porter, Stanley E. "Assessing Translation Theory: Beyond Literal and Dynamic Equivalence." In *Translating the New Testament: Text, Translation, Theology,* edited by Stanley E. Porter and Mark J. Boda, 117–45. Grand Rapids: Eerdmans, 2009.

Punt, Jeremy. "He Is Heavy, and He's My Brother: Unravelling Fraternity in Paul (Galatians)." *Neotestamentica* 46 1 (2012) 153–71.

———. "Rom 1:18–32 Amidst the Gay Debate: Interpretive Options." *Teologiese Studies/Theological Studies* 63 (2007) 965–82.

———. "Sin as Sex or Sex as Sin? Rom 1:18–32 as First Century CE Theological Argument." *Neotestamentica* 42 (2008) 73–92.

———. "Translating the Bible in South Africa: Challenges to Contextuality and Responsibility." In *Bible Translation on the Threshold of the Twenty-First Century: Authority, Reception, Culture and Religion,* edited by Athalya Brenner and Jan Willem van Henten, 94–124. JSOT Supplements 313. Sheffield: Sheffield Academic, 2002.

———. "Whose Bible, Mine or Yours? Contested Ownership and Bible Translation in Southern Africa." *HTS* 60.1–2 (2004) 307–28.

Pym, Anthony. "Review." *Erudit* 6 2 (1993) 184–90.

Rowland, Christopher. "Open Thy Mouth for the Dumb: A Task for the Exegete of Holy Scripture." *BibInt* 1 (1993) 228–45.

Schäffner, Christina. "Third Ways and New Centres. Ideological Unity or Difference?" In *Apropos of Ideology: Translation Studies on Ideology-Ideologies in Translation Studies,* edited by Marie C. Pérez, 23–41. Manchester: St Jerome, 2003.

Schüssler Fiorenza, Elisabeth. *Rhetoric and Ethic: The Politics of Biblical Studies.* Minneapolis: Fortress, 1999.

Segovia, Fernando F. "The Bible as a Text in Cultures: An Introduction." In *The Peoples' Bible,* edited by Curtis Paul DeYoung, et al., 23–30. Minneapolis: Fortress, 2009.

————. *Decolonizing Biblical Studies: A View from the Margins*. Maryknoll, NY: Orbis, 2000.

Smith, Abraham. "Cultural Studies." Paper presented at the SBL International Meeting, Amsterdam, July 2012.

Stanley, Christopher D. "Paul the Ethnic Hybrid? Postcolonial Perspectives on Paul's Ethnic Categorizations." In *The Colonized Apostle: Paul through Postcolonial Eyes*, edited by Christopher D. Stanley, 110–26. Minneapolis: Fortress, 2011.

Stegemann, Wolfgang. "Paul and the Sexual Mentality of His World." *BTB* 23 (1993) 161–66.

Stine, Philip C., ed. *Bible Translation and the Spread of the Church: The Last 200 Years*. 2nd ed. Studies in Christian Mission 2. Leiden: Brill, 1992.

Stone, Ken. *Practicing Safer Texts: Food, Sex and Bible in Queer Perspective*. Queering Theology Series. New York: T. & T. Clark, 2005.

Stowers, Stanley K. "Paul and Self-Mastery." In *Paul in the Greco-Roman World: A Handbook*, edited by J. Paul Sampley, 524–550. Harrisburg, PA: Trinity, 2003.

Swancutt, Diane M. "The Disease of Effemination: The Charge of Effeminacy and the Verdict of God (Romans 1:18–2:16)." In *New Testament Masculinities*, edited by Stephen Moore and Janice Capel Anderson, 193–233. Semeia Studies 45. Atlanta: Society of Biblical Literature, 2003.

Swancutt, Diane M. "Sexy Stoics and the Rereading of Romans 1.18–2:16." In *A Feminist Companion to Paul*, edited by Amy Jill Levine and Marianne Blickenstaff, 42–73. Feminist Companion to the New Testament and Early Christian Writings 6. London: T. & T. Clark, 2004.

Szesnat, Holger. "In Fear of Androgyny: Theological Reflections on Masculinity and Sexism, Male Homosexuality and Homophobia, Romans 1:24–27 and Hermeneutics (A Response to Alexander Venter)." *JTSA* 93 (1995) 32–50.

Thompson, John B. *Ideology and Modern Culture*. Cambridge, MA: Polity, 1990.

Townsley, Jeramy. "Paul, the Goddess Religions, and Queer Sects: Romans 1:23–28." *JBL* 130 (2011) 707–28.

Van der Merwe, Christo H. J. "The Bible in Afrikaans: A Direct Translation: A New Type of Church Bible." http://dx.doi.org/10.4102/hts. v68i1.1204.

Vanhoozer, Kevin J., et al., eds. *Everyday Theology: How to Read Cultural Texts and Interpret Trends*. Cultural Exegesis. Grand Rapids: Baker Academic, 2007.

Van Wijk-Bos, Johanna W. H. "How to Read What We Read: Discerning Good News about Sexuality in Scripture." In *Body and Soul: Rethinking Sexuality as Justice-Love*, edited by Marvin M. Ellison and Sylvia Thorson-Smith, 61–77. Cleveland: Pilgrim, 2003.

Werner, Eberhard. "Toward an Ethical Code in Bible Translation Consulting." *JT* 8 (2012) 1–8.

Whelan, Caroline F. "Amica Pauli: The Role of Phoebe in the Early Church." *JSNT* 49 (1993) 67–85.

White, John L. *The Apostle of God: Paul and the Promise of Abraham*. Peabody, MA: Hendrickson, 1999.

Wright, David F. "Homosexuality." In *Dictionary of Paul and His Letters*, edited by Gerald F. Hawthorne et al., 413–15. Downers Grove, IL: InterVarsity, 1993.

PART III

Savage Readings of Colonialized African Bibles

7

The Bible in the Bush

The First "Literate" Batswana Bible Readers

Musa W. Dube

> "You should know that when we read our Bible we change the let-
> ters with our mouths." —Sebotseng Loatile, Letter to the editor of
> *Mahoko a Becuana* (1890) 33

Introduction: A Storyteller Meets Storytellers!

In this article, I drew my title from Laura Bohannan's celebrated essay,
"Shakespeare in the Bush," which is where I derived the title: "The Bible
in the Bush." It is this essay Laura Bohannan, an American anthropologist from Oxford, who was on her second field trip to the Tiv in Nigeria
to observe some of their rare ceremonies. She had, mistakenly chosen an
inappropriate time for field work. She arrives when the swamps were rising,
which hindered communication and interaction between different homesteads. Up until the swamps drop and ploughing begins, the Tiv, hosting
Bohannan, amused themselves with drinking beer, telling stories, singing
and dancing. There were no ceremonies performed because the swamps
cut communication between various homesteads. And so Bohannan found
herself with plenty of time in her hands and very little to do save to read a
copy of Hamlet that was given to her, following an argument with a friend,
who held that Americans tend to misunderstand Shakespeare, "a very English poet," for they "easily misinterpret the universal by misunderstanding
the particular"[1]. Bohannan protested this perspective holding that, "human
nature is pretty much the same the whole world over, at least the general
plot and motivation of the greater tragedies would always be clear—ev-

---

1. See Laura Bohannan, "Shakespeare in the Bush," 28–33.

erywhere—although some details of custom might have to be explained and difficulties of translation might produce other slight changes. To end an argument they could not conclude, the friend gave Bohannan a copy of *Hamlet* "to study in the African bush," hoping that it would lift her mind "above its primitive surroundings" and that with prolonged meditation she might "achieve the grace of correct interpretation," namely the English one[2]. The more Bohannan read *Hamlet,* the more she got convinced that "*Hamlet* had only one possible interpretation, and that one is universally obvious."[3]

It happened that one morning the Tiv invited Bohannan to tell them a story. Thinking to herself that, "here was my chance to prove *Hamlet* universally intelligible"[4]. Bohannan accepted to tell a story. And so she began in their own style of telling a story, "Not yesterday, not yesterday, long ago a thing occurred. One night three men were keeping watch outside the homestead of the great chief, when suddenly they saw the former chief approach them"[5]. Disruption. They ask. "Why was he no longer their chief?" "He was dead," Bohannan explained[6]. Dead? Dead people do not walk according to the Tiv beliefs. So one of the elders make a point of correction: "Of course, it wasn't the dead chief. It was an omen . . . . Go on"[7]. Altogether, I counted up to nineteen questions they posed by the Tiv to Bohannan, besides commentary, suggestions and co-telling. This was the trend of their listening. They questioned, objected, commented and provided explanations for the events that motivated the plot, quite freely placing the story within their cultural worldviews and then urging Bohannan to continue with the story. Midway through their active listening and the rewriting of Hamlet Bohannan writes "Hamlet was again a good story to them, but *it no longer seemed quite the same story to me.*"[8]

Quite shaken by the elder's self-assured explanation Bohannan continues, "One of these three was a man who knew things"[9]. This was the closest translation that she could find for a scholar, but unfortunately it also meant a witch among the Tiv. When she explained that the scholar associated the appearance of the dead chief with Hamlet, his son, the elders, disapproved that such omens were issues to be handled by chiefs and elders not

2. Ibid., 1.
3. Ibid., 2.
4. Ibid.
5. Ibid., 3.
6. Ibid.
7. Ibid., 4.
8. Ibid., 10; emphasis added.
9. Ibid., 4.

youngsters. They were of the opinion that at the most Hamlet should have consulted a specialized diviner to clarify for him about the death of his father and then approached elders thereafter for them to handle the case for him. They began to debate among themselves and to provide reasons why Hamlet did not follow this path. They concluded that the diviner would have been afraid to divulge information about the most powerful man in the land, King Claudius.

My Response and Implications for Translations

There is so much that can be said about Bohannan's narrative from various perspectives, than I have been able to summarize. Like Bohannan who had crossed many boundaries to reach the Tiv and found herself hedged by the swampy season, "the number of borders being crossed in one translation are always multiple"[10] as *Hamlet* in the bush amply demonstrates.

Maria Tymoczko holds that the case of Hamlet in West Africa . . . illustrates resistance to translation and transfer of concepts ('ghost'), values ('chastity of Ophelia'), customs (the European period of mourning), motivations (Hamlet's madness), material culture (swords for machetes) and plot sequence, as well as rhetorical and linguistic structures. The awareness of such resistance to the uptake and translation of oral material, as well as better understanding of the actual working dynamic between passive and active bearers of traditional cultures has led to re-evaluations of the process of survival, transmission and translation of oral literature"[11]

Tymoczko further underlines that research in translation in the past two decades indicates that "translation is a form of literary refraction: translated texts are processed texts, texts that are manipulated between literary interfacings, illuminating the sociological, ideological and literary constants at work behind the manipulations involved in translation"[12]. Nonetheless, Tymoczko admits that "despite the historical documentation and theoretical build up for more than a decade now, the idea that translation involves manipulation—-ideological and poetic processing remains shocking to traditionalists, students and teachers alike, who persist in the belief in a value-free translation process."[13]

When I first read "Shakespeare in the Bush," I was highly impressed by the Tiv community. They were an empowered audience, who listened

10. See Gentzler, *Contemporary Translation Theories*, 203.

11. See Tymoczko, *Translation in Oral Tradition*, 46–55.

12. Ibid., 46.

13 Ibid.

critically, questioning, commenting, making suggestions, thereby re-writing the story within their own cultural worldview. While initially Bohannan thought her task was merely to find some 'equivalent' words such as using great chief for king or machete for swords, the task involved much more—it was, as the translation studies have underlined that the translation of any work is not just formal, dynamic or functional equivalents of words, phrases, sentences, meaning or effect. Rather translation work or processes involve, "the translation of cultures," fully informed by the agendas of patrons, publishers and purposes they serve. As amply demonstrated by "Shakespeare in the Bush" Translation Studies "no longer defines translation as an activity that takes place between two languages, but views it as an interaction between cultures"[14]. The Tiv had asked for Bohannan's story and threatened not tell her any of their stories unless she tells them stories from her culture. For them it was an exchange of stories, within their space, within their stories and within their own cultures. The Tiv acknowledged Bohannan language limitation, saying, "You must explain what we do not understand, as we do when we tell you our stories."[15] As an anthropologist, Bohannan was a story collector proper. She had not forgotten that as an anthropologist she came to collect primarily the African stories for the European audience. Thus the moment they said madness is caused by witchcraft and creatures in the forest, Bohannan said, "I stopped being a storyteller and took out my notebook and demanded to be told more about these two causes of madness. Even while they spoke," she says, "I jotted down notes, I tried to calculate the effect of this new factor on the plot."[16]

It was quite intriguing to me as an African, when Bohannan reached a point where, while her audience was enjoying the story, to her, it was no longer the same story. At this point I said, "Laura Bohannan welcome to the world!" For us Africans who come from largely oral communities, and in a historical context where the first written stories—whether they are cultures, history, religion, language—were written by westerners, especially during colonial times, it has been an excruciating pain to read the anthropological record, the travellers story, the missionary record, for the most part one cannot recognise herself. It is a different story, precisely because it is an African story that is grafted and interpreted within a western culture. Unfortunately, for the colonial context, which entailed the collection of the stories of the Other, who is different, was a time, when the other was already despised. So

---

14. Gentzler, *Contemporary Translation Theories*, 190.

15. Bohannan, *Shakespeare in the Bush*, 3.

16. Ibid., 8.

the refraction of our stories was not only informed by western cultures, but racism and eurocentrism.

Similarly, when I first read, "Shakespeare in the Bush," I also wondered what kind of Bible translations would we have if our translators and communities were culturally empowered citizens, who were involved in intra and inter-cultural activity; where there is more interactive intercourse between the source and the target text, not in the missionary style; where the target culture is supposedly always, submissively under, receiving male sperms from the source text—-the Biblical/westernised cultures—-but rather in a more interesting love-making were wrestling turns everybody, up down, sideways and all angles. What kind of Bible translations would we have? Well, do we desire this type of translation or do we build a hedge of theories, intuitions, policies, practices, ideologies, agendas, experts, publications and cultures that often mute the targeted communities as subjugated "recipient cultures?" "Shakespeare in the Bush" posits a model of translation as a public hearing. It posits a model that calls us to regard targeted communities and their cultures just as sacred as the stories we bring from other cultures. It posits a model where recipient/targeted communities are not the subjugated Other. Reading this story, I became quiet interested in those historical moments, when culturally-empowered communities first heard the Bible and the translations they embarked upon to bring the story home, and how such translational spaces were negotiated—if we can exegete them from missionary narratives. This, of course, leads me to the second part of my paper; namely, the response of the first literate Batswana readers to the Setswana Biblical translation. I have placed the word 'literate' in quotes to mark the fact that there is literacy in all cultures outside the westernised school system.

The First Batswana Biblical Readers

In this section, I seek to tell the story of the translated Setswana Bible and how the Batswana received the biblical story from the earliest translation presented to them. The translation was in stages, stretching from 1830, when the translation of the gospel of Luke was completed; to 1840 when the New Testament translation was completed to 1857 when the first complete Bible was first printed in Kuruman, located in present day South Africa. Since Translation Studies urges us to study the translators, their time, context, agenda, ideology, and patrons, a brief background of our Bible translator is in order. The Scottish missionary, Robert Moffat, who started his work in Southern Africa in 1817 is credited with translating the first Setswana Bible.

The academic records of Robert Moffat indicate that he was a gardener, who later trained as a farmer. He joined the London Missionary Society in 1816 and arrived in South Africa in 1817 to start his job,[17] obviously, his training was close to nothing—one year or less. As C. Doke points out, "Moffat had never trained as a linguist" (nor a biblical scholar, I must add) and "he came up against intricacies of Tswana"[18]. In addition, Robert Moffat carried out his work and translation during the height of modern colonialism, fully immersed in its thinking and attitudes towards the colonised.

How did the Batswana respond to the translation? To explore the latter, I will largely read the letters Batswana wrote to the editor of *Mahoko a Becwana*, a newspaper that was published by London Missionary Society (henceforth LMS) from Kuruman, between 1883–1896. A number of 'literate' Batswana wrote letters on various subjects, which gives us a window into how they responded to Setswana Bible translation. These letters were recently collected and made available in the volume *Words of Batswana: Letters to Mahoko a Becwana 1883–1896*. I will focus on those letters dealing with correct ways of writing Setswana, since the first written Setswana was associated with Bible translation. Perhaps the reader is wondering, how and why *Hamlet* is comparable to Setswana Bible. Just as *Hamlet* was a work of "a very English poet," the Setswana Bible, too was a work of a Scottish man, who was grafted in his worldview, which, at that time, was that of the British Empire. Would the Batswana readers demonstrate efforts to reclaim the Setswana culture like the Tiv of Nigeria? The analysis of their letters will greatly assist. In reading these letters, I seek to identify ways employed by the earliest Batswana Bible readers to resist colonising translations.

I must admit that comparing the Tiv with Batswana literate writers may be unfair on several levels. First, the Tiv had an opportunity to comment and rewrite the story of Hamlet prior to its written translation. The Batswana writers were only making comments to a completed translation— Robert Moffat does not give us an elaborate description of their engagement with the biblical story in the process of translation. Second, unlike the Tiv that Bohannan characterises as "pagans, who had no belief in individual afterlife"[19] most of the Batswana writers were converted Christians, who had already undergone training in mission schools. Third, while Tiv were seemingly oral, these Batswana were literate since they could write. Fourth, their letters, written between 1883–1896, were drafted almost four decades

17. Doke, *Scripture Translation*, 84–99.

18. Ibid., 85.

19. Bohannan, "Shakespeare in the Bush," explains that the Tiv, "unlike many of the neighbouring tribes . . . didn't believe in the survival after death," 10.

since Robert Moffat's New Testament appeared in 1840. But, since this LMS newspaper allowed them to express their views, was the first of its kind among Batswana speakers, we could say this is the first written response towards the translated version we have addressed to the missionaries and fellow Batswana. Well, forty years after the first New Testament publication and the debate was still hot! We may well say these Batswana writers had been waiting to exhale!

Although I have not had access to Batswana's first oral hearing and response to the biblical story, I, however, read Robert Moffat's 642 page-volume on *Missionary Labours and Scenes in Southern Africa*, a volume he published in 1842 in London, two years after he published the New Testament translation into Setswana. The volume amply indicates that in the first decades Batswana resisted the biblical story, displaying significant indifference, which was frustrating to missionaries. Moffat, thus observed that "although they received much instruction, they appeared never for a moment to have reflected upon it, nor to retain traces of it in their memories, which are generally very tenacious"[20]. To illustrate the point, he cites two examples: one from his friend and another, his adversary, the rain-maker. Munameets, whom he describes as very supportive and intelligent Bechuana man, who always travelled with him, yet just before his death he rhetorically pleaded incapacity to understand Moffat's teaching due to age, deferring such a task to the future generations. Munameets said, "Perhaps you may be able to make children remember your *mekhua* (customs)"[21]. The second case involved the speech of a rainmaker that received great applause leading Moffat to remark that "the poor missionary's argument drawn from the source of Divine truth, were thrown into the shade"[22]. Moffat narrates that "when we attempted to convince them of their state as sinners, they would boldly affirm with full belief in their innate rectitude that there was not a sinner in the tribe"[23] And so Moffat laments that, "Oh when shall the day-star shall arise in their hearts? We preach, we converse, we catechise, we pray, but without the least apparent success . . ."[24] These are largely reported ac-

---

20. Moffat, *Missionary Labours*, 244.

21. Ibid., 246.

22. Ibid., 247.

23. Moffat, *Missionary Labours*, 254. See Robert "Cultural Encroachment and Bible Translation," where he discusses a case of one missionary's attempt to deal with lack of guilt among his targeted audience in Latin America, by making a translation that said, the particular group "killed Jesus."

24. Moffat, *Missionary Labours*, 285. See Jean and Commaroff, *Of Revelation and Revolution*, where they show that in fact Batswana were very resistant to Christian conversion, until a time when they realised that they had lost autonomy to the ever

counts in Moffat's book, but I have not yet come across intense engagement concerning a particular biblical story, displaying dialogue, comparable to Bohannan's Tiv.[25] The letters to the editors, which began to come in 1883, the year that Moffat died, discussed his Bible translation, focusing on the orthography, the various dialects of Setswana, the correct way of writing Setswana and various Christian teachings that clashed with Setswana culture, are thus my source for now.

Setswana Bible Translation: "Whose Interests Are Served?"

Given his accounts of Batswana's disinterest and indifference towards biblical teaching, they hardly asked for the translation. What was the purpose of this translation, where the community was quite indifferent? Who commissioned it and who is served by such a translation? We can hardly place it in the hands and agenda of Batswana. As Part Mgadla and Stephen Volz point out,

> Most African-language publications in the nineteenth century were produced by European missionaries as part of a larger project to make the Bible and other Christian teachings more widely available to potential converts. This process began in southern Africa in the 1820s and 1830s with the publication of biblical excerpts, catechisms and other materials in Setswana, Sesotho, and Isxhosa. The first complete vernacular Bible was in Setswana published in 1857 by the LMS.[26]

The agenda behind the Bible translation lies outside Batswana's interest. It follows that it did not necessarily serve their interest or agenda. Obviously Robert Moffat's Setswana was not perfect when he undertook the translation. I am yet to identity literature that describes the indigenous people who helped him with the task. In his voluminous book, *Missionary Labours and Scene in Southern Africa*, which I as a native of that region can only describe as a "Text of Terror," speaks very disparagingly and bitterly of his interpreter for his poor translations, to a point where Moffat holds that

> a Missionary who commences giving direct instruction to the natives, though far from being competent in the language, is

---

encroaching forces of colonialism of their time.

25. See Comaroff and Comaroff, *Of Revelation and Revolution*, 228, attesting that some Bantu response to the biblical text was to regard the it as "an instrument of divination."

26. See Mgadla and Volz, trans. and eds., *Words of Batswana*.

proceeding on a safer ground than if he were employing an interpreter, who is not proficient in both languages, and who has not a tolerable understanding of the doctrines of the gospel. Trusting an ignorant and unqualified interpreter as attended with consequences, not ludicrous but dangerous to the very objects which lie nearest to the missionary's heart . . . The interpreter, who cannot himself read and who understands very partial what he is translating will as I have afterward heard, introduce . . . into some passages of simple sublimity of the Holy Writ, just because some word in the sentence had a similar sound. Thus the passage, "The salvation of the souls is a great and important subject," (becomes) "The salvation of the soul is a very great sack," must sound strange indeed![27]

But on criticizing the translator for translating the "great and important subject" as *"kgetsi e kgolo"* or a "great sack," Moffat demonstrates that he was quite unqualified to criticise his interpreter, for the latter was correct. An important issue, a court case or task is referred to as *"kgetsi,"* among Batswana to denote its importance and gravity. The interpreter had been spot on to refer to salvation of soul as "a very great sack." On his own ignorance, as one who also could not speak both languages fluently and one who was equally vulnerable to translation blunders, Moffat is apparently self-forgiving and tolerant, arguing that a gross mistranslation is forgiven on the basis of good character! He writes "The natives will smile, and make allowances for the blundering speeches of the missionary and though some may convey the very opposite meaning to that which he intends, they know from his general character what should be, and ascribe the blunder to his ignorance of their language."[28]

It is not only his translator who falls under the mercy of Moffat's eye, the whole of Batswana/Southern African are held to be ignorant and godless. There is, however, hope under the able hand of a gardner-farmer to cultivate their arid souls into the fertile fields of salvation. "Satan," Moffat, says,

is obviously the author of polytheism of other nations, he has employed his agency with fatal success in erasing every vestige of religious impression from the mind of Bechuan, Hottentots and Bushmen, leaving them without a single link to unite them to the skies. Thus the missionary could not make appeal to legends, or altars, or to an unknown God or to ideas kindred, to those he wished to import . . .). Their religious system like those streams in the wilderness, which lose themselves in the

27. Moffat, *Missionary Labours*, 294.
28. Ibid.

sand had entirely disappeared, and devolved on the missionary to prepare for the gracious distribution of the waters of salvation in that desert soil, sowing the seed of the word, breathing many prayers, and shedding many a tear, till the Spirit of God should cause it to vegetate, and yield fruits of righteousness.[29]

And to this major agricultural project of cultivating arid desert soils into life, Moffat had produced a Setswana Bible translation before he grasped the language. First, he had to do the orthography. Five to six decades later different mission centers had used his Bible to develop better Setswana, even within the LMS; hymns and other books had appeared with an improved Setswana orthography. So by 1883 there were varieties of written Setswana, Robert Moffat Bible translation being the crudest of all. With the number of educated Batswana rising, they became dissatisfied with Moffat's translation, as attested by their letters to the editor of *Mahoko a Becwana*. The debate became heated as soon as the newspaper (*Mahoko a Becwana*) was launched on the correct way of writing and pronouncing Setswana. Many Batswana writers insisted that Robert Moffat's earliest translation clearly indicates that he did not understand the language and that they preferred the latest forms of writing and pronouncing Setswana.[30]

Since better ways of writing Setswana had been developed over the years, most Batswana readers also insisted that the latter should be adopted as the standard for the Newspaper. At the center of the debate were the letters *d*, which was translated with *l* or *r*; the consonant *w*, which was written as *oe*; the letter, "*t*" which in some words needed to appear with "*l*" (*tl*), in some words with "*h*" (*th*) and in others with "*lh*" (*tlh*) together. If *l*, *h* or *lh* are left out of the letter "t," where they need to be included—it created different meanings than the intended. A good case in point is the verb "created" in Genesis 1:1. When *h* was left out of *tl*, the verb was written as "*tlola*" (jump?) instead of "*tlhola*" create. The Moffat Bible thus read as follows: "in the beginning God jumped the heavens and the earth," instead of "In the beginning God created the heavens and the earth"[31]. Another debate centered around the vowels *o* and *e*, whether they should be aspirated/hyphenated or not. In each case, using or not using the letter *d*, *w* or the hyphenated *e* and *o*, did not only change the pronunciation of Setswana words, in some cases, it changed the meaning, as elaborated above. In his letter to the editor, Gomotsegang Magonaring,[32] underlined that even though there are a

29. Ibid., 244.

30. Mgadla and Volz, *Words of Batswana*, 7–42.

31. Ibid., 29.

32. Gomotsegang Magonaring (December 1889).

number of Setswana dialects "the letters *d, o, e* and *w* are the ones with which the language of Setswana is spoken, throughout the entire language of Setswana."[33] The letter dated December 1889, written by Sekaelo Piti, captures and illustrates the general concern. He wrote,

> We have complained much about our language in the books, be- cause they have not been representing true Setswana but rather Setswana and English—an English Setswana—that is read as only a reminder of the real thing.[34] For example, "*go diha*" to make has been written as "*go riha*," "*didimala*" [be quiet] as "*ririmala*" or "*lilimala*," also "*Modimo*" [God] as "*Morimo*," and "*legodimo*" [heaven], as "*legorimo*." But when we saw hymn books in the year 1883, we were very happy because a mission- ary had arrived who speaks the language of our mothers and who speaks proper Setswana. He says, "*Yesu kwana ea Modimo*" Jesus lamb of God and not "*Yesu koana*" or "*kuana*."

This missionary also printed a spelling book in the year 1885. He is the one who knows the true language of Setswana."[35]

These concerns were quite legitimate for in some cases the changing or leaving out of one letter, dramatically changed the meaning of the verses (eg *kuana* for lamb, written without a *w* could mean hat. Verses that should read as "Jesus the lamb of God, or "behold the lamb of God" would read as "Behold the Hat of God." If "*go diha*" is used for the verb "to make," it would easily heard and understood as "to drop something down" instead of mak- ing or creating). Going back to Genesis 1:1 suppose the translation chose the word "to make" for "to create," the Setswana translation could read: "In the beginning when God dropped (*diha*) the earth and the heavens, instead of make (*dira*). In other cases, the translation created meaningless new words, such as "*ririmala*," for *didimala*/be quite. The new word, *ririmala*, could possibly be read as referring to a hairy stomach; if at all. In the same letter to the editor Gomotsegang Magonaring (December 1889) outlines

---

33. Mgadla and Volz, *Words of Batswana*, 31.

34. This writer was spot on for indeed when Moffat discusses how he designed the written Setswana, it is clear that he based it on western languages and sounds. Giving guidance of how to pronounce Sestswana, he says, "*CH* is represented in Bechuana by Italian *C*, is sounded like *ch* in chance . . . *tl* like Welsh *ll* . . . preceded by a t; *ng* which is represented in the written language by the Spanish n, has a ringing sound of *ng* in sing. This outline will enable anyone to read the language with tolerable correctness," said Moffat, in *Missionary Labours and Scenes,* 224. He goes on to discuss, how the word Botswana was spelt differently among the Dutch or English, depending on whether they found an equivalent sound or not in their languages!

35. Mgadla and Volz, *Words of Batswana*, 31.

many examples to illustrate how substituting the consonant *d* with *r* created new unintended meanings. For example, the word for thundering/sounding, *duma*, when its *d* was dropped and written with *r* (*ruma*) it means "to devour." With the *d* replaced with *r* in the verb *duela*, meaning to pay it reads as *ruela*, *which* means to keep, domesticate, or possess something for someone.[36] One can imagine that if a verse said Jesus paid (*duela*) for our sins it would now be read to mean *he kept* (*ruela*) our sins. Similarly, the word *dumela*, which is used in Setswana for greeting, meaning lets agree or peace among us, written with an *r*, instead of *d* would read *rumela*, which now means send!

Second, Batswana were unhappy for through translation and the written books (hymns, spelling books, dictionaries, Bible), their language was now infused with "English and was now an English version of Setswana. Piti called it "an English Setswana—that is read only as a reminder of the real thing.[37]As Banani Diphafe would state in his letter of January 1890, "I see us becoming confused, only parallel to the language and speaking it like a white person who is just learning Setswana. He says "*Modimo*" [God] as "*Morimo*," and "*dilo*" [things] as "*lilo*." Speaking with a "*d*" sounds right but "*l*" is ridiculous'[38]. In Setswana only little children, who are learning to speak, are expected to be unable to be pronounce words and say such as things "*lilo*," instead of "*dilo*." The Moffat's translation thus introduced changes that made readers sound like stuttering and stammering little babies who are still learning how to talk. The translation had infantilized them. Hence each time they had to read the Bible they had to put a persona of infants. Age among Batswana is traditionally an important social marker, in fact, far above gender. Any time one fails to recognise an elderly person and treats them as children it is regarded as great disrespect and insult. Naturally Batswana readers would be upset by their Bible reading experience.

In a letter dated June 6, 1883, the missionary editor (Alfred Gould), though patronizing, acknowledged that there is indeed an issue that needs to be attended concerning the correct way of writing and pronouncing Setswana.[39] He then promised to include the issue for consideration by the general missionary council. This he did, although three years later. On his return, he reported that the missionary council had voted to return to the most "original" written Setswana—one that was consistent with the earliest Bible translation of Robert Moffat, and to suppress the newer ways of writ-

36. Ibid.
37. Ibid., 36.
38. Ibid., 35.
39. Ibid., 15–16.

ing, which were more appreciated by Batswana. This meant the retention of the most corrupted written Setswana. The report on the response of missionaries, dated September 2, 1889, is worth quoting at length:

In March this year, missionaries of the LMS who teach in the language of Setswana gathered at Kuruman. As they met, they took up the issue of the letters that are used for printing and writing. Many missionaries of other missions oppose some of the letters with which they have been writing. They reject them because they have never liked them. They reject the letter *d* and they reject the letter *w*. These missionaries like the old way of printing, the one that still used today for the Bible and the Testament. They also argue that the old printing is known by many more people. So these things were discussed and it was agreed that those letters should not be changed and that writing and printing should be done only with old letters. Now *w* has been dropped so that it will be written "*banoe*," (others) not "*banwe*," and it will be written "*rumela*" [greet] not as "*dumela*" and "*Morimo*" God not "*Modimo*," and "*lilo tse di thata*" [difficult things] not "*dilo tse di thata*" It was agreed that e' and o- (aspirated//hyphenated) should be changed and instead put as plain *e* and plain *o*. Some letters will for the time being still be published as they are. The letter "*h*" will be used to differentiate "*tlala*" [hunger] from "*tlhala*" [divorce].[40]

The report indicates that one little, but significant victory, was won, concerning the inclusion of *h* in the syllable *tl*. This meant that at last Genesis 1:1 could be read as, "In the beginning God created *(tlhola)* the heavens and the earth, instead of "In the beginning "God jumped *(tlola)* the heavens and the earth." Indeed the Alfred Wookey's revised version of the Setswana Bible of 1908 did just that. The report from the missionary council meeting, however, had more bad news than good ones. The overall concerns with other central consonants and vowels such as (*d, l, w*, and hyphenated *o, e*) were rejected. The reasons given are quite telling and patronising to say the least. It was the views and feelings of missionaries that mattered. It was what they liked which would stand. The prevailing/current and better ways of writing, appreciated by Batswana speakers, were to be reversed. The protests of Batswana about their distorted, meaningless language, which was now reduced to "an English–Setswana—that is as only a reminder of the real thing"[41] did not matter, "for these missionaries like the old way of printing."[42] The report goes on to say, "so these things were discussed and it was agreed that those letters should not be changed and that writing and

40. Ibid., 27.

41. Ibid., 29.

42. Ibid., 27.

printing should be done only with old letters," that is, the Robert Moffat Setswana bible translation. The missionary like the English–Setswana and insist it should be the standard way of writing. Their response assists us to answer better, in so far as the agenda of the translation is concerned.

Decolonizing the English–Setswana: Subversive Ways of Reading

Following this report, the letters to the editor indicate that many Batswana objected to this decision and others pleaded for the decision to be re-considered to no avail. They were, in fact, protesting to what was concluded, a nonnegotiable issue—until such a time that it would please the missionaries to reverse it. Shot down, forced to write and read Setswana according to the stuttering tongue of a child; forced to read and write in English Setswana, the Batswana were nonetheless, not helpless. In fact, they had already developed strategies of reading that circumvents the imposed discourse of the "English–Setswana." Yet they had hoped it could be corrected, but now that they had been informed that what will be maintained as the standard way of writing the Setswana language was what the the missionaries liked. The Batswana readers fell back to their strategies of reading as resisting readers. Dikokwane Gaboutlwelwe, who wrote in response to the report using the example of Genesis 1, illustrates the point.

"I see the old written Setswana in the Bible as we read in Genesis chapter one. There we find it written like this: '*Morimo o lo ua tlola magorimo le lehatsi mo tsimologong;*' . . . but when we read it aloud we say, '*Modimo o lo wa tlhola magodimo le lehatshe mo tshimologong.*'"[43] In the quote, Gaboutlwelwe says their reading strategy overlooks the colonial missionaries' constructed English–Setswana language. Instead they read the Moffat Bible from their oral base, putting back all the excluded consonants *d, h, w,* and ignoring the new creations of *r, l, ua,* that infantilizes the readers, creates confusion, meaningless and induces wrong meanings. So, in fact, even if the verse said in the beginning "God jumped the heavens and the earth" they read it as "in the beginning God created (*tlhola*) the heavens and the earth." (I have to say there was more that was problematic in the translation than the verb create/jump debate. While I do not know how to name it, I think it is best noted that what we have here was "Setswana English//English Setswana.) This reading strategy is further confirmed by Sebotseng Loatile who also responded to the missionary's report saying,

43. Ibid., 29.

I am very happy to receive the newspaper and to hear the words that I have been hearing. I hear news about other nations and the word of God. But about the letters that has been taken out, I am very concerned. I assumed that our Bible was printed as it is because the missionaries had not quite grasped our language. But now they understand our language and they speak it very well. So I am surprised they are removing core letters [d, w, aspirated o and e]. Here everyone who reads books is not happy about the removal of the letters that have been removed. *You should know that when we read our Bible we change the letters with our mouths.*[44]

This reading strategy of reading from the base of the oral tradition is quite significant. What is in the oral base is the whole culture, another Canon, embodied by the community. The refusal to change what was overtly wrong assisted Batswana readers to openly assert their oral tradition and understanding as the main reference point, than to take the English–Setswana Bible as the final authority on their culture. This was crucial since, the English–Setswana translation of the Bible involved more than just the replacement of key consonants and vowels with newly created *(li ri)* ones. It also included changing the Batswana spiritual world from sacred to evil, in order to supplant it with Christianity. An excellent example, which I have written about, was the translation of *Badimo* as demons[45]. I re-narrate my encounter with this translation in order to illustrate how the Batswana ways of reading from the Setswana oral tradition base, subverts the colonial discourse of darkness and heathens.

Reclaiming *Badimo* as Sacred Figures: Batswana Reading Strategies

In 1995, I carried out fieldwork research, seeking to read Matthew 15: 21–28 with Batswana women. In the process, I discovered something else.[46] The ancestors had been translated as demons in the Alfred Wookey's revised Setswana Bible of 1908. I did not have access to Robert Moffatt's original Bible of 1857 to verify where this use of ancestors for demons originated. Where the Matt 15:21 woman said, "My daughter is severely possessed by demons," in the Setswana translation it said my daughter is severely pos-

44. Ibid., 33; emphasis added.

45. See Dube, "Consuming a Colonial Cultural Bomb," 33–59.

46. For the original description see Dube, "Consuming a Colonial Cultural Bomb," 37–42.

sessed by *Badimo/*Ancestors. Where Jesus cast out demons, Jesus cast out the *Badimo/*Ancestors. I was so shocked by this translation so much so, that I virtually scrambled all over the New Testament pages to other passages where Jesus cast out demons to verify my stunning discovery.

And yes I discovered a very sad story. The ancestors had been translated as demons in the Setswana Bible. It was shocking. Almost desperately, I turned to Mark 5, where Jesus cast out the Legion demons that possessed and maddened a man in Gadarene. I found out that in the Setswana Bible of 1908 Jesus cast out the legion of *Badimo/*Ancestors, who ran into the sea and got buried. It was a textual burial of *Badimo/*Ancestors. I was virtually trembling, shocked that Batswana who first read the so-called word of God were made to discover that what they venerated as sacred figures, were in fact, just demons. Ancestors being the extended memory of the families with their departed members, could not be reduced to demons, without reducing everyone to the same. What a perfect way of proving that Batswana were helpless heathens lost in the darkness. I thought, to myself, and for more than a century and half Batswana Bible readers consumed this colonial bomb, planted to explode their cultures away, and they could not read Greek for themselves to check it out if this was representative, or the closest "equivalent" term. I was deeply shaken. But that was before I discovered that the first Batswana readers had long leant to read the Bible from their oral cultural base than the missionaries' perspective of heathens in the darkness. As expressed by Gaboutlwelwe and Loatile: "*You should know that when we read our Bible we change the letters with our mouths.*" But how would they reinstate the demonized *Badimo/*Ancestors?

Again, this was a separate but pleasant surprise and discovery. In the process of reading the Bible with non-academic women, who were church leaders in African Independent Churches, I found out that they read/use the Bible as a divination set. Now divination among Batswana involves consulting *Badimo* about all situations of concern for the living and finding useable solutions. It involves recognizing *Badimo/*ancestors as mediators between the living, the dead and God. So, far from *Badimo* functioning as demons, in the Batswana ways of reading, *Badimo* together with Jesus, were divine forces of positive power than negative power. I could not have imagined this U-turn. This strategy of resistance depends on reading the Bible with and through Batswana oral cultures. It depends on using the authority of African traditions than giving the English–Setswana Bible the final word. It is a strategy of the Tiv, taking a story that conflicted with their values and retelling it such that to them it was "a good story again" although to Bohannan "it no longer seemed quite the same story." I want to believe that Bible translation has been on the road for so long. Like Bohannan, the travelling anthropologist, Bible translation and translators, have long crossed many boundaries, they are already perched among elders and communities, who seek to hear more stories told according to their own terms, even if the story may no longer seem quite the same story to its bearers. Such decolonising community rewritings are long overdue.

Bibliography

Bassnett, Susan, and Andre Lefevere A. *Translation, History and Culture*. London: Cassell, 1990.

Bohannan, Laura. "Shakespeare in the Bush: An American Anthropologist Set Out to Study the Tiv of West Africa and was Taught the Meaning of Hamlet." *Natural History* 75 (1966) 28–33.

Bailey, Randall, and Tina Pippin. *Semeia 76: Race, Class, and Politics of Biblical Translation*. Atlanta: Society of Biblical Literature, 1998.

Carroll, Robert P. "Cultural Encroachment and Bible Translation: Observations on Elements of Violence, Race, and Class in Production of Bibles in Translation." *Semeia 76* (1996) 39–54.

Comaroff, Jean, and John Comaroff. *Of Revelation and Revolution: Christianity, Colonialism and Consciousness in South Africa*. Vol. 1. Chicago: University of Chicago Press, 1991.

———. "Through the Looking Glass: Colonial Encounters of the First Kind." *Journal of Historical Sociology* 1 (1988) 6–30.

Doke, Clement M. "Scripture Translation into Bantu Languages." *African Studies* 17/2 (1958) 84–99.

Donaldson, Laura. *Decolonising Feminisms: Race, Gender, and Empire Building*. Chapel Hill: University of North Carolina Press, 1992.

Dube, Musa W. "Consuming a Colonial Cultural Bomb: Translating *Badimo* into 'Demons' in the Setswana Bible." *JSNT* (1999) 33–59.

Gentzler, Edwin. *Contemporary Translation Theories*, 2nd ed. Clevedon, UK: Multilingual Matters, 2001.

Mgadla, T. Part, and Stephen C. Volz, trans. and eds. *Words of Batswana: Letters to Mahoko a Bechwana, 1883–1896*. Van Riebeeck Society, 2nd series 37. Cape Town: Van Riebeeck Society for the Publication of South African Historical Documents, 2006.

Moffat, Robert. *Missionary Labours and Scenes in Southern Africa*. London: John Sow, Paternoster-Row, 1842.

Noss, Phillip A., ed. *A History of Bible Translation*. Roma: Edizioni di Storia e Letteratura, 2007.

Smith, Abraham. "The Productive Role of English Bible Translators." *Semeia 76* (1996) 69–80.

Sugirtharajah, R. S. "Textual Cleansing: A Movement from Colonial to the Postcolonial Version." *Semeia 76* (1996) 7–20.

Tymoczko, Maria. "Translation in Oral Tradition as a Touchstone for Translation Theory and Practice." In *Translation, History and Culture*, edited by Susan Bassnett and André Lefevere, 46–55. London: Pinter, 1990.

Volz, Stephen C. "Written on Our Hearts: Tswana Christians and the Word of God in the Mid 19th Century." *JRA* 38 (2008) 112–40.

8

Novel Biblical Translation of Ngugi wa Thiong'o

Malebogo Kgalemang

Introduction

Translation takes a double form in Ngugi wa Thiong'o's novel, *Devil on the Cross* (1982).[1] Firstly, is the language transcription in which the English text was translated from: Ngugi's vernacular, Kikuyu.[2] Second, the novel is a cultural and postcolonial translation of certain biblical and Christian symbols. In the process of this translation, new meanings are produced. Translation, in postcolonial theory is an event, a political and resistance process in which the postcolonialist subverts the initial or original processes.

Translation is not the simple act of one foreign language text into another language. Translation as advanced by Andre Lefevere "is a rewriting of an original text."[3] By this, Lefevere means translation is

> All rewritings, whatever their intention, reflect a certain ideology and a poetics and as such manipulate literature to function in a given society in a given way. Rewriting is manipulation, undertaken in the service of power, and in its positive aspect

---

1. During December 31, 1977—December 12th, 1978, the Arap Moi administration imprisoned Ngugi for his political and anti-government writings. While in prison he began penning the novel on a piece of toilet paper. The process of writing *Devil on the Cross* is diarized in his memoir *Detained: A Writer's Diary*.

2. Writing the book in Kikuyu was part of Ngugi's project of decolonizing the mind as the title of his book astutely observes. His argument was that English should not be the reference point from which we think about languages but should be grouped with other languages.

3. Lefevere, *Translation, Rewriting and the Manipulation of Literary Fame*, vii. Language Education Process, 2004a: viii. See the following Ren Shuping. "Translation as Rewriting." *International Journal of Humanities and Social Science* 3.18 (2014) 55–59.

can help in the evolution of a literature and a society. Rewriting can introduce new concepts, new genres, new devices and the history of translation is the history also of literary innovation, of the shaping power of one culture upon another. But rewriting can also repress innovation, distort and contain, and in an age of ever increasing manipulation of all kinds, the study of the manipulation processes of literature are exemplified by translation can help us towards a greater awareness of the world in which we live."[4]

Rewritings are not innocent endeavours neither pure matters but contain "certain ideologues and poetics."[5] Translators also "manipulate literature"[6] for a particular purpose and function. From the above, translation as a rewriting process is not an easy and simple matter or process, neither a pure one. It is a complex process that "involves factors such as power, ideology, poetics and patronage, etc."[7] As rewriting, translation is not an "isolated activity"[8] for there is "always a context in which translation takes place, a history from a text emerges and another one into which a text is transposed."[9]

Since translation is not an isolated activity, it means the translation of *Devil on the Cross* takes place within a specific context. The appropriation of another literature into a contextual specificity means power and ideology are at work in the production of new meanings in the *Devil on the Cross*. The manipulation process of literature Ngugi appropriates become key to the translation processes. I argue that through an appropriation of certain and specific biblical texts, Ngugi creates an innovative form of translation as rewriting. His translation appropriates texts from another culture for his own ideological courses and purposes. Given that this translation of a text from another culture forms the crux of *Devil on the Cross*, I argue further that translation as rewriting in Ngugi's *Devil on the Cross* takes place in the third space.

According to Homi Bhabha most translations take place in the third space.[10] The third space is a "limitless composition of life worlds that radically open and openly radicalizable."[11] It is a politically focused and

4. Lefevere, *Translation,* 12–13.

5. Ibid., 15.

6. Ibid., 14–18.

7. Shuping, "Translation as Rewriting," 55.

8. Aksoy, "Translation as Rewriting."

9. Lefevere, *Translation.*

10. Bhabha, *The Location of Culture,* 53–56.

11. Soja, "Thirdspace," 54.

susceptible to strategic choice. This third space is not completely tamed but its "knowledge nevertheless guides our search for emancipatory change and freedom from domination."[12] The third space can be defined as just that, a space, that is neither geographical nor tangible. This article will read translation taking place in *Devil on the Cross*-a novel about a postcolonial nation, Kenya, struggling to survive after acquiring its independence.

In Ngugi's novel translation, the third space implies a "new view on the world and the production of knowledge."[13] The third space is a "mutual political strategy against all forms of oppression; and a starting point for many new approaches."[14] Therefore, to unravel and discuss the new world, or revolutionary world and one with which is a "site of production, the production of anxiety, an untimely place."[15] The third space is a sociopolitical, economic and religious space. It is where "issues of race, class, and gender can be addressed simultaneously without privileging one over the other; where one can be Marxist and post-Marxist, materialist and idealist, structuralism and humanist, disciplined and transdisciplinary at the same time."[16]

The third space is where Ngugi's novel translation takes place. It is negotiated through an appropriation of the significant biblical narratives which are the following: the parable of the talents; the replacement of Jesus on the cross by the devil, and the translation of the crucifixion as a revolution measure against the brutalities and barbarism of the capitalism.

The structure and plot of *Devil on the Cross* is based on the logic of Christian discourses. It employs satiric elements to mock and make critical commentary on the barbaric nature of the bourgeoisie. It translates the gospel of Matthew parable of the talents to explain the capitalist ideology dominating the postcolonial context of Kenya. On the other hand, it calls for a revolution by translating the crucifixion of Jesus into the crucifixion of the devil as a symbol and representation of capitalism. Through the crucifixion, it advocated for an alternative world in which emancipation, liberation and a communal spirit drives the unity and materialist needs of the people.

Therefore, it is these three key biblical narratives that this chapter will focus on. Thus Ngugi creates a third space to resist the Christian symbol and utilization of the ideology of crucifixion. The third space, is a critical location and starting point for Ngugi's novel translation strategy. As Bhabha

12. Ibid., 55.
13. Ibid.
14. Ibid., 54.
15. Ibid.
16. Ibid., 44.

says, the third space represents the unpresentable constituting the discursive conditions of enunciation that ensure that the meaning and symbol of culture have no primordial unity or fixity; that even the same signs can be appropriated, translated, historicised and read anew[17] leading to the negotiation of cultural contradictions and misapprehensions.

What does such translation achieve? Does the author's reading indicate those who claimed to be liberators are just devils? What is the connection of the devil to the Kenyan postcolonial, neo-colonial, socioeconomic, and political conditions? Who is the devil? How does this rewriting of a major Christian symbol recast the meaning of the crucifixion? This chapter will attempt to answer these questions by insisting that the translation of the (greatest) Christian symbol creates an alternative ethical and political authority against the dogmatism of prevailing power.

Bhabha has also proposed hybridity in addition to the idea of the third space where translation takes place. Hybridity is not cultural merging in the "traditional sense of the word."[18] It can also be described in Mary Louise Pratt's[19] words as the "contact words."[20] According to Michaela Wolf, hybridity becomes the product of "translation between cultures"[21] and can generate "borderlines affects and identifiers."[22] Thinking with the "third space" in Ngugi's *Devil on the Cross* is to claim that "thinking and writing are acts of translation."[23]

Below I will discuss the translations the parable of the talents from Matthew's gospel; the crucifixion of Jesus changed into the translation of the crucifixion of the devil. I will commence with the Matthew Parable of the talents and its translation in *Devil on the Cross*.

The Translation of the Gospel of Matthew in *Devil on the Cross*

Since translation is rewriting of the original text, the rewriting of Matthew's parable of the talents reveals the purpose and ideology to the relationship of the local bourgeoisie and its partners. Their connection, tie, link and imitation of their master-servants relation is an important measure for

17. Bhabha. *The Location*, 111.

18. Ibid., 111.

19. Pratt, *Imperial Eyes*.

20. Ibid.

21. Wolf, "Translation-transculturation."

22. Ibid.

23. Bhabha, "In the Cave of Making," ix–xiv.

Ngugi's translation. Ngugi's own appropriation is driven by a certain ideology; an ideology that strives for the liberation and emancipation of the postcolonial nation of Kenya. Below is a parallel table to illustrate the parable of the talents in the book of Matthew 25:14–46 and the kingdom of Wiles Parable from *Devil on the Cross*.

Matthew 25:14–46	*Devil on the Cross'* Kingdom of Wiles
14 "For it (the kingdom of God) will be like a man going on a journey, who called his servants and entrusted to them his property.	And it came to pass that as the ruler was about to return to his home abroad, he again called together all his servants and gave them the key to the land.
	Then he gave them his property and goods to look after and even to increase and multiply.
15 To one he gave five talents, to another two, to another one, to each according to his ability. Then he went away.	To one he gave capital amounting to 500,000 shillings, to another 200,000 shillings, and to another, 100, 000 shillings;
16 He who had received the five talents went at once and traded with them, and he made five talents more. 17 So also he who had the two talents made two talents more. 18 But he who had received the one talent went and dug in the ground and hid his master's money.	To every servant according to how loyally he has served his master, and followed his faith, and shared his outlook.
	And so he went away, leaving by the front door. And the servant who had received 500,000 shillings immediately set out and bought things cheaply at a higher price, and in this way made a profit of 500,000 shillings.
19 Now after a long time the master of those servants came and settled accounts with them.	

| | *Devil on the Cross'* |
| Matthew 25:14–46 | Kingdom of Wiles |

And the one who had received 200,000 shillings did the same: he bought cheaply from producers, and sold dearly to consumers, and so he made a profit of 200,000 shillings. But he who has received only 100,000 shillings thought he was clever, and he reviewed his life and that of the masses of the land, and that of the master who had just left for a foreign country.

And he began to talk to himself, saying: This lord and master has always bragged that he alone developed this country with the aid of the small amount of money that he came with, shouting, 'Capital! Capital!'

Now let me see whether capital will yield profit without being watered with the sweat of the worker or buying cheap the labour of the peasant and worker. If it produces profit by itself, then I shall know beyond all doubt that it is money that develops a country. So he went, and he put the 100,000 shillings in a tin, and covered it well, and then dug a hole by a banana plant, and buried the tin there.

20 And he who had received the five talents came forward, bringing five talents more, saying, and 'Master, you delivered to me five talents; here I have made five talents more.' 21 His master said to him, 'Well done, good and faithful servant. [c] You have been faithful over a little; I will set you over much. Enter into the joy of your master.'

And the one who had been given 500,000 shillings came and said: 'My lord and master, you left me with capital of 500,000 shillings. I have doubled it.' And the lord was truly amazed, and he exclaimed, 100 per cent profit? A fantastic rate of profit. You have done well, you good and faithful servant.

Matthew 25:14–46	*Devil on the Cross'* Kingdom of Wiles
22 And he also who had the two talents came forward, saying, 'Master, you delivered to me two talents; here I have made two talents more.' 23 His master said to him, 'Well done, good and faithful servant. You have been faithful over a little; I will set you over much. Enter into the joy of your master.'	And the one who had been given 200,000 shillings came and told his master: 'My lord and master, you left me with 200,000 shillings. Behold, your capital has yielded another 200,000 shillings.' And the lord spoke and said: 'Wonderful, this is really wonderful: such a rising rate of profit! A stable country for investment. You have done well, you good and faithful servant.
24 He also who had received the one talent came forward, saying,	
'Master, I knew you to be a hard man, reaping where you did not sow and gathering where you scattered no seed, 25 so I was afraid, and I went and hid your talent in the ground. Here you have what is yours.' 26 But his master answered him, 'You wicked and slothful servant! You knew that I reap where I have not sown and gather where I scattered no seed? 27 Then you ought to have invested my money with the bankers, and at my coming I should have received what was my own with interest. 28 So take the talent from him and give it to him who has the ten talents. 29 For to everyone who has will more be given, and he will have an abundance. But from the one who has not, even what he has will be taken away. 30 And cast the worthless servant into the outer darkness. In that place there will be weeping and gnashing of teeth.'	And the one who had been given 100,000 shillings stepped forward and told his master: You, lord and servant, member of the white race, I have discovered your tricks! I have also discovered your real name. Imperialist, that's your name, and you are a cruel master. Why? Because you reap where you have never sown. You grab things over which you have never shed any sweat. You have appointed yourself distributor of things which you have never helped to produce.

The parallel reveals a rewriting of the foreign text to illustrate Kenya's domestic and political culture and conflict. A closer scrutiny at the parallel structure reveals three scenes:[24]

> **Scene 1:** the master gives talents or shilling to his subjects and goes away
>
> **Scene 2:** the slaves attend to their responsibilities
>
> **Scene 3:** the master returns and rewards two of the slaves while he punishes the third.

Ngugi uses the Parable of talents to portray the practices and conflict created by capitalists and their "subject colleagues" in post-independence Kenya defined and dominated by former imperialists and local bourgeoisie. He rewrites the parable to reflect the political and ideological analysis of the postcolonial nation of Kenya. Ngugi's rewriting or translation is particular in that "there is always a context in which translation takes place, a history from which a text emerges and another one into which a text is transposed."[25] He rewrites the parable to demonstrate the logic of empire of capital, logic of profit making and of economic and political power.

What exactly transpires in this process of translation? The kingdom of God is elided for the Kingdom of Wiles. God is displaced for the devil. The first two servants in both parables are subject and obedient to the master and the ruler. In both parables and the third servant in the novel is a replica of the parable of the Matthean parable. Moreover the language the third servant uses "to legitimise his refusal of the master's claim remains consistent between the two accounts."[26] The third servants in both resist their master and ruler's agenda. Both deliver the ultimate: "because you reap where you have never sown. You grab things over which you have never shed any sweat. Master, I knew you to be a hard man, reaping where you did not sow and gathering where you scattered no seed, so I was afraid, and I went and hid your talent in the ground. Here you have what is yours" Matthew 25:25–26.

Ngugi's translation has a displacement slant to it. It reflects the "process of displacement that paradoxically, makes the presence of the book (bible) wondrous to the extent to which it is repeated, translated, misread, (and)

---

24. Carter, *Matthew and the Margins*, 487–97.

25. Andre Lefevere, "Translation Practice(s) and the Circulation of Cultural Capital. Some Aeneids in English," in Susan Bassnett, ed., *Constructing Cultures: Essays on Literary Translation*, Topics in Translation 11 (Clevedon: Multilingual Matters, 1998), 59.

26. Ibid., 489.

displaced."[27] The appropriation of the parable subverts the foundation of the parable as an allegory of the kingdom of God. This displacement repeats this with a difference. But what and where are the differences? The difference begins with the narrator stripping the supposedly or seemingly spiritual aspect of the Matthew parable of the talents. Where Matthews parable uses "talents" which in essence is "capital," with both "monetary and spiritual connotations;" and "to the one he gave five talents, to another two and to another one, to each according to his own ability; and immediately he on a journey" Matthew 25:15. Therefore the appropriation of the parable displaces and dislocates in its repetition the 'original' understanding of the parable of the talents as an allegory of the kingdom of God. In fact Bart DiFiore contends that parallels serve "only as the framework around which Ngugi hybridises the parable."[28]

Thus Ngugi's rewriting and translation of Matthew's Parable of the talents "adapted the other text to a certain ideology or to a certain poetics, and usually to both."[29] Furthermore, the parable of the talents reflects the "nature of the political independence granted to African countries and the relationship existing between the former colonial masters and the African elites."[30]

Not only does Ngugi satirize capitalism through political translation of the parable of talents, there are other translation of Christianity key themes, religious idioms and language that kiss and stain the pages of the novel. Ngugi, as already noted appropriates Christ on the cross and the crucifixion. The next section will therefore, explore Ngugi's translation of Christ on the Cross and the crucifixion, particularly their function in the satirising of capitalism through religious lingo and ideology.

The Crucifixion of Revolution

The thieves and robbers' testimonies at the feast focus on their worship at the altar of capitalism and their subject to the empire of capital. It also marks how they have been dehumanised by their accumulation and exploitation of the peasants. Ngugi calls to wage a war against the empire of capital. The call to overthrow and undo the emperor of capital, represented as the devil, is made through the appropriation of the Christian crucifixion of Jesus. The devil is the harbinger of evil. Throughout the novel's plot, the

27. Bhabha, *Location*, 145.

28. DiFiore, "Ngugi's Hybridization."

29. Ibid., 8.

30. Balogun, "Ngugi's Devil on the Cross," 76–99.

devil is deployed in various scenes. The devil is ever present right from the beginning of the plot.[31]

The devil is an imperial export to colonies of empire. The devil is the "redolent of the power of evil."[32] Through the devil, we get to understand the fetishizing of evil in the form of the devil. The devil, according to Michael Taussig is the "creator of commodities"[33] and "the commodity fetishism of capitalist's cosmography."[34] Therefore, the devil's feast of thieves and robbers is to celebrate the empire of capital's fetishism of commodities. It is organised for "money's and capitalism's sake"[35] that the feast the "Devil's feast is organised."[36]

The devil's feast of thieves and robbers is dominated with the Christian religious lingo. Commenting on the religious lingo, F. Odun Balogun's observes that the meeting portrays an image of an "international conference of financers conducted in the form of a Sunday church service."[37] God is evoked to "pour blessings on (their) proceedings!"[38] The devil's feast, like a church service, commences with a song; "the Hell's Angels band struck up a tune . . ."[39] The "congregation's" singing is described thus; "The tune did not have a lilting rhythm. It was more like a psalm or a hymn. After a few minutes, everybody turned towards the band, and they started to sing, as if they were in church";[40]

> Good news has come
> To our country!
> Good news has come

---

31. The devil is first hinted at in a note thrown to the female protagonist Wariinga- from the thugs hired by Her landlord- "We are the Devil's Angels: Private Businessman, Make the slightest move to take this matter to the authorities," further revelation are to Wariinga again and the invitation she receives regarding the devil's feast of thieve and robbers is written "the devil's feast," (28, 68). Ngugi, *Devil on The Cross*, 28, 68.

32. Michael T. Taussig. *The Devil and Commodity Fetishism in South America* (Chapel Hill: The University of North Carolina Press, 1980), 28.

33. Ibid., 94–95.

34. Ibid., 94.

35. Muzigirwa, "Devil on the Cross," 1–11.

36. Ibid., 9.

37. Balogun, "Ngugi's Devil on the Cross," 80.

38. Ngugi, *Devil*, 87.

39. Ibid., 90.

40. Ibid. See also Balogun, "Ngugi's Devil on the Cross," 80. During the Roman empire's rise, the term goodnews (eugellion) associated with the goodnews of the empire, who was during the golden years of his rule, called a savior. It is initially a term of empire that the writers of the new testament appropriated when writing the Gospels.

About our Saviour![41]

The thieves and robbers participating at the feast are imagined as worshippers at the altar of capitalism, and are subjects to the empire of capital. For example, the character Mwaura describes his commitment to the "god of modern theft and the lord of modern robbery."[42] Mwaura confesses that "Business is my temple, and money is my God . . . Show me where money is and I'll take you there."[43] Another businessman, Nding'uri's accumulation is grotesquely described thus; when he became rich, "he began to fart property, to shit property, to sneeze property, to scratch property, to laugh property, to think property, to dream property, to talk property, to sweat property, to piss property. Property would fly from other people's hands to land in Nding'uri's palms."[44]

To dispose the empire of capital and its subjects is to decry the empire and its effects. It is to also show "a social form that undermines the basis of social unity."[45] On the other hand, there is need to subvert a "System that puts profit seeking ahead of people and that makes man an appendage of the economy and a slave to the work process instead of the master of it."[46] (29) Ngugi calls for the crucifixion of the devil since the devil is responsible for capitalist development, for injustices, exploitation and marginalisation of the peasant.[47] The "devil, who would lead us into the blindness of the heart and to the deafness of the mind, should be crucified, and care should be taken that his acolytes do not lift him down from the cross to pursue the task of building hell for the people of the earth."[48] Moreover, the crucifixion of the devil is advocated through the female protagonist, Wariinga, a spectator at the devil's feast of thieves and robbers.

It is when Wariinga a secondary school student, and a member of Church of the Holy Rosary, Wariinga was visited by a nightmare.[49] Nightmares are horrific tales.

41. Ngugi, *Devil*, 90.

42. Ibid., 193.

43. Ibid., 56.

44. Ibid., 64.

45. Michael T. Taussig. *The Devil and Commodity Fetishism in South America.* (Chapel Hill: The University of North Carolina Press), 1980: 28.

46. Taussig, *The Devi and Commodity*, 29.

47. See Ngugi, *Devil*, 33–55 where passengers representative of various Kenyan economic groups narrate the state of the nation. The majority represent the peasantry of Kenya postcolony.

48. Ibid., 4.

49. Ibid., 13.

(Waringa) saw a crowd of people dressed in rags walking in the light, propelling the devil towards the Cross. The Devil was clad in a silk suit, and he carried a walking stick shaped like a folded umbrella. On his head there were seven horns, even trumpets for sounding infernal hymns of praise and glory. The Devil had two mouths, one on his forehead and the other at the back of his head. His belly sagged, as if it were about to give birth to all the evils of the world. His skin was red, like that of a pig. Near the cross he began to tremble and turned his eyes towards the darkness, as if his eyes were being seared by the light. He moaned, beseeching the people not to crucify him, swearing that he and all his followers would again build Hell for the people on the Earth.

But the people cried in unison: 'Now we know the secrets of all the robes that disguise your cunning. Your commit murder, then you don your robes of pity and you go to wipe the tears from the faces of orphans and widows. You steal food from people's stores at charity and you offer them a calabash filled with the grain that you have stolen. You encourage lasciviousness solely to gratify your own appetites, then you put on robes of righteousness and urge men to repent, follow you so that you may show them paths of purity. You seize men's wealth, then you dress in robes of friendship and instruct them to join in the pursuit of the villain who has robbed them.

And there and then the people crucified the Devil on the Cross, and they went away singing songs of victory.[50]

Two key Christian texts are appropriated: the crucifixion of Christ and the beastly language of Revelation. Both are used to "think with" the destruction of the capitalist devil. The crucifixion and beastly languages are "sign(s) taken for wonders"[51]-of the crux of Christian faith. Ngugi's appropriation of New Testament narratives "re-embodies and rearticulates his political themes and resistances."[52]

The appropriation of the crucifixion of Jesus to that of the devil is an intention of forcing the Christian religion into a non-traditional role: instead of Jesus on the cross, it is the devil on the cross.[53] Jesus who historically we know as saviour for Christians is displaced on the cross and replaced with the devil. What does this displacement mean? Where then

50. Ibid., 13.

51. Bhabha, *The Location*, 122.

52. DiFiore, "Ngugi's Hybridization," 4.

53. Balogun, "Ngugi's Devil," 77.

do we locate salvation? The crucifixion or in the unity of the crucifiers? The identities of the people at the crucifixion are through social and political identities: devil is "clad in a silk suit."[54] He carries a "walking stick shaped like a folded umbrella"[55] and his "skin was red, like that of a pig."[56] The devil is a representative of the empire of capital, its emperor. A "crowd of people dressed in rags walking in the light"[57] drive him "towards the cross."[58] This is an encounter of two classes; the peasants identified in rags, and the bourgeoisie who is identified in his garb and race. The "crowd of people"[59] have taken an initiative to crucify the devil. Through the crucifixion of the devil, there is new meaning and understanding of salvation. Salvation is liberation, emancipation, and freedom from the empire of capital and its local subjects. It is not found in the cross or the crucifixion. Liberation or emancipation is through the proletariat's initiative. The spectacular execution of the empire of capitalism is also a theatrical enactment of a quest for revolution.

The portrayal of the devil is where an innovative or novel translation takes place. The call and demand for the crucifixion of the devil, takes place in the third space. In that third space is where the hybrid of the crucifixion is located. Bhabha articulates a point relevant to this third space. He notes, "to that end we should remember that it is in the "inter"-the cutting edge of translation and negotiation, the in-between, the space of the entire that Derrida has opened up in writing itself-that carried the burden of the meaning of culture."[60] The crucifixion is the "cutting edge of translation . . . the in-between space"[61] where the burden of the meaning of suffering, of marginalization and exploitation of the ordinary people is carried.

The replacement of Jesus by the devil is a translation into a "hybrid displacing space."[62] This space recalls efforts of "challenge and resistance"[63] to the empire of capital. Furthermore, it is at this moment of change where "transition of difference into sameness, and sameness into difference."[64]

54. Ngugi, *Devil*, 13.

55. Ibid.

56. Ibid.

57. Ibid.

58. Ibid.

59. Ibid.

60. Young, "The Void of Misgiving," 81–95.

61. Ibid., 82.

62. Ibid., 81.

63. Ibid., 82.

64. Ibid.

Ngugi repeats the Christian crucifixion discourse with a difference. Through the devil on the cross, Ngugi creates "repetition and difference"[65] in that salvation is not on the cross as already pointed out. The crucifixion of the devil is to "construct a hybrid work as a postcolonial response to identity repression . . ."[66]

Therefore, the space where the devil's crucifixion takes place is a postcolonial space. It turns the crucifixion of Jesus on its head. Ngugi subverts Jesus crucifixion by seemingly saying, it is not Jesus who deserves to be crucified but the devil, the harbinger of evil. Therefore, this is a hybridized moment: "if hybridity is heresy, then to blaspheme is to dream."[67] Thus through heresy and hybrid construction in the third space, Wariinga's nightmare is a revolution.

The Devil Beast and Apocalypse

> "On his head there were seven horns, seven trumpets for sounding infernal hymns of praise and glory. The devil had two mouths, one on his forehead, and the other at the back of his head. His belly sagged, as if it were about to give birth to all the evils of the world."[68]

> "And I stood upon the sea, and saw a beast rise up out of the sea, having seven heads and ten horns, and upon his horns ten crowns, and upon his heads the name of blasphemy.[69]

Through Wariinga's nightmare, we are drawn into the power of the prophetic vision of future events from the New Testament book of Revelation. The devil is doubly represented or doubly split. On the one hand, he is a male representative who wears suits. On the other, the devil is articulated through the beastly language of the Revelation of John., "The bestial language leaps"[70] from the pages of Revelation to Ngugi's novel translation. Revelation's bestial language reveals aspects of the spectacular: "On his head there were seven horns, seven trumpets . . . the devil had two mouths, one on his forehead, and the other at the back of his head."[71] Wariinga's nightmare has shifted

65. Ibid., 81.

66. Ibid.

67. Bhabha. *The Location*, 324.

68. Ngugi, *Devil*, 13.

69. See The New Testament Book of Revelation, 13.

70. Pippin, *Apocalyptic Bodies*, 78.

71. Rev 13:1; and Ngugi, *Devil*, 13.

from capitalist man to capitalist beast. This beast is "about to give birth to all the evils of the world."[72] Apocalypse is revelation. It is a "revealing of and a revelling in the end time horrors:"[73] the "end of time horrors"[74] of capitalism.

The irony of Wariinga's nightmare is that it has an "aspect of hope"[75] in its quest to crucify the devil. Apocalypse, theologians noted, is also eschatological especially for its "indignation in the face of injustice, that is, its prophetic critique of the status quo, its privilege of the future as the horizons of renewal and its historicizing account of its time."[76] The "Crowd in rags[77]" defied the devil-in the end-or must defeat the devil. What is impossible in real life-the destruction of the colonizing government and all that is evil in the world-is possible in the realm of the horror of fantasy."[78]

Conclusion

So, the translation of the parable of the talents, the crucifixion of Jesus, and the beastly language of Revelation occupies the third space of enunciation. Ngugi's novel translation in the third space defines *Devil on the Cross* (1982) as a postcolonial and decolonizing text. The appropriation of biblical language affirms Ngugi's position that "language embodies the thought process and values of a culture."[79] Therefore, appropriating biblical language is to translate language into the Kenyan postcolonial and decolonial context. A new culture translated out of the parable, the crucifixion and beast language carries a culture of revolution, destabilisation, resistance, emancipation, and decolonization in the third space of enunciation. The third space is a translation for a new world order. Unfortunately, the call to crucify the devil doesn't end with a free, emancipated and liberated world. The devil is brought down from the cross and resurrects after three days.[80] By this Ngugi indicates that the fight to rid the world of imperialism is a long drawn battle that does not end in one single victory. It is an ongoing

---

72. Ngugi, *Devil*, 13.

73. Pippin, *Apocalyptic Bodies*, 78.

74. Ibid., 79.

75. Ibid.

76. Keller, *Apocalypse Now and Then*, 20.

77. Ngugi, *Devil*, 13.

78. Pippin, *Apocalyptic Bodies*, 79.

79. wa Thiong'o. *Decolonizing the Mind*, 13.

80. Ngugi, *Devil*, 13.

battle with foreign imperialists and their surrogates resurfacing in ever changing newer forms.

Bibliography

Aksoy, Bernin. "Translation as Rewriting: The Concept and Its Implications on the Emergence of a Natural Literature." *Translation Journal* 5/3 (July 2001). http://www.bokorlang.com/journal/.

Balogun, F. Odun. "Ngugi's Devil on the Cross: The Novel as Hagiography of a Marxist." *Ufahamu: A Journal of Africa Studies* 16/2 (1987–88) 76–92.

Bhabha, Homi. *The Location of Culture*. London: Routledge & Kegan Paul, 1994.

Carter, Warren. *Matthew and the Margins: A Socio-Political and Religious Reading*. Bible & Liberation Series. Maryknoll, NY: Orbis, 2005.

Lefevere, Andre. *Translation, Rewriting, and the Manipulation of Literary Frame*. London: Routledge & Kegan Paul, 1992.

Keller, Catherine. *Apocalypse Now and Then: A Feminist Guide to the End of the World*. Boston: Beacon, 1996.

Muzigirwa, Bonaventure. *Devil on the Cross: Ngugi's Marxist Invitation*. Munich: Grin, 2012.

Ngugi wa Thiong'o. *Decolonizing the Mind: The Politics of Language in African Literature*. London: Curry, 1981.

———. *Devil on the Cross*. London: Heinemann, 1982.

———. *Detained: A Writer's Prison Diary*. Nairobi: Heinemann, 1981.

Pippin, Tina. *Apocalyptic Bodies: The Biblical End of the World in Text and Image*. London: Routledge, 1999.

Pratt, Mary Louise. *Imperial Eyes: Travel Writing and Transculturation*. London: Routledge, 2008.

Shiping, Ren. "Translation as Rewriting." *International Journal of Humanities and Social Science*. Vol. 3 No. 18; October 2013, 55–59.

Soja, Edward W. "Thirdspace: Toward a New Consciousness of Space and Spatiality." *Communicating in the Thirdspace*, edited by Karin Ikas and Gerhard Wagner, 49–61. Routledge Research in Cultural and Media Studies 18. New York: Routledge, 2009.

Taussig, Michael T. *The Devil and Commodity Fetishism in South America*. Chapel Hill: University of North Carolina Press, 2010.

Wolf, Michaela. "Translation-transculturation: Measuring the Perspective of transcultural Political Actions." Borders, Nation, Translations: www. translate.epicp.net.

Young, Robert J. C. "The Void of Misgiving." In *Communicating in the Third Space*, edited by Karin Ikas and Gerhard Wagner, 81–95. Routledge Research in Cultural and Media Studies 18. New York; London: Routledge, 2009.

9

On Reading the Enculturated–Hybridized Bibles of the African Postcolony

Charting the Way Forward

R. S. Wafula

Luther College
Decorah, Iowa, USA
wafuro01@luther.edu

"Savages" Can Read Too: Theorizing "Savage" Readings

In order to appreciate African Bible Translation contestations represented in this volume, one needs to understand the current status of knowledge production, consumption, and distribution in the world. In *Orientalism*, Edward Said shows a Western discourse that represents non-Western peoples as different—as the "Other."[1] This Otherness is depicted in binary contrasts. Whereas non-European people are depicted as irrational, slow thinkers, inaccurate in their intellectual propositions, unreasonable, and illogical—at best representing anarchy and chaos, the European, in contrast, is depicted as rational, logical, and intelligent in all their dealings—the very embodiment of order and civility.[2] From Said's analysis one can deduce the sustained effort to represent non-European peoples as primitive and backward. This primitiveness demarcates their episte-

1. Said, *Orientalism*, 2.
2. Ibid. 38.

192

mological systems as useless in the imagined European epistemological world. European knowledge is therefore marketed as the lifeline for the survival of non-European peoples.

Walter Mignolo makes the same claim as Said. He shows how binary otherness between Europeans and non-Europeans is passed on as unqualified truth.[3] With such overwhelming power, machinery, and resources, the West constructed what it purported to be all there is to know about oriental peoples. As V.Y. Mudimbe points out, this construction of the Other was no mean narrative. It constituted a body of knowledge that has governed Western understanding of the Other for generations.[4] As a result the European epistemological framework did not only deprive the non-European people the right to represent themselves, but also the legitimacy to be heard should they ever represent themselves. This twin agenda was then calculatedly filtered into all fields of academic discourses (biology, geography, history, sociology, anthropology, linguistics, religious/theology, and so forth) and sociopolitical and economic systems. The combined bodies of knowledge marketed the idea that the Other is incapable of self-government, self-determination, self-advancement, and self-representation—that everything they do is doomed to fail.[5] Thus in the process of knowledge production, distribution, and consumption, the European epistemological frameworks practiced what Paulo Freire calls 'the banking concept' of education. The 'teacher', in this case the European, possessing all knowledge deposits it in the empty bank account (the heads of non-Europeans). Thus the non-Europeans are perceived as empty vessels with no intelligence—savages with no learning, no culture and no contribution to the future of humanity. As a result knowledge and its acquisition becomes a European gift to the non-European peoples.[6] For Africa, the Europeans followed the well outlined European world-view in Joseph Conrad's novel (*Heart of Darkness*) of a dark continent inhabited by savage-like human beings. According to this world-view the African subhuman species, being at the very lowest level of Darwinian developmental scale, would forever be lost without European intervention.

However, while the European narratives wanted to shut down and shut out any 'savages'' significance in Knowledge production, distribution, and consumption, the resilience of African bible translation theorists as represented in this volume, stands as an enduring testament that these

---

3. Mignolo, *Local Histories/Global Designs*, ix.

4. Mudimbe, *The Invention of Africa*, 1–16.

5. Said, *Orientalism*, 12, 32–34.

6. Freire, *Pedagogy of the Oppressed*, 71–72.

'savages' can never be shut out. They can read and re-read too, and do so damn well. Their intellectual prowess is exhibited in an endless stream of efforts in defining and redefining African destiny as well as contesting any external encroachment on that destiny.

"Savages" Reading the Bible

The papers in this volume demonstrate an African 'savage' spirited effort to deny the white man the last word on the religio-cultural norms and values of African/Africana peoples. In her article "Consuming a Colonial Cultural Bomb," Musa Dube returns to the vexing question of cultural colonization. She shows how in her meetings with local present day Batswana women she found out that they had been, linguistically, brainwashed to the extent that they preferred older European translations of the Bible (Wookey's Bible of 1908), over and against newer and Batswana translations (like the 1992 Morolong Bible, or the Sandilands' Setswana New Testament, completed in 1970).[7] Unfortunately, as Dube finds out, the preferred colonial translations had distorted the Batswana religio-cultural meanings.[8] Dube discovered that cultural colonization was not limited to the educated elite who readily embraced Western values, including English as a medium of communication, but also with uneducated masses (like some of the women who belonged to African Independent Churches, that had broken ties with missionary Christianity). In her research, Dube discovered rather that cultural colonization was deeply embedded in the fabric of all of Setswana culture. This embeddedness challenged the Setswana people to hate and reject their own cultural values (including ancestor veneration) in exchange for European religio-cultural values.[9] Thus the translation politics was a colonial instrument to force the Batswana people to accept that they are a lost people and in darkness—a people who need the European light clothed in the garment of Christianity.

As though a double tragedy, it wasn't just the Bible that distorted Setswana religio-cultural values, Setswana language also suffered a linguistic calamity. The European dictionary translations of the Setswana language followed the European missionary cultural colonization. For example the word *Badimo* (ancestral spirit) was translated as evil spirits or demons. However, Dube shows that the Batswana people have not taken the mutilation of their language and religious ideals kindly. In 1993, a Batswana

7. Dube, "Consuming a Colonial Cultural Bomb," 33–59.

8. Ibid., 41.

9. Ibid., 41–42.

translator set out to deconstruct the colonial cultural imperialism inherent in European dictionary translations of Setswana. The translator changed the colonial *Badimo*-demons translation to *Badimo*-ancestors designation. By so doing this Batswana reader destabilizes the European narrative by restoring the originally defaced African religio-cultural understanding of *Badimo*. These decolonizing efforts continued with subsequent Batswana dictionary translators. In relation to the Bible Dube's own reading is not only a powerful protest against imperial cultural colonialism, but a call to revisit Bible translation projects Among Batswana people—a call that sublimely envisions a program for decolonization of the mind of Batswana people so that they can embrace their religio-cultures again. But more importantly Dube shows that the Bible is hybridized among the AIC Christians. This hybridization plays an instrumental destabilizing role in contesting European mutilation of African religio-cultural values. Whereas the European missionary narrative defines *Badimo* as evil spirits, the AIC Christians, without imagining it as a contradiction, consult diviners (who are representatives of *badimo*) who use the bible in their divination. Thus the Bible's antagonistic position against the *Badimo* is subverted. The AICs decolonize the Bible hence reclaiming the use of *Badimo* for healing against missionary Christianity's death sentence imposed upon the *Badimo*.[10]

Musa follows this up with another essay in this volume where she makes a case for the role of African orality to resist Eurocentric and dogmatic translations of biblical texts into African languages. Using Laura Bohannan's encounter with the Tiv people of Nigeria and her discovery of their unique re-reading of Hamlet, Dube points out how Batswana readers resist passivity in the European Bible translation and mutilation of Setswana language. Whereas the Eurocentric epistemology had led Bohannan to a resigned fate of non-activity among the Tiv people—a people regarded as living in the bush with no intelligence. But when Bohannan read Hamlet with them she discovered that the bush people were alive, inquisitive, and involved. The bush was on fire! Within it was the Moses-God like epiphany of re-creating a new Hamlet. To the Tiv, Hamlet was no longer a dead-lettered book. It became a living organism, changing and gaining new nuances from the orality prowess of the Tiv people. Dube points out that like the Tiv, the Batswana people, use orality as a tool to listen critically, question assumptions, give comments and suggestions, and in the process end up re-writing the biblical texts within their own cultural worldview. As a result translation becomes no longer an exercise of translating words from one language to another, but it becomes rather a translation of one culture into another with the recipient

10. Ibid., 53–56.

culture taking an active role to shape the final product of what now becomes their biblical texts.[11]

In his essay, "Postcolonial Translation Theory and the Swahili Bible," Aloo O. Mojola argues that Western colonial presuppositions let them to a belief that Swahili people and hence Kiswahili language was primarily an Arab language infused by African local dialect words. Due to this misconception the translation of the Bible into Kiswahili was based on Arabic morphology and only secondarily on African languages. As a matter of fact the missionaries who attempted the first translations relied on the support of Arab elites in Mombasa and other East African coastal towns. The same was the case in developing the first Kiswahili dictionaries. As a result of this the first Kiswahili Bible translations were heavily interpolated with European as well as Arabic religio-cultural values.[12]

It wasn't until 1995 that the first complete Kiswahili Bible was translated by Kiswahili speakers of native African origin (commonly known as Biblia Habari Njema). It is here that the seeds of decolonizing the Kiswahili Bible began. Although, as Mojola argues, this translation did not engage into de-Arabizing the translation, it nevertheless allowed into its translation theory contemporary standardized Kiswahili as spoken, particularly among native African peoples in Tanzania, rather than following the older European missionary Arabized Kiswahili translations.[13]

Mojola's efforts to point out missionary privileging of Arabic religio-cultural values over and against native African values in orginal Kiswahili Bible translations is geared towards his reflection on the possibilities that lie within postcolonial translation theories to decolonize that process and establish a Kiswahili Bible that is cognizant of the religio-cultural values of native African Kiswahili speaking peoples of East Africa. In other words, the 19th century missionary imperial legacy is not left to call the last shot on African's religio-cultural self-definition. Mojola's reading demonstrates new efforts that are propelling more and more African scholars, not only to critique cultural imperialism, but to chart ways for re-doing what was done by these missionaries.

Johnson Kĭriakŭ Kĩnyua starts by a forceful statement that Bible translation into African languages was a colonial praxis. Using the translation of the New Testament Bible into Gikuyu language he shows how 19th Century European missionaries' practices were a mediating urgency for colonization. The missionaries played into the colonial hegemonic power whereby

11. Dube, "The Bible in the Bush," 79–103.

12. Mojola, "Postcolonial Translation Theory and the Swahili Bible," 77–104.

13. Ibid., 99–101.

rather than depending on Gikuyu speaking translators (or interpreters) the missionaries translated the Bible themselves using very limited Gikuyu language skills that they personally gained. Feeding into the colonial strategy of unifying all people for easy control, the missionaries formed what they called the United Kikuyu Language Committee to help create a unified Kikuyu language orthography at a great disadvantage to the different dialects of Gikuyu language. To compound the problem, this committee had no single original Gikuyu language speaker.[14] Needless to say, the committee made many mishaps in its work as they imposed on the diverse Kikuyu people a unified orthography. They realized along the way that the words they had chosen would often render totally different meanings (in different Kikuyu dialects) than the intended meanings. But the missionaries insisted on their understanding over that of native Gikuyu speakers who pointed these mistakes out to them.

However, Kĩnyua points out how the Gikuyu Bible translation opened up not only a space for Eurocentric colonization but also in-between spaces that allowed for native Gikuyu speakers' resistance through questioning the missionary word choices. Thus the few Gikuyu people that missionaries consulted during the translation process of particularly difficult and untranslatable Gikuyu words became active translation participants by default. By taking advantage of missionary language limitations these Kikuyu people understood and effectively exploited their window of opportunity as a space for transformative acts of decolonization.[15] Kĩnyua also points out a more active resistance whereby ordinary readers like Charles Mũhoro and Bildad Kaggia resisted the missionary translated Gikuyu New Testament by taking upon themselves to re-translate the parts they felt violated Gikuyu religio-cultural values as well as argue with missionaries to reconsider/revise their translations.[16] These early resistance has given impetus for contemporary Gikuyu Christian translators to re-translate the entire Gikuyu Bible—one that is attuned to and sensitive to Gikuyu religio-cultural values.

On her part, Gomang Seratwa, Ntloedibe-Kuswani contests missionary translations of the concept of demons in Setswana. She argues that the missionaries took the Setswana word for the deity and the spirit world (dead ancestors) *Modimo* (*Badimo*, in plural), and used it to translate the Hebrew Bible word God. The problem is that unlike the Hebrew Bible where God (Yahweh) is male, in Setswana language Modimo is genderless. Thus by using the word to translate God of the Hebrew Bible, the Setswana God

14. Kĩnyua, "A Postcolonial Analysis of Bible Translation," 58–95.

15. Ibid., 84–85.

16. Ibid., 87–91.

became masculinized hence opening a window for patriarchy to commit violence against women with an argument that even God is male.[17] However, Ntloedibe-Kuswani, like the rest of our contributors show how Setswana Bible translators from 1992 onwards started a decolonizing Bible translation praxes whereby they purged the Bible of missionary demonization of Batswana religio-cultural values.[18] It is this resistance, according to Ntloedibe-Kuswani, that represents the best hope to create a meaningful Bible for the Batswana people—a Bible that does not superimpose its religious claims on other people's religious traditions—but one that dialogues with other religious practices. The future Setswana Bible therefore, is not one that seeks to coopt/submerge Batswana religio-cultural norms and values but one that starts with Batswana religio-cultural norms and then borrows from the biblical world to enrich itself. Thus this reverses the process of translation hermeneutics. Rather than Setswana being the receptor language it becomes the source (primary) language while the Bible becomes the receptor language in the process of creating the Setswana Bible.

Dora R. Mbuwayesango takes up the question of the nineteenth-century European missionary suppression of the Shona God *Mwari*. Like *Modimo* discussed above, Mbuwayesango points out that *Mwari* was a genderless God. But when the Europeans equated Yahweh (male gendered Hebrew God) with *Mwari* they transformed the understanding of the Shona God into European machinations. Mbuwayesango argues that this usurpation allowed the Europeans to have the Bible speak as the authentic voice of *Mwari* even though Yahweh's ways and dealings were not identical with Mwari's ways.[19] All over a sudden *Mwari* became human (as Yahweh in Gen 2) as opposed to Shona religious worldview that depicted *Mwari* as a spirit with no human form.[20] Thus the European missionaries colonized the Shona God and used that God as a weapon to invalidate Shona religious practices that did not align with the Yahweh-*Mwari*.[21] As a remedy to this problem Mbuwayesango proposes direct translation of the Bible from original Hebrew and Greek texts rather than through the medium of English. In the new translations, Yahweh should be transliterated rather than be called *Mwari*. In this way the Shona can maintain their God distinct from the Hebrew God.[22] By making this radical proposal, Mbuwayesango joins already

---

17. Seratwa, Ntloedibe-Kuswani, "Translating the Divine," 78–97.

18. Ibid., 91.

19. Mbuwayesango, "How Local Divine Powers Were Suppressed," 63–77.

20. Ibid., 69.

21. Ibid., 70–73.

22. Ibid., 75.

loud 'savage' voices that are calling for the emancipation of African religious values from Eurocentric epistemologies.

Jeremy Punt works on the premise that both an acknowledgement of the effects of cultural gender constructions in biblical texts and the urge to create gender-neutral biblical texts firms the status quo of these constructions. He shows, for example, how the Greek term διάχονος (one who serves) in the New Testament has far reaching meanings including servant, helper, agent, and so forth, but when used in reference to women such as Phoebe in Rom 16:1–3, it is normally rendered as deaconess hence limiting the role of women in the Jesus movement to one (feminized) role. This translation ignores the patronage system within which Paul uses the term to refer to Phoebe. Punt argues that in the wider Roman Imperial cultural milieu the word διάχονος that Paul uses for Phoebe is better translated as minister rather than deaconess. As a result texts and translations that render Phoebe as a διάχονος (deaconess) rather than a minster (a term reserved for men) do so purely on the basis gendering differentiation of Phoebe (as a woman) as opposed to men rather than on the faithful translation of the whole range of the meaning of the word διάχονος. This cultural differentiation was operative in the Roman imperial context within which Paul wrote his letter as well as modern day translational contexts. As such Punt urges translators to take into consideration the import of cultural studies on translational practices.[23] In so doing he implicitly contests translations (like the 19th century missionary Bible translations) that ignored the cultural forces that impinge on translation and Bible interpretation practices.

"Savages" Interrogating Sociopolitical and Cultural Differences in Bible Translation Politics

In this section I explore the idea already argued in some of the essays in this volume that translation of the Bible is not just about the translation of words. Informed translation is also about understanding and appropriating the culture, politics, economics and social forces inherent in the texts being translated. As a result of this Bible translation theory/theories need to take into account the sociopolitical and economic forces behind the words of the Bible. Here I would suggest that all African Bible translations should have lengthy introductions to clarify the history, culture, politics, economics and social forces that influenced the writing of the Bible. In the case of the Hebrew Bible this introduction should include an assessment of the enduring influence of the Ancient Near East empires on the Bible; particularly how

23. Punt, "(Con)figuring Gender in Bible Translation," 1–10.

the Israelite exile influenced the concepts of power struggles in the Hebrew Bible texts. The New Testament introduction should include the role and influence of the Greco-Roman empire on the New Testament Writings. Let me illustrate the importance of these introductions by using the Lubukusu Bible translation.[24]

Saving "Wele" (Bukusu God) from "Yahweh" (The Hebrew God)

When the Bible was finally translated into Lubukusu the Hebrew God Yahweh was translated as "Wele" the name for Bukusu God. Thus the translation made Yahweh and Wele synonymous—one name for one God just in different languages. At once the god of the Hebrews became the god of Bukusu people. But is Yahweh synonymous with Wele? The following discussion will show that the answer to this question should be in the negative.

Who Is Yahweh?

In the Hebrew Bible Yahweh is characteristically known as God of Abraham, God of Isaac, and God of Jacob (and later as 'God of our ancestors,' referring to these three) or God of the Israelites. Let me examine the import of some of these associations.

Yahweh God of Abraham

Yahweh first appears to Abram (later called Abraham) in Gen 12 in the context of a family journey that starts in Gen 11:27. Yahweh's first conversation with Abram is a command for him to continue his father's journey to an unknown destination. After the command Yahweh adds the following words of blessing:

> I will make of you a great nation, and I will bless you, and make your name great, so that you will be a blessing. I will bless those who bless you and the one who curses you I will curse; and in you all the families of the earth shall be blessed (Gen 12:2–3).[25]

24. The first complete Lubukusu Bible was completed and published by the Bible Society of Kenya in 2010. Lubukusu is a language spoken by a Luhya subgroup that lives primarily in Bungoma County, Western Kenya.

25. NRSV. Unless otherwise stated, all bible passages will utilize this translation.

We can see that Yahweh's blessing personalizes Yahweh's relationship with Abram in exclusivity of all others including Abram's companions. Despite the fact that Abram has a wife and a nephew (Lot) with him (Gen 12:5), Yahweh speaks blessings over him in a singular "you" in a manner that puts him in a class of his own against his relatives. Furthermore Yahweh's words that he would curse those who curse Abram put Abram in a privileged status over and against others, particularly those who would cross Abram's line. Indeed later when Abram lies to Pharaoh that his wife Sarai is his sister and Pharaoh takes her for a wife, Yahweh punishes Pharaoh instead of Abram (Gen 12:10–20). Thus for Yahweh Abram is a larger than life character to the extent that his evils bear no moral and ethical consequences against him. Yahweh's silence seems to ignore and treat lightly the grievous crime that Abram has committed not only against Pharaoh but also against his wife. In other words, Yahweh is a very exclusive God who is 'madly' in love with Abram. He is Abram's personal God conferring benefits on Abram and those who are in Abram's league. As a matter of fact Yahweh hostages all humanity to Abram by stating that it is only through or by Abram that anyone can be blessed.[26]

Yahweh and Land Ownership

In Gen 15:18–21, Yahweh makes a covenant with Abram and promises him the land saying:

> To your descendants I give this land, from the river of Egypt to the great river, the river Euphrates, the land of the Kenites, the Kenizzites, the Kadmonites, the Hittites, the Perizzites, the Rephaim, the Amorites, the Canaanites, the Girgashites, and the Jebusites.

Yahweh affirms this covenant later in Gen 17:8 with the words:

> And I will give to you and to your offspring after you, the land where you are now an alien, all the land of Canaan, for a perpetual holding; and I will be their God.

In keeping with his character as Abram's personal God, Yahweh has no regard for other groups of people. He promises Abram other people's land. In spite of the fact that the land is occupied, Yahweh grants it to Abram as a perpetual holding. However, it is what should happen to the people who own the lands that describe to us the extent of pure evil that Yahweh can

---

26. See also Wafula, *Biblical Representations of Moab*, 83.

commit in order to keep his promises to Abraham and his descendants. Yahweh states in Exod 23:23–33:

> When my angel goes in front of you, and brings you to the Amorites, the Hittites, the Perizzites, the Canaanites, the Hivites, and the Jebusites, and I blot them out, you shall not bow down to their gods, or worship them, or follow their practices, but you shall utterly demolish them and break their pillars in pieces . . . And I will send the pestilence in front of you, which shall drive out the Hivites, the Canaanites, and the Hittites from before you. I will not drive them out from before you in one year, or the land would become desolate and the wild animals would multiply against you. Little by little I will drive them out from before you, until you have increased and possess the land. I will set your borders from the Red Sea to the sea of the Philistines, and from the wilderness to the Euphrates; for I will hand over to you the inhabitants of the land, and you shall drive them out before you. You shall make no covenant with them and their gods. They shall not live in your land, or they will make you sin against me; for if you worship their gods, it will surely be a snare to you.

Yahweh's words close completely the door to negotiations and common grounds for interethnic peaceful coexistence in the land. When Yahweh brings Abraham's descendants into the land of others, he not only dispossesses them, but he also kills them or allows the Israelites to kill them. Yahweh carries out this removal systematically and slowly, in a sadistic manner—almost as a spot, allowing the Israelites to give birth and increase in number to be able to control the land resources. Yahweh is categorical about Israel living an exclusive life on the lands of the others. In Deut 7:1–11 the Israelites are told to have no covenants, no inter-marriages and no interactions with the people of the land. Thus Yahweh plants the seeds of segregated living in the social fabric of his people Israel. Apparently, to use modern terms, Yahweh is not averse to racism and apartheid. He in fact is the creator of these vices. The people of the land are demarcated as evil and hence unwanted by Yahweh. Deut 20:16–18 even goes on to make a case that to get rid of these people through violence is to do Yahweh's work. Annihilation of the people of the land is a divine command. The culmination of this gruesome violence against the people of the land is recorded in the book of Joshua with the total destruction of the cities of Ai (Josh 7) and Jericho (Joshua 8) as symbols of unimaginable violence that characterizes much of the Hebrew Bible.

Yahweh Against his own Creation

There are other stories that characterize who Yahweh is that are important. But let it suffice for me to simply mention them here in passing. In Genesis 3 after Adam and Eve had eaten the forbidden fruit, Yahweh apportions differentiated punishments that raptures the relationship between man and woman (both initially touted as the epic of God's creation). In Genesis 4, for no apparent reason, Yahweh accepts the offering of Abel over and against that of Cain leading to the first human murder. In a sense Yahweh's action implicitly puts him at the center of blame for the death of Abel. The stories of Yahweh's complicity in setting one kin over and against another are a common leitmotif in the Hebrew Bible. For example Yahweh decrees that Adam will rule over Eve (Gen 3:16), he partners with Abraham against Lot (Gen 12:1—19:38),[27] he disinherits Ishmael in preference for Isaac (Gen 21:12–14), and he subordinates Esau to Jacob (Gen 25:22–23).

In Gen 7 God becomes angry at his creation and decides to wipe out all life through a great flood except Noah and his family and one kind of each animal, male and female. As humanity begins to heal from the trauma of the flood and to organize themselves against the unknown dangers, including their first skyscraper, Yahweh is annoyed with their efforts. He creates language confusion to thwart human development saying:

> "Look, they are one people, and they have all one language; and this is only the beginning of what they will do; nothing that they propose to do will now be impossible for them. Come, let us go down, and confuse their language there, so that they will not understand one another's speech.'" So the Lord scattered them abroad from there over the face of all the earth, and they left off building the city. Therefore it was called Babel, because there the Lord confused the language of all the earth; and from there the Lord scattered them abroad over the face of all the earth. (Gen 11:9)

This division sows discord and hatred among human beings making it impossible not only to build the tower but for human beings to live together in harmony as well. Thus, according to the Hebrew Bible, God is the creator of racial categories as is manifested in language differentiations.

The above picture gives us a taste of the character and nature of Yahweh in the Hebrew Bible. The question then is; is this Yahweh equivalent to Wele? Let me now briefly address this question by a discussion of who Wele is.

27. See Wafula, *Biblical Representations of Moab*, 82–91.

Who Is Wele?

The Bukusu God Wele, who is genderless, expresses self through three manifestations: *Wele Khakaba* (meaning God who creates and apportions livelihood to various peoples), *Wele Mukhobe* (meaning Wele's manifestation through elders, both dead and alive, seers, and diviners) and *Wele We luchi* (the expression of Wele who dispels evil).[28] In all of the above manifestations Wele does not bless any one Bukusu more or over and against other Bukusu people. Wele does not put a wedge between kinsmen. Rather Wele is always invoked as the reconciler of those that have differences in the community. Similarly Wele does not dispossess other people in order to give Bukusu people land. In the Bukusu narratives concerning land acquisition and disputes diplomacy and dialogue were the primary channels of solving any conflicts. Such conversations would always begin with the dictum, "There is enough land for all of us." Once the reconciliation conversations were concluded, the parties in a land dispute would put their weapons together before the elders (arbitrators on behalf of Wele). The elders would then pronounce the end of dispute by uttering the following proverb: *Owikana kamaya ora esimbo.*" The transliteration is, "He/she who denounces violence burns their weapon." In terms of external interactions the Bukusu believed that Wele who gave them land and blessings also gives others their land and resources. This giving is a divine gift that cannot be violated without incurring the wrath of Wele. So Bukusu people would never violet other people's rights to land in the name of Wele.

Thus when you look at the manifestations, and understandings, and historical processes that created Yahweh and Wele as described above you begin to notice that translating Yahweh as Wele is doing a great disservice to the religious understanding of God among the Bukusu people. The Bukusu people did not experience the exilic/postexilic historical developments that affected the Israelites. For this reason to name Yahweh as Wele is to impose not only a foreign God on the Bukusu people, but is also to impose the Israelite sociohistorical and economic processes on the Bukusu people. By naming Yahweh Wele, you impose upon the Bukusu people the violent legacy of a highly exclusive Yahweh who is a creation and a weapon of the Israelite ruling elite against those they wanted to imperialize. Seen from this perspective, I don't think it is asking too much to argue that we need to decolonize the Lubukusu Bible (and by implication all other Bibles) to correct the imputations of Yahweh on a people who had nothing to do with the practices of this violent God.

28. Oruka, *Sage Philosophy,* 35.

Thus following up on Mbuwayesango's argument earlier in this paper, I agree that Yahweh should be transliterated rather than translated to avoid importing Hebrew Bible 'baggage' into other languages. But in order for this kind of decolonization to take place the Bukusu people (as is the case for other African peoples with translated Bibles) have to be let into the inside story of the sociopolitical and economic understanding of Yahweh's ways. In other words, it is not enough to translate the Bible words, we also need to translate the socio-cultural, economic, and political forces that shaped the words of the Bible. We need translate the biblical philosophy—of exclusivity, violence against all groups of people that were non-Israelites, and voices of contest against this exclusivity calling for inclusivity. In addition we need to translate the mutation of biblical texts beyond their original contexts; particularly how European missionaries and colonialists used them as a weapon for taking away African lands. These various translations will help us draw a line between the usefulness and harmfulness of the Judeo-Christian texts for our African religio-cultural contexts. As Mbuwayesango eloquently states we must look back to recover our Wele, Modimo, Mwari, Ngai, and so forth, from European shackles.[29] But this Bible decolonialization project is going to be like walking a long road that would require taking one step at a time towards our wholeness. This journey will require education that is beyond knowledge on the Bible. It will require knowledge of the Bible that allows people to understand the texts on their own terms.

"Savages" Charting the Way Forward for African Bible Translations

Most of the problems inherent in African Bible translations have to do with the Eurocentric epistemological framework that continues to place the white male 'expert' at the top of the African Bible translation hierarchal structure. As Aloo O. Mojola points out the first stage of this process, in the late 1800s and early 1900s was characterized with missionary translators who learned African languages and then translated the Bibles into these languages. The second stage was characterized by missionary translators who relied on local language speakers. But they exercised the power over all matters related to translations. The third stage is characterized by a growing number of African translators but with the white missionary 'expert' serving as a consultant. The missionary expert exercised 'quality control' on the translation and in some circumstances as stated earlier in this paper, called the shots on the final meaning of the translation, even when the "expert" had limited knowledge

29. Mbuwayesango, "How Local Divine Powers Were Suppressed," 74.

of the meaning and nuances that he advanced. The fourth and final group is composed of African translators who, seemingly exercised some authority over the final meaning of the texts, but not above the White male 'expert' who takes a role insidiously slated as advisory role but for all purposes gave him implicit power over the translation.[30]

Although Mojola is of the opinion that the majority of United Bible Societies' work falls in group three and four, and that this allows Africans to control the final meaning of the biblical texts, the reality is that the European "expert" does not play a limited role as Mojola would like it. More often than not the European "expert" continues to call the shots, often subtly influencing the final meaning of the words by nudging the translators towards certain conclusions. With the power differential between the "expert" and African Bible translators, the African Bible translators find themselves often times having to decide between keeping a job by following the dictates of the European "expert" or challenging the "expert" with the possibility of losing their jobs.

Behind this structural hierarchy that maintains the need for a European "expert" is the insidious Eurocentric epistemological framework that makes a false argument to the effect that that there aren't enough African biblical and linguistic scholars who can do what the European 'expert' does. Of course the reality is totally different. The pool of African linguistic expertise goes way back into the early 1960s with the likes of Chinua Achebe, Wole Soyinka, and Ngũgĩ Wa Thiong'o, just to name a few. The same can be said of African biblical scholars.[31] With many African scholars out there in almost any field related to Bible translation, it is untenable and indefensible to have European "experts" hovering over African Bible translations. This protest should be taken up seriously, especially if one considers that translation is not a value free enterprise and that everyone involved often leaves their religio-cultural imprints on the translations. As a result of this, decolonizing the African Bible would require that all African Bible translation projects be managed by African experts.

Conclusion

All the above is possible because, as DeGruy argues we may be brutalized, stripped of our identity, tortured, dispersed, and vandalized by colonialism

---

30. Mojola, "Bible Translation in Africa."

31. See Holter, "Sub-Saharan African Doctoral Dissertations in Old Testament Studies," who documents the history of African biblical scholarship that goes back into the early 1960s, particularly in the Old Testament Studies.

and postcolonialism, but African/Africana people are a strong resilient breed. We have always risen again and again from the ashes to assert ourselves, our independence, and our need to be dignified human beings. We have done it in the past we are doing it now, and our generations after us will continue to do it.[32] Nothing will stop us until all forces of racialized epistemologies are no longer part of humanity. When this is finally achieved, we will not only have healed ourselves from our colonial legacy, but we will also have healed the colonizers as well from their superiority and called them to a humanity that we all share as equal creatures regardless of the color of our skin.

Bibliography

DeGruy, Joy Angela. *Post Traumatic Slave Syndrome: America's Legacy of Enduring Injury and Healing*. Oregon: Joy DeGruy Publications, 2013.

Dube, Musa W. "The Bible in the Bush." *Translation* 2 (2013) 79–103.

———. "Consuming A Colonial Cultural Bomb: Translating '*Badimo*' into 'Demons' in Setswana Bible." *JSNT* 73 (1999) 33–59.

Freire, Paulo. *Pedagogy of the Oppressed*. Translated by Myra Bergman Ramos. New York: Herder & Herder, 1970.

Holter, Knut. "Sub-Saharan African Doctoral Dissertations in Old Testament Studies." In *Biblical Interpretation in African Perspective*, edited by David Tuesday Adamo, 99–116. Lanham, MD: University Press of America, 2006.

Kĩnyua, Johnson Kiriyaku. "A Postcolonial Analysis of Bible Translation and Its Effectiveness in Shaping and Enhancing the Discourse of Colonialism and the Discourse of Resistance: The Gikuyu New Testament—A Case Study." *Black Theology: An International Journal* 11 (2013) 58–95.

Mbuwayesango, Dora R. "How Local Divine Powers Were Suppressed: The Case of Mwari of the Shona." In *Other Ways of Reading: African Women and the Bible*, edited by Musa Dube, 63–77. Global Perspectives on Biblical Scholarship 2. Atlanta: Society of Biblical Literature, 2001.

Mignolo, Walter D. *Local Histories/Global Designs: Coloniality, Subaltern Knowledges, and Border Thinking*. Princeton Studies in Culture/Power/History. Princeton: Princeton University Press, 2000.

Mojola, A. O. "Bible Translation in Africa: What Implications Does the New UBS Perspective Have for Africa? An Overview in Light of the Emerging New UBS Translation Initiative." *Acta Theologica, Supplement* 2 (2002) 202–13. http://www.ajol.info/index.php/actat/article/viewFile/5460/29598.

———. "Postcolonial Translation Theory and the Swahili Bible." In *Bible Translation and African Languages*, edited by Gosnell L. O. R. Yorke and Peter M. Renju, 77–104. Bible Translation in Africa. Nairobi: Acton, 2004.

Mudimbe, V. Y. *The Invention of Africa: Gnosis, Philosophy, and the Order of Knowledge*. African Systems of Thought. Bloomington: Indiana University Press, 1988.

32. DeGruy, *Post Traumatic Slave Syndrome*, 181.

Ntloedibe-Kuswani, Gomang Seratwa. "Translating the Divine: The Case of Modimo in the Setswana Bible." In *Other Ways of Reading: African Women and the Bible,* edited by Musa W. Dube, 78–97. Global Perspectives on Biblical Scholarship 2. Atlanta: Society of Biblical Literature, 2001.

Oruka H., Odera. *Sage Philosophy: Indigenous Thinkers and Modern Debate on African Philosophy.* Philosophy of History and Culture 4. Leiden: Brill, 1990.

Punt, Jeremy. "(Con)figuring Gender in Bible Translation." *HTS Teologiese Studies / Theological Studies* 70/1 (2014) 10pp. doi: 10.4102/hts.v70i1.2051.

Said, Edward. *Orientalism.* New York: Pantheon, 1978.

Wafula, R. S. *Biblical Representations of Moab: A Kenyan Postcolonial Reading.* Bible and Theology in Africa 19. New York: Lang, 2014.

Made in the USA
Middletown, DE
04 August 2017